Lecture Notes in Computer Science 13927

Founding Editors

Gerhard Goos
Juris Hartmanis

Editorial Board Members

The series Lecture Notes in Computer Science (LNCS), including its subseries Lecture Notes in Artificial Intelligence (LNAI), and Lecture Notes in Bioinformatics (LNBI), has established itself as a medium for the publication of new developments in computer science and information technology research, teaching, and education.

LNCS enjoys close cooperation with the computer science R & D community, the series counts many renowned academics among its volume editors and paper authors, and collaborates with prestigious societies. Its mission is to serve this international community by providing an invaluable service, mainly focused on the publication of conference and workshop proceedings and postproceedings. LNCS commenced publication in 1973.

Pierre Collet · Latafat Gardashova ·
Samer El Zant · Ulviya Abdulkarimova
Editors

Complex Computational Ecosystems

First International Conference, CCE 2023
Baku, Azerbaijan, April 25–27, 2023
Proceedings

 Springer

Editors
Pierre Collet ⓘ
Strasbourg University
Strasbourg, France

Samer El Zant ⓘ
Strasbourg University
Strasbourg, France

Latafat Gardashova ⓘ
Azerbaijan State Oil and Industry University
Baku, Azerbaijan

Ulviya Abdulkarimova ⓘ
French Azerbaijani University
Baku, Azerbaijan

ISSN 0302-9743   ISSN 1611-3349 (electronic)
Lecture Notes in Computer Science
ISBN 978-3-031-44354-1   ISBN 978-3-031-44355-8 (eBook)
https://doi.org/10.1007/978-3-031-44355-8

This Springer imprint is published by the registered company Springer Nature Switzerland AG
The registered company address is: Gewerbestrasse 11, 6330 Cham, Switzerland

Paper in this product is recyclable.

Preface

CCE 2023 initiated a series of triennial international conferences on *Complex Computational Ecosystems*, within a series of annual conferences organized by the French–Azerbaijani University (UFAZ), the Azerbaijan State Oil and Industry University (ASOIU) and the University of Strasbourg (UNISTRA). It was also organized as an event of the E-laboratory on Complex Computational Ecosystem (ECCE) of the Complex Systems Digital Campus (CS-DC) UNESCO UniTwin. The conference took place on April 25–27, 2023, in Baku, the capital of Azerbaijan, in the Caucasus.

The main objective of CCE 2023 was to bring together scientists from various fields to explore trans-disciplinary challenges that crossed theoretical questions with empirical observations of multi-level and multi-modal computational ecosystems. Complex Computational Ecosystems are ecosystems implementing complex emergent behaviour out of the interaction of their constituting elements. They are "computational" in the sense that their emergent properties can be modelled by mathematical expressions that can be run on computers for the purpose of simulating or improving their models by comparing their output on previously collected observed data.

They are therefore constitutive of the 4 "P"s of complex systems: **P**articipative by the collection of data that will be used to model the complex ecosystem, **P**redictive in the sense that the elaborated model be used for simulation of a digital twin of the ecosystem, **P**reventive if running simulations could show that modifying initial conditions could thwart potential catastrophic events predicted by the simulation of the ecosystem, and **P**ersonalized because due to their emergent nature, the sensitivity to initial conditions makes it necessary to specialize the model to the specific case that is studied.

The conference received 46 submissions from co-authors from 15 different countries, covering 11 different topics. The selection used an innovative 3-phase collaborative double-blind author/reviewer procedure similar to the one implemented by *Frontiers* and also used in the CS-DC 2015 UNESCO UniTwin world conference:

1. The topic chairs manually anonymously assigned each anonymous paper to 3 to 6 recognized experts in their domains holding at least a PhD and asked them for a first review to be handed back within 15 days, as is the common practice in double-blind reviewed international conferences.
2. Then, a second 15-day collaborative phase started during which authors were given the opportunity to improve the papers with the help of reviewers with a catch:
3. At the end of the improvement process, the last version was sent back to the reviewers and in order to be accepted, the improved papers had to be deemed at least "acceptable" by at least 3 reviewers.

This innovative procedure is not as harsh on the authors as the standard one, in the sense that during the collaborative work with the reviewers, they can exchange points of view with the reviewers, but also should take their remarks into account. As a result, the paper is improved and more papers get accepted, without any compromise on the quality of the accepted papers, as in the end they must meet the minimum requirements of at least 3 reviewers.

CCE 2023 also accepted submissions by co-chairs, in which case the selection of reviewers was delegated to other co-chairs of the conference. The papers submitted by co-chairs were then anonymously reviewed during the first phase and went through the described procedure up to the online Program Committee paper selection meeting, to which all reviewers were invited and that was recorded in case of litigation. Co-authors of discussed papers (including co-chairs) were asked to disconnect when acceptation of the papers they co-authored was discussed.

The selected papers presented in these proceedings belong to:

Theoretical approaches:

1. Symbolic Artificial Intelligence,
2. Machine Learning, Artificial Evolution and Genetic Programming
   with papers studying ontologies alignment, reinforcement learning, image processing, evolutionary reduction, genetic programming, fuzzy patterns and business ecosystems, as well as to:

Empirical approaches:

3. Agro-ecological computational ecosystems, with papers presenting Monte Carlo simulations, augmented ecosystems, globally coupled map lattices and plant growth dynamics.
4. Security for complex computing systems, with papers presenting graph-based analytics to model and analyze cyber-situational awareness, such as network security management and cyber-attacks.
5. Educational computational ecosystems, with papers using predictive patterns and data mining to improve higher education systems.
6. Satellite and climate ecosystems, with a paper using evolutionary algorithms to model El Niño and La Niña climatic events,
7. Geosphere computational ecosystems, also using evolutionary algorithms to estimate Seismic Phase Delays.

In addition, CCE 2023 featured four keynote speakers who delivered insightful presentations to give attendees some inspiration for new research directions:

- Pierre Collet on a Diachronic Epistemology of Complex Systems, introducing the series of CCE triennial conferences,
- Anne Håkansson on Volatile Multiple Smart Systems Networks,
- Jacques Demongeot on Complex Systems and Epidemic Modelling, and
- Latafat Gardashova and Babek Guirimov on Fuzzy Logic to Process Complex Numerical Data in Business Applications.

The last keynote presenters offered to contribute a paper the content of which was validated by Latafat Gardashova, co-author of the contribution and co-chair of CCE 2023.

With a combined online/offline format, the conference allowed scientists who physically came to Baku and scientists connected worldwide to present their work, attend and ask questions on other presentations. All presentations were recorded with the assent of the presenters and available on the website of CCE 2023: https://cce-2023.ufaz.az/.

Finally, we would like to express our deepest gratitude to all the authors, reviewers, and topics chairs, and to all who contributed to the success of CCE 2023. We would also like to thank Springer for publishing these proceedings and making them available to the broader scientific community.

May 2023

Pierre Collet
Latafat Gardashova
Samer El Zant
Ulviya Abdulkarimova

Organization

Conference Host

Mustafa Babanlı — Azerbaijan State Oil and Industry University, Azerbaijan

Program Committee Chairs

Pierre Collet — University of Strasbourg, France
Latafat Gardashova — Azerbaijan State Oil and Industry University, Azerbaijan
Samer El Zant — University of Strasbourg, France
Ulviya Abdulkarimova — French-Azerbaijani University, Azerbaijan

Conference Organization

Elizaveta Bydanova — French-Azerbaijani University, Azerbaijan
Kamil Piriyev — French Azerbaijani-University, Azerbaijan
Gadir Rustamli — French Azerbaijani-University, Azerbaijan

Topic Chairs

Rodrigo Abarca del Rio — Universidad de Concepcion, Chile
Habib Abdulrab — INSA Rouen, France
Chun-Yen Chang — National Taiwan Normal University, Taiwan
Masatoshi Funabashi — Sony Computer Science Laboratories, Japan
Pierre Parrend — EPITA Strasbourg, France
Conor Ryan — University of Limerick, Ireland
Mathieu Schuster — Strasbourg University, France
Cécilia Zanni-Merk — INSA Rouen, France

Keynote Speakers

Pierre Collet	University of Strasbourg, France
Jacques Demongeot	Université Grenoble Alpes, France
Latafat Gardashova	Azerbaijan State Oil and Industry University, Azerbaijan
Babek Guirimov	Azerbaijan State Oil and Industry University, Azerbaijan
Anne Håkansson	UiT, The Arctic University, Norway

Steering Committee

Mustafa Babanli	Azerbaijan State Oil and Industry University, Azerbaijan
Pierre Collet	Strasbourg University, France
Latafat Gardashova	Azerbaijan State Oil and Industry University, Azerbaijan
Jean Marc Planeix	Strasbourg University, France
Cécilia Zanni-Merk	INSA Rouen, France

Program Committee

Martin Husak	Masaryk University, Czech Republic
Sofiane Lagraa	Fujitsu, Luxembourg
Cécilia Zanni-Merk	INSA Rouen, France
Ali Ayadi	Strasbourg University, France
Samer El Zant	Strasbourg University, France
Smita Kasar	Maharashtra Institute of Technology, India
Godai Suzuki	Synecoculture Association, Japan
Karim Tout	Uqudo, UAE
Amel Borgi	ISI/LIPAH, Université de Tunis El Manar, Tunisia
Gopinath Chennupati	Amazon, USA
Matthieu Dien	GREYC - UNICAEN, France
Nabil El Kadhi	Vernewell Academy, UAE
Franco Giustozzi	INSA Strasbourg, ICube Laboratory, France
Ting Hu	Queen's University, Canada
Tatsuya Kawaoka	Synecoculture Association, Japan
Meghana Kshirsagar	University of Limerick, Ireland
Mohamed Lamine	University Lumière Lyon2, France
Nuno Lourenço	University of Coimbra, Portugal

Pedaste Margus	University of Tartu, Estonia
Darian Reyes	University of Limerick, Ireland
Lina Soualmia	Normandie University, France
Sam Tseng	National Taiwan Normal University, Taiwan
Shane Tutwiler	University of Rhode Island, USA
Ying-Tien Wu	National Central University, Taiwan
Francisco Alvial	Universidad de la Frontera, Chile
Hernan Astudillo	Universidad Técnica Federico Santa María, Chile
Romi Banerjee	Indian Statistical Institute, India
Mathieu Bourgais	INSA Rouen, France
Stefano Cagnoni	University of Parma, Italy
Pierre Collet	Strasbourg University, France
Valentina Dragos	Office national d'Etudes et de Recherches Aérospatiales, France
Salah Elfalou	Lebanese University, Lebanon
Ghada Gharbi	EPITA Strasbourg, France
Mario Giacobini	University of Torino, Italy
Badis Hammi	Télécom ParisTech, France
Malcolm Heywood	Dalhousie University, Canada
Mariem Jelassi	Ecole nationale des Sciences de l'Informatique, France
Ibrahim Jrad	Bourgogne University, France
Maarten Keijzer	Hydroinformatics Institute, Singapore
Benjamin Kellenberger	Yale University, USA
Yannick Kergosien	Université de Cergy-Pontoise, France
Wissame Laddada	INSA Rouen, France
Olivier Lengliné	Strasbourg University, France
Marie-Jeanne Lesot	LIP6 - UPMC, France
Penousal Machado	University of Coimbra, Portugal
Abdenacer Makhlouf	Université de Haute Alsace, France
Nidà Meddouri	LRE, EPITA, Kremlin-Bicêtre, France
Eric Medvet	University of Trieste, Italy
Kanak Moharir	Babasthali Vidyapeeth University, India
Douglas Motadias	State University of Rio de Janeiro, Brazil
Rene Noel	Universidad de Valparaiso, Chile
Mahammad Nuriyev	Khazar University, Azerbaijan
Takuya Otani	Waseda University, Japan
Chaitanay Pande	IITM Pune, India
Pierre Parrend	EPITA Strasbourg, France
James Patten	Lero, Science Foundation Ireland Research Centre for Software, Ireland
Lukas Rosenauer	BSH Home Appliances

Keynotes

Volatile Multiple Smart Systems Network

Anne Håkansson

UiT The Arctic University of Norway

Abstract. Cyber-physical systems, CPS, like self-driving vehicles, e.g., cars, drones, and water vessels, are common in society, today. AI is used to enable the CPS to autonomously carry out tasks in society. But fully autonomous CPS can currently not be accepted in heavy traffic and dynamic environments. In this talk Professor Anne Håkansson describes Volatile Multiple Smart Systems Network and how this kind of network can be applied to deploy fully autonomous CPS in society.

Complex Systems and Epidemic Modeling

Jacques Demongeot

Université Grenoble Alpes

Abstract. Epidemic modeling and more, pandemic modeling, involves a mathematical approach using complex systems architectures at two levels: i) for representing the contagion process between susceptible individuals and ii) for simulating the efficiency of mitigating and/or curative measures based on prevention, vaccination and therapy policies. For the first level, we will take as example the COVID-19 outbreak and for the second the obesity spread, both declared worldwide pandemic by the World Health Organization (WHO).

A Diachronic Epistemology of Complex System

Pierre Collet

University of Strasbourg

Abstract. The science of Complex Systems is a «new» science born in the middle of the XXth century, but is it really the case? This keynote will present how the understanding of science has evolved in the Western World since Parmenides of Elea (6th century BCE) and Leucippus (5th century BCE) to the beginning of the 20th century with Poincaré and the advent of the 3rd meta-ethics in the 1970s, and the latest understanding of Loop Quantum Gravity as an attempt for a Theory of Everything (TOE).

Method Based on Alpha-Level Fuzzy Model to Efficiently Process Z-Numbers in Business Applications

Latafat Gardashova and Babek Guirimov

Azerbaijan State Oil and Industry University

Abstract. The research considers an approach to processing data described as Z-numbers, which is efficient in business applications. Zadeh's Extension principle is used as a general framework for solution. Alpha-level based fuzzy number model is used for both Value (A) and Reliability (B) parts of Z-number. The evolutionary DEC algorithm developed by the authors is suggested for optimization tasks. The performance and accuracy of the Approach is demonstrated on example problems. The software implemented on the basis of the suggested method has demonstrated excellent performance, which allows its potential use for complex processing problems involving Z-numbers.

Contents

Agro-Ecological Computational Ecosystems

Security for Complex Computing Systems

Education Computational Ecosystems

Satellite and Climate Ecosystems

Geosphere Computational Ecosystems

Symbolic Artificial Intelligence

Automation of User Interface Testing by Reinforcement Learning-Based Monkey Agents

Daniel Gerber[1]([✉]), Urwashi Kapasiya[1], Lukas Rosenbauer[1], and Jörg Hähner[2]

[1] BSH Hausgeräte GmbH, Im Gewerbepark B10, 93059 Regensburg, Germany
{daniel.gerber,urwashi.kapasiya,lukas.rosenbauer}@bshg.com
[2] University Augsburg - Chair for Organic Computing, Am Technologiezentrum 8, 86159 Augsburg, Germany
joerg.haehner@informatik.uni-augsburg.de

Abstract. The complexity of *Graphical User Interfaces* (GUIs) in consumer applications such as home appliances has significantly risen in recent years. For example, the number of different views in the GUIs has increased from simple selection views to complex sub-menu structures. Alongside the development, both testing complexity and cost have risen drastically. A way of handling this increase is test automation by the use of machine learning algorithms. This work focuses on reinforcement learning-based autonomous grey-box monkey testing for consumer GUIs. As a monkey tester, a Deep Q-Network is interacting with the device under test. Experiments are performed on an oven GUI as well as on a desktop training environment. A known feature representation for monkey testing is compared to three alternative representations, as well as a random agent. A careful selection of the feature representation can improve the exploration performance. Empirical results for the autonomous exploration of GUIs show the usefulness of reinforcement learning-based monkey testing over pure random testing on consumer GUIs. This can lead to an efficiency advantage in practice, as pure random testing is often the status quo in many well-known GUI test-frameworks such as Squish.

Keywords: Monkey Testing · Reinforcement Learning · Machine Learning · Human Machine Interface · User Interface Testing

1 Introduction

Machine Learning methods can provide substantial support to software testing [7]. Especially, for testing industrial *Graphical User Interfaces* (GUIs) [21]. A starting point for monkey testing of such *User Interfaces* (UIs) is random testing with the benefit of testing an UI without knowing further insides into the internal workings of the device under test [18]. In recent years variations of random testing have been employed as can be seen in the survey of Huang et

© The Author(s), under exclusive license to Springer Nature Switzerland AG 2023
P. Collet et al. (Eds.): CCE 2023, LNCS 13927, pp. 3–15, 2023.
https://doi.org/10.1007/978-3-031-44355-8_1

al. [9]. Such techniques create randomized interactions and inputs in order to validate a device [9]. A form of random testing is monkey testing, where a subset of approaches employ methods of *Reinforcement Learning* (RL) to facilitate better coverage of the target environment, i.e., UIs [24,30]. For example, these methods have been successfully used for testing Android applications [1,5,22,27]. Wetzlmaier et al. have brought the monkey testing idea to industrial applications [30]. The approach of Saber et al. [24] is focusing as well on RL-based Monkey testing on industrial desktop applications and yields a starting point for investigation.

The contribution of this work is to bring RL-based monkey testing to the domain of consumer products such as home appliances. The experiments are performed on an embedded GUI, i.e., a GUI of an oven device, as well as, on a desktop training environment. Different feature representations are compared against each other, as well as, a pure random agent in two different environments. Overall, the explorational aspect of monkey testing is in the center of the analysis.

This paper is organized as follows: After a recap on related work (Sect. 2), the used setup for monkey testing is introduced in Sect. 3. In the next section, the formal problem statement, as well as, the transition to the used machine learning algorithm is described (Sect. 4). Several variants of the algorithm and the experiments are discussed in Sect. 5, which is followed by a brief summary (Sect. 6) that concludes this paper.

2 Related Work

Validation is vital part of modern software development and has a significant impact on total project cost [4,8,32]. Thus testing has gotten into focus of various researchers [31]. Many subproblems such as test selection are examined for example in [17]. Our use case is located in the validation of user interfaces. UI testing has been pursued both by companies such as the Qt Group [20] as well as by academia (consider the survey of Pingfan et al. [12]). Modern UIs offer more and more (sub)-menus, options, and apps, with which the possible usage paths grow exponentially. This issue has been recognized by the scientific community [22,24] which propose validation methodologies using machine learning.

Our solution is based on RL. This subcategory of machine learning has its roots in Bellman's theory of dynamic programming [26]. We rely on an adaptation of deep Q-learning which combined traditional Q-learning with artificial neural networks [14]. We are not the first to employ reinforcement learning to testing problems in general. Not only UI testing has been examined using RL. For example regression testing has been addressed using RL methodologies [23,25]. Zheng et al. [33] use deep Q-Learning to validate computer games. Kim et al. [11] use the techniques to create vital test data. Moghadam et al. [16] proposed a solution for performance testing.

In contrast to the domain of android applications [22] and the domain of industrial applications [24,30], this paper focuses on the domain of consumer products, i.e., an embedded oven GUI of a home appliance. Additionally, We compare five different feature variants against each other on the task of monkey testing, including the variant of Saber et al. [24]. Another new aspect is the validation methodology of the different approaches on the absolute numbers of explored UI states – oppose to relative ones in [24]. The embedded GUI is interfaced via manufacturer's diagnosis software framework. Therefore, the overall approach can be categorized as grey-box testing [10] – oppose to a white box [19] or a black box [22] monkey approach.

3   Test Bed

Two different environments are built up and described in the following to verify the monkey testing approach: The first setup is an oven UI which represents a consumer application. Figure 1 provides an overview on the experimental setup. The hardware is a front panel of an oven appliance, which is a standalone electronic unit without the rest of the appliance. The electronic unit is ran by an embedded software, which in return can be interfaced from the testing PC. Part of the proprietary software testing framework is also the possibility to introduce touch inputs such as touches or slides gestures to the device. It is also possible to extract screenshots of the current view of the display. An exemplary screenshot of the oven display can be observed in Fig. 2. We coin this setup the *oven environment*. The second environment is a simple artificial desktop application, which is referred to as *buttongrid environment*. Figure 3 provides a screenshot of the application. The different states of the environment are organized in groups of $n = 3$ nodes in $L = 4$ levels, which results in a total of $\sum_{l=0}^{L-1} n^l = \sum_{l=0}^{4-1} 3^l = 40$ UI states. The 4 buttons 'Button1', 'Button2', 'Button3', and the 'Back' button allow to navigate through those states. The states are indicated by three letters 'AAA', 'BBB', 'CCC', etc., as visualized in Fig. 3. Via the 'Home' button the environment can be reset to its initial state 'AAA'. The 'Dummy' button results in no state transitions and the 'Back' button enables the return to the respective previous state. Overall, a software framework was developed (https://github.com/pmdg2226/explorational_monkey_testing), which allows to select either environment for RL-based monkey testing.

4   Problem and Algorithm Description

The main objective is the increase of test coverage during UI testing. Similar to Saber et al. [24], the aim of this work is to ideally explore all possible UI states. We limit ourselves to that, because the actual target of discovering software bugs occurs to infrequently in order to form a proper feedback signal. Let $U \subset \mathbf{N}$ be the set of discovered unique states of the environment. In the wider sense, our goal is to maximize the number of discovered states given a policy π, where

$$\max_{\pi} |U_\pi(t)|. \tag{1}$$

With π being a policy describing a mapping from the states s to probabilities of possible actions a in that particular state. The interested reader is referred

Fig. 1. Overview testbed of oven environment with standalone GUI (1), USB hardware interface adapter (2), testing PC (3), and power supply (4).

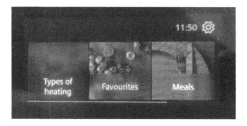

Fig. 2. Screenshot of the oven environment.

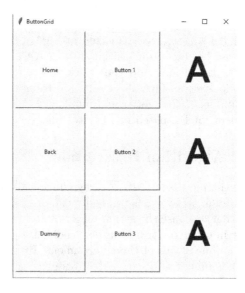

Fig. 3. Screenshot of buttongrid environment. On the left, the 6 buttons allow to navigate through the underlying UI states. On the right, the current UI state is indicated by the three letters 'AAA' distributed over 3 individual labels.

to [26] for a detailed introduction. The different screenshots or UI states are our observable part of the environment. Thereby, the question arises how to differentiate one image from another. A *Structural Similarity Index Measure* (SSIM) [28] was employed in order to asses the similarity. On top, two adequate thresholds ξ_1, ξ_2 were chosen per environment such that the current UI state u_t and previous UI state u_{t-1} could be effectively differentiated.

- If $SSIM(u_t, u_{t-1}) < \xi_1$ a major state change occurred,
- $\xi_1 \leq SSIM(u_t, u_{t-1}) < \xi_2$ a minor state change occurred, and if
- $\xi_2 \leq SSIM(u_t, u_{t-1})$ no state change has occurred.

The latter describes a case when an agent has chosen an action, such that the UI stays after action execution in the same UI state. SSIM was chosen over other metrics like the *Mean Squared Error* (MSE), as MSE turned out to be too sensitive to minimal changes, i.e., two screenshots can differ very slightly on the pixel level, but still represent the same state. This can translate to relatively large errors in terms of MSE. SSIM seems to be more robust in that regard.

Each environment has a discrete action space, which is predefined in the beginning. The represented actions can be performed on the environment, i.e., mouse clicks for the buttongrid environment and touch and slide gestures for the oven environment. l indicates thereby the number of actions for the respective environment. Let a be an arbitrary action from the corresponding action space and A_t the chosen action at time step t in the following.

The previously introduced UI states $u \in U$ can be related to a state representation s in the RL-sense. Different kinds of representations are possible in order to do so. In order to investigate the influence of the different representations, the following features are formed:

$$\mathbf{s}_1 = [\mathbf{s}_{bin}, \mathbf{0}] \tag{2}$$

$$\mathbf{s}_2 = [\mathbf{0}, \mathbf{s}_{pot}] \tag{3}$$

$$\mathbf{s}_3 = [\mathbf{s}_{bin}, \mathbf{s}_{pot}] \tag{4}$$

$$\mathbf{s}_4 = [\hat{\mathbf{s}}_{bin}, \mathbf{0}] \tag{5}$$

One way might be a numbering of the different UI states and a binary representation of the number in form of a vector $\mathbf{s}_{bin} \in \{0,1\}^b$ (Eq. 2). Let M be the maximum number of discover-able UI states and $b = \lceil \log_2 M \rceil$. Another option ($\mathbf{s}_{pot}$) is the approach of Saber et al. [24]. Each action is represented as a vector entry of $\mathbf{s}_{pot} \in \{0,1\}^l$ (Eq. 3). The i-th element of this vector is either 1 if the corresponding action count $x_a^i < 5$ or 0, else. In this way, the information about which action is most promising for further exploration is encoded. The authors denoted these actions *potential* actions. In case of a length mismatch between b and l, zeroes are padded in such a way that $\mathbf{s}_{bin}$ and $\mathbf{s}_{pot}$ have same length to form a matrix representation (Eq. 4). Additionally, let $\hat{\mathbf{s}}_{bin}$ (Eq. 5) be a binary representation of an entire sequence of UI states (oppose to a binary representation of single UI states as in $\mathbf{s}_2$). During runtime all occurring UI states u are recorded. The consecutive states can be grouped to sequences of $m = 5$ UI states and stored as well. The individual stored index number of the current sequence is represented as a binary number and brought to vector form $\hat{s}_{bin} \in \{0,1\}^{\hat{b}}$, where $\hat{M}$ represents the maximum number of discover-able sequences of UI states and $\hat{b} = \lceil \log_2 \hat{M} \rceil$. This representations allows to take more than one UI state into account for decision making.

In order to encourage an exploration behavior of the agent, the reward R_t is defined as (adopted from [24]):

$$R_t := \begin{cases} \frac{1}{x_u} \times v_u, & SSIM(u_t, u_{t-1}) < \xi_1, \\ \frac{1}{x_a^i}, & \xi_1 \leq SSIM(u_t, u_{t-1}) < \xi_2, \\ -1, & \xi_2 \leq SSIM(u_t, u_{t-1}). \end{cases} \quad (6)$$

The following nomenclature is used:

– u_t denotes the current UI state and u_{t-1} the previous UI state.
– $SSIM(u_t, u_{t-1})$ denotes the Structured Similarity Index Measure.
– x_u denotes how often the current UI state u_t was visited and x_a^i expresses the count of the action that was taken under this UI state (the count for the i-th action in the corresponding action space).
– v_u denotes the number of potential actions that are available.

The defined reward function (Eq. 6) delivers a balanced reward with respect to the number of potential actions available, limited by the number of visits of the UI state (major state change). The second statement lowers the reward the more often a particular action has been taken in the past (minor state change). And the third statement punishes the agent when it is not moving to another state. Overall, the reward definition aims at encouraging an agent to choose its policy in such a way that it moves to more and more unseen states and therefore maximizes test coverage. To determine a policy π that maximizes the overall rewards, the Bellman equation [26] comes into operation. The corresponding Q-value function can be defined as

$$q_\pi(s, a) = \mathbb{E} \left[\sum_{k=t+1}^{T} \gamma^{k-t-1} R_k \mid S_t = s, A_t = a \right], \quad (7)$$

with $t = 0, 1, ..., T$, where T denotes the last time step and γ the so called discount factor. The sum term expresses the accumulated future rewards, which are considered to assess the value of the different actions to be chosen in each particular state [26, p.58].

The *Deep Q-Network* (DQN) algorithm tries to estimate the optimal Q-function (Eq. 7) by the use of a general function approximator [14]. This reinforcement learning agent goes beyond a Q-learning approach, were states are simply encoded as entries in a table [29]. The main reason to choose a DQN network over a Q-learning approach in this work is the possibility to allow more general inputs in form of different feature representations. As a network architecture serve two feed-forward layers with 64 neurons and *Rectified Linear Units* (ReLU) activation functions [2], followed by a linear output layer.

Algorithm 1: Deep Q-learning algorithm for UI monkey testing as simplified pseudocode

---

1 Initialize the main network weights with random values
2 Update target network weights with main network weights
3 Initialize state and action counts to zero
4 **for** *episode* ← 1 **to** *max_episodes* **do**
5   Reset the environment to the initial state u_0
6   **for** *step* ← 1 **to** *max_steps_per_episode* **do**
7   Represent the current UI state u_t as state s_t
8   Select action a_t through roulette wheel strategy
9   Apply selected action a_t to the environment, which results in u_{t+1}
10   Increment state and action counts accordingly
11   Determine next state s_{t+1} and reward r_{t+1} from u_{t+1}
12   Add entry $(s_t, a_t, r_{t+1}, s_{t+1})$ to replay memory
13   Sample a random batch of entries from replay memory
14   Update the main network weights based on the batch
15   **if** *step* % *target_update_rate* = 0 **then**
16   Update target network weights with main network weights
17
18   **end**
19 **end**

For the algorithm (Algorithm 1), we are widely following the procedure of Mnih et al. [14]. The authors employ a reinforcement learning approach (similar to control tasks, where a joint training and testing phase is employed), which is based on interactions with the environment (contrary to supervised learning, where a split of training and testing phases is used). In detail, non-prioritized *Experience Replay* [13] and a target network alongside the main network comes into operation [15]. For action selection, we differ slightly by using a roulette-wheel strategy [6]. Based on the Q-value estimates (Eq. 7), the DQN algorithm determines a policy π that maximizes the overall goal (Eq. 1).

5   Experiments

Different kinds of features come into operation and are evaluated against each other in two environments. Since state discovery is in the focus, the total number of unique states is tracked throughout the experiments. There is one dedicated experiment for each of the two environments. The experiments are performed multiple times (denoted as *runs*) and contain five different agent configurations (denoted as *variants*). Each run of each variant consists of several *episodes* of a sequence of *steps*. Algorithm 1 provides an overview of the experimental procedure, i.e., a single run. A step represents thereby one interaction with the environment – taking an action, retrieving the new state, and receiving a reward. For every episode, the environment is reset to its initial state u_0. These UI states are the defined entry points to the environments visualized in Fig. 2 and Fig. 3.

The episodic process prevents that the agent gets stuck at a specific state. It is worth mentioning that state tracking and internal state/action counts (e.g. for potential features, or the reward) are not reset across multiple episodes. The reason for this organisation is to evaluate the progress across episodes.

For buttongrid, $l = 20$ was used. It is also possible to assign multiple predefined actions to click on the 'dummy'-button in order to simulate an even bigger action space (Sect. 3). The predefined action space consists of 4 meaningful clicks and 16 dummy clicks. Please note that the 'home'-button is only used to reset the environment. The 'dummy'-button was introduced in order to simulate a more complex environment (not only $l = 4$) that is closer to the oven environment, because only a fraction of the actions in the action space lead in each UI state to a state transition. For the oven environment $l = 40$ is chosen. Typical positions of UI elements were selected as possible actions. These positions are fixed for most of the UI elements, e.g., a back arrow is most of the time on the top left corner of the screen. A few elements can have non-fixed positions, such as a selection icon that is placed after a title element (different lengths of text elements introducing variability).

For the buttongrid experiment, 10 runs of 5 variants in 50 episodes with 50 steps were performed, resulting in 125000 interactions. For the oven experiment, 10 runs of 5 variants in 30 episodes with 100 steps were performed. In total this results in 150000 touch interactions with the oven GUI. These variants are listed in the following:

- *binary* (variant 1, Eq. 2) - Only binary state features s_1 are used as network inputs.
- *potential* (variant 2, Eq. 3) - The network inputs contain only potential features s_2.
- *bin&pot* (variant 3, Eq. 4) - Both potential and binary state features s_3 are fed to the network.
- *memory* (variant 4, Eq. 5) - A binary state representation of the last $m = 5$ states s_4 is given to the DQN.
- *random* (variant 5) - The respective actions are picked randomly on the basis of an uniform distribution. Please note, that there is no state representation needed for a random selection of actions.

Figure 4 visualizes the results of the two experiments for oven and buttongrid environments. The graphs show the mean and standard deviation of the total number of unique UI states. In Fig. 4a, the potential features show a superior exploration performance in the first half of the episodes on the oven environment, on average. In the second half of the episodes the binary state features seem to be the better choice. It is also worth mentioning, that the random policy for the oven environment is not far apart from the leading curve. Ultimately, the total number of discovered states at the end of the experiments is most important to the overall task, which deems the binary features the best performing representation for the oven environment. Figure 4b shows a more distinct separation of the DQN-based approaches against the random agent for buttongrid. Here, the potential features (variant 2) show the best performance on average. For example, 30 unique states

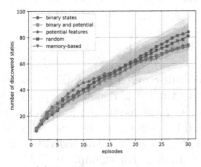
(a) Results oven environment

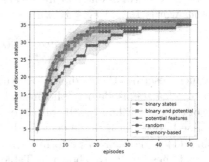
(b) Results buttongrid environment

Fig. 4. Results of the two experiments for oven and buttongrid environment. The graphs represent mean and standard deviation of the total number of discovered UI states over episodes for the different algorithmic variants.

Table 1. Results table of p-values for the oven environment with values rounded to third digit and bold entries for $p < 0.05$.

	binary	potential	bin&pot	memory	random
binary	–	0.078	**2.964e-09**	**5.792e-10**	**4.698e-05**
potential	0.922	–	**2.627e-06**	**7.559e-07**	0.201
bin&pot	1.0	1.0	–	**0.015**	0.998
memory	1.0	1.0	0.985	–	0.999
random	1.0	0.799	**0.002**	**0.001**	–

Table 2. Results table of p-values for the buttongrid environment with values rounded to third digit and bold entries for $p < 0.05$.

	binary	potential	bin&pot	memory	random
binary	–	1.0	0.869	1.0	**1.034e-42**
potential	**8.467e-17**	–	**3.075e-14**	**3.844e-08**	**4.248e-62**
bin&pot	0.131	1.0	–	1.0	**1.265e-37**
memory	**4.307e-09**	1.0	**0.000**	–	**2.190e-54**
random	1.0	1.0	1.0	1.0	–

are on average reached after about 12 episodes, whereas the random agent needs about 22 episodes to reach the same amount of discovered states.

To provide further insights, statistical tests were performed on the data visualized in the graphs before. In particular, Wilcoxon tests [3] were employed on the discovered number of unique states. Each pair of algorithmic variants are tested against each other (example for variant pair 1, 2). As a null hypothesis servers the criteria of one feature variant (2) outperforms the other variant (1). In other words $H_{0,12} : \tilde{x}_1 \leq \tilde{x}_2$ with

$$\tilde{x}_1 = \underset{\forall n_{run}, \forall n_{eps}}{med} \{|U_{1,n_{run}}(n_{eps}T_{eps})|\}, \tag{8}$$

which describes the median of the amount of discovered unique UI states at the end of each episode over all runs. The product $n_{eps}T_{eps}$ denotes the point in time of the end of the n_{eps}-th episode of one experiment, because T_{eps} represents the time budget for a single episode. If the null hypothesis can be rejected, one variant (1) is deemed to perform better than the other (2). The individual p-values of these tests are shown in Table 1 and Table 2. For example in Table 1, the value $4.698e^{-05}$ (first row, last column) represents the p-value of the null hypothesis $H_{0,15}$. The value indicates that the binary features (variant 1) are outperforming a random action selection approach (variant 5).

The statistics indicate, that the recommended features for the oven environment are binary state features. For this environment a random testing policy is only slightly worse. For the buttongrid environment, the potential features show the best performance among the variants and the second best variant is the memory-based approach, which also leads to the most discovered states on average at the end of the experiments.

Overall, the results from the experiments show a mixed picture. The choice of the features depends on the respective environment and need to be determined individually. The usefulness of potential features could be verified for buttongrid and partially for the oven environment. The binary states features led to overall better results on the oven environment with a random policy slightly worse. Depending on the time budget for testing, it can be beneficial to either use the potential features or the binary state features in the oven setup. However, the recommended representation are the binary state features due to the most significant results in Table 1 and the highest number of discovered states on average at the end of the oven experiment.

6   Conclusion

The presented work focuses on the automation of UI testing for graphical user interfaces. As a main contribution, Reinforcement learning-based monkey testing is brought to the area of consumer applications. Experiments on an oven home appliance indicate the applicability of monkey testing to this area. The number of discovered UI states can be increased by a careful selection of the state representation. For practical implementations, the binary state features showed the best explorational performance on the consumer user interface in the experiments.

Scientific Validation

This paper has benefited from the remarks of the following reviewers:

- Ali Ayadi, Strasbourg University, France
- Lina Soualmia, Normandie University, France
- Mathieu Bourgais, INSA Rouen, France

The conference organisers wish to thank them for their highly appreciated effort and contribution.

References

1. Adamo, D., Khan, M.K., Koppula, S., Bryce, R.: Reinforcement learning for android gui testing. In: Proceedings of the 9th ACM SIGSOFT International Workshop on Automating TEST Case Design, Selection, and Evaluation, pp. 2–8 (2018)
2. Agarap, A.F.: Deep learning using rectified linear units (relu). arXiv preprint arXiv:1803.08375 (2018)
3. Conover, W.: Practical nonparametric statistics. Wiley, New York (1971)
4. Fraser, G., Wotawa, F.: Redundancy Based Test-Suite Reduction. In: Dwyer, M.B., Lopes, A. (eds.) Fundamental Approaches to Software Engineering, pp. 291–305. Springer, Heidelberg (2007)
5. Gao, Y., Tao, C., Guo, H., Gao, J.: A deep reinforcement learning-based approach for android gui testing. In: Web and Big Data: 6th International Joint Conference, APWeb-WAIM 2022, Nanjing, China, November 25–27, 2022, Proceedings, Part III, pp. 262–276. Springer, Cham (2023). https://doi.org/10.1007/978-3-031-25201-3_20
6. Golberg, D.E.: Genetic algorithms in search, optimization, and machine learning. Addion wesley **1989**(102), 36 (1989)
7. Hourani, H., Hammad, A., Lafi, M.: The impact of artificial intelligence on software testing. In: 2019 IEEE Jordan International Joint Conference on Electrical Engineering and Information Technology (JEEIT), pp. 565–570. IEEE (2019)
8. Hsu, H.Y., Orso, A.: MINTS: a general framework and tool for supporting test-suite minimization. In: 2009 IEEE 31st International Conference on Software Engineering, pp. 419–429 (2009)
9. Huang, R., Sun, W., Xu, Y., Chen, H., Towey, D., Xia, X.: A survey on adaptive random testing. IEEE Trans. Software Eng. **47**(10), 2052–2083 (2019)
10. Khan, M.E., Khan, F.: A comparative study of white box, black box and grey box testing techniques. Int. J. Adv. Comput. Sci. Appl. **3**(6) (2012)
11. Kim, J., Kwon, M., Yoo, S.: Generating test input with deep reinforcement learning. In: 2018 IEEE/ACM 11th International Workshop on Search-Based Software Testing (SBST), pp. 51–58 (2018)
12. Kong, P., Li, L., Gao, J., Liu, K., Bissyandé, T.F., Klein, J.: Automated testing of android apps: a systematic literature review. IEEE Trans. Reliab. **68**(1), 45–66 (2019)
13. Lin, L.J.: Self-improving reactive agents based on reinforcement learning, planning and teaching. Mach. Learn. **8**(3), 293–321 (1992)

14. Mnih, V., Kavukcuoglu, K., Silver, D., Graves, A., Antonoglou, I., Wierstra, D., Riedmiller, M.: Playing atari with deep reinforcement learning. arXiv preprint arXiv:1312.5602 (2013)
15. Mnih, V., et al.: Human-level control through deep reinforcement learning. Nature **518**(7540), 529–533 (2015)
16. Moghadam, M.H., Saadatmand, M., Borg, M., Bohlin, M., Lisper, B.: Poster: performance testing driven by reinforcement learning. In: 2020 IEEE 13th International Conference on Software Testing, Validation and Verification (ICST), pp. 402–405 (2020)
17. Note Narciso, E., Delamaro, M., Nunes, F.: Test case selection: a systematic literature review. Int. J. Softw. Eng. Knowl. Eng.**24**, 653–676 (2014)
18. Patel, P., Srinivasan, G., Rahaman, S., Neamtiu, I.: On the effectiveness of random testing for android: or how i learned to stop worrying and love the monkey. In: Proceedings of the 13th International Workshop on Automation of Software Test, pp. 34–37 (2018)
19. Paydar, S.: Automated gui layout refactoring to improve monkey testing of android applications. In: 2020 CSI/CPSSI International Symposium on Real-Time and Embedded Systems and Technologies (RTEST), pp. 1–9. IEEE (2020)
20. Qt: Squish. https://www.qt.io/product/quality-assurance/squish (2003). Accessed 1 Dec 2022
21. Ramler, R., Buchgeher, G., Klammer, C.: Adapting automated test generation to gui testing of industry applications. Inf. Softw. Technol. **93**, 248–263 (2018)
22. Romdhana, A., Merlo, A., Ceccato, M., Tonella, P.: Deep reinforcement learning for black-box testing of android apps. ACM Trans. Softw. Eng. Methodol. (2022)
23. Rosenbauer, L., Stein, A., Pätzel, D., Hähner, J.: XCSF with experience replay for automatic test case prioritization. In: Abbass, H., Coello, C.A.C., Singh, H.K. (eds.) 2020 IEEE Symposium Series on Computational Intelligence (SSCI), virtual event, Canberra, Australia, 1–4 December 2020. IEEE (2020)
24. Saber, S., et al.: Autonomous gui testing using deep reinforcement learning. In: 2021 17th International Computer Engineering Conference (ICENCO), pp. 94–100 (2021)
25. Spieker, H., Gotlieb, A., Marijan, D., Mossige, M.: Reinforcement learning for automatic test case prioritization and selection in continuous integration. CoRR abs/1811.04122 (2018)
26. Sutton, R.S., Barto, A.G.: Reinforcement Learning: An Introduction. A Bradford Book, Cambridge, MA, USA (2018)
27. Vuong, T.A.T., Takada, S.: A reinforcement learning based approach to automated testing of android applications. In: Proceedings of the 9th ACM SIGSOFT International Workshop on Automating TEST Case Design, Selection, and Evaluation, pp. 31–37 (2018)
28. Wang, Z., Bovik, A., Sheikh, H., Simoncelli, E.: Image quality assessment: from error visibility to structural similarity. IEEE Trans. Image Process. **13**(4), 600–612 (2004)
29. Watkins, C.J., Dayan, P.: Q-learning. Mach. Learn. **8**(3), 279–292 (1992)
30. Wetzlmaier, T., Ramler, R., Putschögl, W.: A framework for monkey gui testing. In: 2016 IEEE International Conference on Software Testing, Verification and Validation (ICST), pp. 416–423. IEEE (2016)
31. Yoo, S., Harman, M.: Regression testing minimization, selection and prioritization: a survey. Softw. Test. Verif. Reliab. **22**(2), 67–120 (2012)

32. Yu, Y., Jones, J.A., Harrold, M.J.: An empirical study of the effects of test-suite reduction on fault localization. In: Proceedings of the 30th International Conference on Software Engineering, ICSE 2008, pp. 201–210. Association for Computing Machinery, New York, NY, USA (2008)

33. Zheng, Y., et al.: Wuji: automatic online combat game testing using evolutionary deep reinforcement learning. In: 2019 34th IEEE/ACM International Conference on Automated Software Engineering (ASE), pp. 772–784 (2019)

New Siamese Neural Networks for Text Classification and Ontologies Alignment

Safaa Menad[(✉)], Wissame Laddada, Saïd Abdeddaïm, and Lina F. Soualmia

Univ. Rouen Normandie, LITIS UR4108, 76000 Rouen, France
{safaa.menad1,wissame.laddada,said.abdeddaim,soualfat}@univ-rouen.fr
https://www.litislab.fr/

Abstract. Integrating heterogeneous and complementary data in clinical decision support systems (e.g., electronic health records, drug databases, scientific articles, etc.) could improve the accuracy of these systems. Based on this finding, the PreDiBioOntoL (Predicting Clinical Diagnosis by combining BioMedical Ontologies and Language Models) project aims at developing a computer-aided clinical and predictive diagnosis tool to help clinicians to better handle their patients. This tool will combine deep neural networks trained on heterogeneous data sources and biomedical ontologies. The first obtained results of PreDiBioOntoL are presented in this paper. We propose new siamese neural models (BioS-Transformers and BioS-MiniLM) that embed texts to be compared in a vector space and then find their similarities. The models optimize an objective self-supervised contrastive learning function on articles from the scientific literature (MEDLINE bibliographic database) associated with their MeSH (Medical Subject Headings) keywords. The obtained results on several benchmarks show that the proposed models can solve different biomedical tasks *without examples* (zero-shot). These results are comparable to those of other biomedical transformers that are fine-tuned on supervised data specific to the problems being addressed. Moreover, we show in this paper how these new siamese models are exploited in order to semantically map entities from several biomedical ontologies.

Keywords: Language Models · Transformers · Contrastive Learning · Siamese Neural Networks · Zero-shot Learning · Biomedical Texts · Biomedical Ontologies · Ontology Alignment

1 Introduction

Clinical decision support systems help clinicians in the diagnosis process. However, most of these systems are based on limited data, such as Electronic Health Records (EHRs) or drug databases, which can increase the risk of diagnosis errors. Between 2% and 5% of hospitalizations are due to drug-related iatrogenesis [2]. To improve the accuracy of these systems, integrating complementary and heterogeneous data, such as biomedical scientific literature and domain knowledge representations such as ontologies, may be useful. Based on these hypotheses, the project PreDiBioOntoL (Predicting Clinical Diagnosis by combining

P. Collet et al. (Eds.): CCE 2023, LNCS 13927, pp. 16–29, 2023.
https://doi.org/10.1007/978-3-031-44355-8_2

BioMedical Ontologies and Language Models) aims at developing a computer-aided clinical and predictive diagnosis tool and platform founded on Artificial Intelligence in order to help clinicians from University Hospitals to better handle their patients. The diagnostic tool will combine machine learning, deep neural networks trained on heterogeneous data sources, such as medical databases, scientific literature, and real life data, but also biomedical ontologies, and semantic web technologies. In this paper we detail the already obtained results, mainly the development of new siamese neural [4] models and their exploitation in the context of aligning heterogeneous biomedical ontologies. These alignments will enable us to achieve good interoperability within the system that predicts a diagnosis and proposes a potential drug for a given disease.

Ontology alignment plays a critical role in knowledge integration. It aims at matching semantically related entities from different ontologies. Real-world ontologies often contain a large number of classes, which not only causes scalability issues, but also makes it harder to distinguish classes with similar names and/or contexts but representing different objects. Usual ontology alignment solutions typically use lexical matching as their basis and combine it with structural matching and logic-based mapping repair. Recently, machine learning has been proposed as an alternative way for lexical and structural matching. For example, DeepAlignment [16] relies on word embeddings to represent classes and compute two classes' similarity according to their word vectors' Euclidean distance. Nevertheless, these methods adopt traditional non-contextual word embedding models such as Word2Vec. Pre-trained transformer-based language representation models such as BERT [7] can learn robust contextual text embeddings, and usually require only moderate training resources for fine-tuning. Although these models perform well in many Natural Language Processing (NLP) tasks, and are effective at predicting semantic similarity between sentence pairs [22], they have not yet been sufficiently investigated in ontology alignment task and concept mapping.

The abundance of available biomedical data, such as scientific articles, has also made it possible to train these models on corpora for biomedical applications [1,17,18]. However, these language models require fine-tuning on precise and rarely available supervised data for each task, which strongly limits their use in practice. Since most biomedical NLP tasks (e.g., relation extraction, document classification, question answering) can be reduced to the computing of a semantic similarity measure between two texts (e.g., category/article summary, query/results, question/answer), we propose here to build a new pre-trained Siamese model that embeds pairs of semantically related texts in the same vector representation space, and then it measures the similarity between them. These models can be applied in the ontology alignment task to measure the similarity between concepts.

In this paper, we also bring transformers to the ontology alignment task by (i) detailing our models BioSTransformers and BioS-MiniLM capable of solving several NLP tasks without examples (zero shot); (ii) showing experimentally on several biomedical benchmarks that without fine-tuning for a specific task, comparable results with biomedical transformers fine-tuned on supervised data can be obtained; and (iii) presenting how these models could be used in order to semantically map entities from different biomedical ontologies.

2   Related Work

Several domain and application ontologies are used for the same purpose. However, redundancy and missing links between concepts from different ontologies may occur due to the heterogeneity of ontology modeling. In the literature, ontology alignment is proposed to overcome this heterogeneity and allows semantic interoperability.

2.1   Ontology Alignment and Semantic System

Considering an application, ontology alignment can be defined as a semantic enhancement between concepts, roles, and instances from several ontologies. In [33], the authors defined a distributed system as a system interconnecting two ontologies. Considering this definition, three semantics of a distributed system are specified: simple distributed semantics where knowledge representation is interpreted in one domain; integrated distributed semantics where each local knowledge representation is interpreted in its own domain; and contextualized distributed semantics where there is no global domain of interpretation. In this paper, since we mapped two ontologies from a single domain (biomedical ontologies) by means of pre-trained transformers, we consider simple distributed semantics.

2.2   Matching System and Background Knowledge for Alignments

Ontology alignment results from an important task known as the Ontology Matching (OM) where a matcher is developed to identify similarities between ontologies. With regards to the classification of matching systems presented in [28], a matcher can be based on terminological (e.g. labels, comments, attributes, etc.), structural (ontology description), extensional (instances), or semantics (interpretation and logic reasoning) similarities. Moreover, because of the low level of semantic expressiveness of some ontologies, external resources can be exploited in the matching approaches. It was for example the case in the study [19] when they align the SNOMED CT with BioTopLite2 an upper level ontology.

Considering OM, an extensive survey is presented in [26] to describe this external background knowledge and its usage. Furthermore, the authors distinguish four categories of matching approaches using background knowledge: factual queries, where the data stored in the background knowledge is simply requested; structure-based approaches, where structural elements in the background knowledge are exploited; statistical/neural approaches (Fine-TOM [12], DAEOM [32]), where statistics or deep learning are applied on the background knowledge; and logic-based approaches where reasoning is employed with the external resource. For example, in [5] terminological, structural with background knowledge based on statistical strategies were employed to map biomedical ontologies. Like with CIDER-LM [29], our matching system depends on terminological similarities with a neural approaches to propagate a contextual similarity between elements (properties and classes) from two biomedical ontologies. The difference between the two approaches occurs in the embedding model used. In [29], they used the S-BERT [27] model, which is a generalist model trained on large corpus from Wikipedia. Whereas, in our work we apply the BioSTransformers models that we have proposed. These models are trained on our specific unsupervised biomedical data that we have prepared enabling us to achieve semantic similarity within the context of biomedical text.

3   Transformers

In this section, we provide some definitions to clarify our approach, which entails aligning ontologies using sentence transformers.

Transformers are neural networks based on the multi-head self-attention mechanism that significantly improves the efficiency of training large models. They consist of an encoder that transforms the input text into a vector and a decoder that transforms this vector into output text. The attention mechanism performs better in these models by modeling the links between the input and output elements. A pre-trained language model (PLM) is a neural network trained on a large amount of unannotated data in an unsupervised way. The model is then transferred to a target NLP task (downstream task), where a smaller task-specific annotated dataset is used to fine-tune the PLM and to build the final model capable of performing the target task. The process is called fine-tuning a PLM.

3.1   Pre-trained Language Models

Pre-trained language models such as BERT [7] have led to impressive gains in many NLP tasks. Existing work generally focuses on general data. In the biomedical domain, pre-training on PubMed texts leads to better performance in biomedical NLP tasks [3,17,24]. The standard approach to pre-training a biomedical model starts with a generalized model and continues the pre-training using a biomedical corpus. For this purpose, BioBERT [17] uses abstracts retrieved from PubMed and full-text articles from PubMed Central (PMC). BlueBERT [25] uses both PubMed text and MIMIC-III (Medical Information Mart for Intensive Care) clinical notes [14]. SciBERT [3] is an exception; the pre-training is done from scratch, using the scientific literature.

3.2   Siamese Models

Sentence transformers have been developed to calculate a similarity score between two sentences. They are models that use transformers for tasks related to sentence pairs: semantic computing similarity between sentences, information retrieval, sentence reformulation, etc. These transformers are based on two architectures: cross-encoders that process the concatenation of the pair, and bi-encoders siamese models that encode each pair element in a vector. Sentence-BERT [27] is a BERT-based bi-encoder for generating semantically meaningful sentence embeddings that are used in textual similarity comparisons. For each input, the model produces a fixed-size vector (u and v). The objective function is chosen so that the angle between the two vectors u and v is smaller when the inputs are similar. The objective function uses the cosine of the angle: $cos(u, v) = \frac{u.v}{|u|||v||}$, if $cos(u, v) = 1$, the sentences are similar and if $cos(u, v) = 0$, the sentences have no semantic link.

Other sentence transformers models have been developed [6, 9, 30], among them, MiniLM-L6-v25[1] is a bi-encoder based on a simplified version of Mini-LM [31]. This fast and small model has performed well on different tasks for 56 corpora [20].

4   Proposed Models: BioStransformers and BioS-MiniLM

In this section, we provide a detailed description of our proposed models that constitute a fundamental contribution to the architecture of our project as shown in Fig. 1.

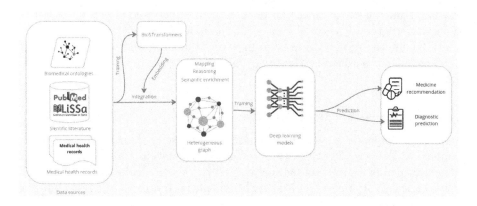

Fig. 1. The overall architecture of PreDiBioOntol.

Siamese transformers perform well in the general domain, but not in specialized ones (such as the biomedical). Here we propose new siamese models pretrained on the PubMed corpus. Siamese transformers were originally designed to transform (similarly sized) sentences into vectors. In our approach, we propose to transform MeSH terms, titles, and abstracts of PubMed articles in the same

---

[1] https://huggingface.co/sentence-transformers/all-MiniLM-L6-v2

vector space by training a siamese transformer model on these data. We want to ensure a match space between the short text and the long text in this vector. Therefore, we trained our models with pairs of inputs (title, MeSH term) and (abstract, MeSH term). Based on these data, we have built two models: the first one is our Siamese transformer (BioSTransformers) built based on a transformer pre-trained on biomedical data, and the second one is a siamese transformer already pre-trained on generalized data (BioS-MiniLM).

BioSTransformers. To build BioSTransformers, we were inspired by the Sentence-BERT [27] model by replacing BERT by other transformers. We used transformers that have been trained on biomedical data (bio-transformers) to create siamese transformers by adding a pooling layer and changing the objective function. The pooling layer computes the average vector of the transformer's output vectors (token embeddings). The two input texts pass successively through the transformer producing two vectors u and v at the output of the pooling layer, which are then used by the objective function. We selected the best performing bio-transformers models after the initial tests we have done: BlueBERT [25], PubMed BERT [10], BioELECTRA [15] and BioClinicalBERT [1]. These models were trained on PubMed except for BlueBERT and BioClinicalBERT, which were also trained on clinical notes.

Table 1. The biomedical transformer models used to create BioSTransformers.

Model name	Size	Datasets
BlueBERT	441 MB	PubMed abstracts and clinical notes
BioELECTRA	438 MB	PubMed and PubMedCentral full texts
PubMedBERT	440 MB	PubMed and PubMedCentral full texts
BioClinicalBERT	436 MB	BioBERT trained on clinical notes

BioS-MiniLM. In this model, we used a siamese transformer pre-trained on general data and then trained it on our data. Several general sentence-transformer models already pre-trained are available. They differ in size, speed, and performance. In those which obtained the best performances, we used MiniLM-L6-v2 (see Sect. 3) which has been pre-trained on 32 general corpora (Reddit comments, S2ORC, WikiAnswers, etc.).

Objective function. In a sentence transformer, supervised data are represented by triplets (sentence 1, sentence 2, similarity score between the two sentences). In our case, since we do not have any score for abstracts nor titles and their corresponding MeSH terms, we consider that:

- an abstract, a title, and the MeSH terms associated with the same article (identified by a PMID) are similar, and the score is equal to 1;
- an abstract (or a title) with MeSH terms not associated with the same article are not similar, and the score is therefore equal to 0.

We use a self-supervised contrastive learning objective function based on the Multiple Negative Ranking Loss (MNRL) function in the Sentence-Transformers package[2]. The MNRL only needs positive pairs as input (the title (or abstract) and a MeSH term associated with the article in our case). For a positive pair (title_i or abstract_i, MeSH_i), MNRL considers that each pair (title_i or abstract_i, MeSH_j) with $i \neq j$ in the same batch is negative. Since an article can be associated with several MeSH terms, we ensured in the batch generation that an abstract (or title) associated with a MeSH term in PubMed is never taken as a negative pair.

5   Models Evaluation by NLP Tasks

5.1   Experiments

At first, to quickly test the different transformers and the objective function to choose, we used only titles and reduced the number of MeSH terms. We selected 1,402 MeSH terms and 3.79 million pairs (title, MeSH) and used 18,940 articles with their titles and MeSH terms for validation.

In the second step, once we selected the transformer models and the MNRL objective function, we evaluated our BioSTransformers and BioS-MiniLM models on the (title, MeSH) and (abstract, MeSH) pairs generated from all MeSH terms used in PubMed. Since we realized that using all pairs from the 35 million articles in PubMed is unnecessary for improving the results in term of F1 score, we used only 6.75 million pairs for fine-tuning. A total of 18,557 articles were used for validation.

The two NLP tasks and the data used are described below:

1. Document classification: the Hallmarks of Cancer (HoC) corpus consists of 1,852 abstracts of PubMed publications manually annotated by experts according to a taxonomy composed of 37 classes. Each sentence in the corpus is assigned zero to several classes [11];
2. Question answering (QA):
   (a) PubMedQA: a corpus for Question answering specific to biomedical research. It contains a set of questions and an annotated field indicating whether the text contains the answer to the research question [13];
   (b) BioASQ: a corpus that contains several QA tasks with expert annotated data, including yes/no, list, and summary questions. We focused on the "yes/no" question type (task 7b) [21].

We consider the two tasks (document classification and question answering) as a text similarity problem in order to retrieve the closest results for each query. We consider the k closest results for each query, where k is the number of results attributed to the query by the expert. The similarity between the query and the results is measured by the cosine similarity between the query vector and the

---

[2] https://www.sbert.net/docs/package_reference/losses.html# multiplenegativesrankingloss.

result vectors. In a classification task, the query is the category, and the results are the documents classified in that category. In a question answering task, the query is the question, and the results are an answer.

5.2   Results

We evaluated our models according to the F1 score used in the benchmarks HoC [11], PubmedQA [13], and BioASQ [21] in [10]. The results obtained by our siamese transformers models without example (without fine-tuning) are given in Table 2.

Table 2. Evaluation results (F1 score) of our models on different benchmarks.

Corpora/Model	BioS-MiniLM	S-Bio ELECTRA	S-PubMed BERT	S-Blue BERT	S-BioClinical BERT
HoC	0.492	**0.499**	0.489	0.468	0.457
PubMedQA	0.649	0.675	**0.729**	0.652	0.652
BioASQ	0.747	0.694	**0.751**	0.713	0.714

Table 3 shows the results obtained on the same tasks by models that are explicitly fine-tuned to these tasks [10]. These models are fine-tuned for each benchmark with the supervised data available in each case. These results show that the proposed models can solve these tasks in a comparable way to biomedical models fine-tuned on supervised data specific to the addressed problems that we did not use in our zero shot approach.

Table 3. Evaluation results (F1 score) of the models fine-tuned specifically for these tasks on different benchmarks [10].

Corpora/ Model	BERT +fine-tuning	RoBERTa +fine-tuning	BioBERT +fine-tuning	SciBERT +fine-tuning	ClinicalBERT +fine-tuning	BlueBERT +fine-tuning	PubMedBERT +fine-tuning
HoC	0.802	0.797	0.820	0.812	0.808	0.805	**0.823**
PubmedQA	0.516	0.528	**0.602**	0.574	0.491	0.484	0.558
BioASQ	0.744	0.752	0.841	0.789	0.685	0.687	**0.876**

For the HoC benchmark, the results obtained by our best S-BioELECTRA model are far below the results obtained by PubMedBERT+fine-tuning (0.499 vs. 0.823). This may be explained by the fact that the models in [10] were fine-tuned specifically for each task, including document classification, by modifying the model architecture and adding specific layers for each case.

On the other hand, for the PubMedQA benchmark, the results obtained by our best S-PubMedBERT model are better than those obtained by BioBERT+fine-tuning (0.729 vs. 0.602). Finally, for the BioASQ benchmark, the results obtained by our best S-PubMedBERT model are comparable to the results obtained by the fine-tuned models, even though PubMedBERT+fine-tuning gives better results (0.751 vs. 0.876). All this done without re-adapting the architecture of our models for each task and without fine-tuning them on the specific data of the mentioned benchmarks.

6 Ontology Alignment

In the previous section, we demonstrated that our models achieved good results for document classification and QA. Therefore, our models perform well in semantic similarity comparison and can be applied to ontology alignment.

To better understand our use case, which illustrates an ontology alignment considering a biomedical domain of interest, we present in this section, some definitions inspired from [8,23,26]. Although, we adapt these definitions to our purpose. Figure 2 summarizes the process of an ontology matching following the definitions presented in this section.

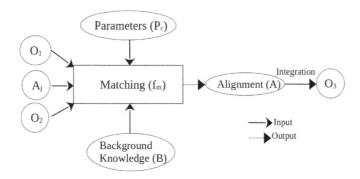

Fig. 2. The matching process of ontologies (inspired from [28]).

Ontology definition: an ontology O_i is a set of vocabularies (eg. Drugs, Disease, Chemical Entities, etc.) defined by means of taxonomies to describe a given domain of interest. A vocabulary is considered as a set of elements $e_i = < C_i, R_i, I_i >$; with C_i being the set of concepts, R_i aggregates relations to connect concepts, and I_i gathers the set of instances to interpret concepts and relate them with R_i. Thus, each element gathers Concepts, Relation, and instances. An ontology O_i is also semantically enriched with X_i to define axioms that formalize concepts based on logic languages such as Description Logics or First Order Logic.

Ontology alignment and OM: an alignment describes the correspondence between two ontologies. Formally, given two ontologies O_1 and O_2, we limit the definition of an alignment A to a set of triples. Each triple is specified by the terminology of the binary relation $r(e_1, e_2)$; where r depicts the relation between the two elements $e_1 \in O_1$ and $e_2 \in O_2$. Accordingly, the OM is the process of finding these sets of correspondence. For instance, if the concept *Mother* $\in O_1$ and the concept *Parent* $\in O_2$ then an alignment may be applied between the two elements *Mother* and *Parent* through the relation of inclusion $r = \sqsubseteq$ i.e. *Mother* $\sqsubseteq$ *Parent*. A confidence score c may also be added to the correspondence triple to check the similarity between e_1 and e_2 (e.g. the value of $c \in [0,1]$).

Matching system: it may be defined as a matcher function having several parameters to compute the similarity between entities. Let $F_m(O_1, O_2, A_j, P_c, B)$ with P_c as a parameter that holds the confidence value of similarity and B the set of external resources background knowledge) used to find (or not) an alignment A_j between the element e_1 and e_2.

Ontology integration: following the work presented in [23], we define an ontology integration as a semantic enhancement of a target ontology O_1 using elements from a source ontology O_2. The result may be seen as a new ontology O_3 developed through the alignment $A = < r_j, e_{1,j}, e_{2,j}, c_j >$. Wich means that the alignment is expressed by the relation r_j between the two elements $e_{1,j}$ and $e_{2,j}$ via the concept c_j (semantically the same).

7   Ontology Alignment with BioSTransformers

In this section, we describe our approach to map elements from different biomedical ontologies using our siamese models. Thus the latter is a core system of the matching process. Given that transformer models function as language models, it is mandatory that the elements within the ontology gather labels (or comments) enriched through relations (properties). We consider the matching process as a similarity problem where our model receives elements (concepts and relations) retrieved from the ontologies as inputs, and computes the similarity between them. Based on the output score, we decide if the element corresponds to the other or not.

Our use case is the mapping of elements from two biomedical ontologies: DOID (Human Disease Ontology[3]) and DrOn (Drug Ontology[4]) to propose an ontology integration in which each disease gathers a list of potential drugs. We followed the steps according to [23].

7.1   The Pre-processing Phase

Since we used the DOID and the DrOn ontology, we retrieved textual data from both of them using SPARQL queries. Thus, we extracted: (*i*) classes as elements from DOID that defined a disease (Disease names space[5]) and (*ii*) metadata of Chemical Entities of Biological Interest (ChEBI) in which medicines are mainly composed from DrOn. These metadata describe information about a disease through a comment property definition (Meta Data of ChEBI[6]). However, there

---

[3]   https://bioportal.bioontology.org/ontologies/DOID.
[4]   https://bioportal.bioontology.org/ontologies/DRON.
[5]   http://purl.obolibrary.org/obo/.
[6]   http://purl.obolibrary.org/obo/IAO_0000115.

is no existing association between DOID and DrOn ontologies. We were able to extract a sum of 13,678 diseases and 3,295 metadata.

7.2   The Matching Phase

The BioSTransformers model is exploited as a matching function where the background knowledge represents the data on which the model is trained: PubMed first and then on MIMIC III (a database containing patients' electronic health records). For this step, we chose the SBio_ClinicalBERT model. Compared to others, this model obtains good results for labels comparison. This is due to the fact that this model is trained on all notes from MIMIC III.

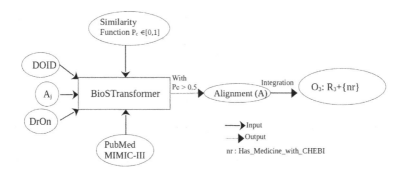

Fig. 3. The matching process of DOID and DrOn using BioSTransformers.

7.3   The Merging Phase

The generated alignments are one-to-one mappings between a single element from DOID and a single element from DrOn. The type of the correspondence is an *inclusion* ($\sqsubseteq$) between the metadata that defines a ChEBI class and a disease concept. This alignment is held when the confidence score (the similarity score) is greater than the threshold 0.5. If an alignment exists, then a new relation is defined between the disease class and the ChEBI concept. This new relation forms a third merging ontology in which both DrOn and DOID are defined. We label this relation as *Has_Medicine_with_CHEBI*. Figure 3 illustrates how BioSTransformers are used in ontology alignment task. We obtain very encouraging results when using it to find a similarity. For instance, in DrOn, the *"CHEBI_27779"* that composes the drug named *"Griseofulvin"* is defined by the metadata *"An oxaspiro compound produced by Penicillium griseofulvum. It is used by mouth as an antifungal drug for infections involving the scalp, hair, nails and skin that do not respond to topical treatment"*. In DOID the disease *"DOID_3136"* is defined by *"scalp dermatosis"*. The matching process gives a similarity score of 0.561. Since the confidence score is greater than 0.5 we create a new relation *"Has_Medicine_with_CHEBI(DOID_3136, CHEBI_27779)"*. All the new relations may be fetched through a simple SPARQL Query. We were able to generate 615 alignments with a confidence score greater than 0.5.

The next step to validate the alignments will be to use structural methods based on the existing concept hierarchies in each of the two ontologies used. Another possible approach is to use the UMLS (Unified Medical Language System) Metathesaurus[7] as an evaluation resource. By searching for the corresponding drug of each disease in the UMLS using its CUI (Concept Unique Identifier) and the UMLS API[8], one can retrieve the treatment of the disease using the semantic relation *may_be_treated_by*. Subsequently, the comparison of the drug recommended by our model with the drug mentioned in the UMLS is straightforward.

8 Conclusion

This paper outlines the PreDiBioOntoL project, which seeks to advance the development of a computer-aided tool for clinical and predictive diagnosis that can assist clinicians in enhancing patient care. The project integrates deep neural networks trained on heterogeneous data sources and biomedical ontologies. As a first step, we have proposed new siamese models BioSTransformers and BioS-MiniLM that can solve several biomedical tasks without example (zero shot). These models embed text pairs in the same representation space and compute the semantic similarity between texts of different lengths. Then, we have evaluated our models on several biomedical benchmarks and showed that without fine-tuning for a specific task, we obtain results comparable to biomedical transformers fine-tuned on supervised data specific to the tasks addressed. Subsequently, we proposed to exploit our models in a practical scenario that entailed the mapping of entities from two distinct biomedical ontologies in order to establish new relationships. The approach was instanced between DOID and DrOn, with the aim of proposing a candidate drug for a given ailment. A further evaluation of the obtained alignments is in progress and the integration of other ontologies (e.g., adverse drug events) is planned.

Scientific Validation

This paper has benefited from the remarks of the following reviewers:

- Valentina Dragos, Office National d'Etudes et de Recherches Aérospatiales, France
- Samer El Zant, Strasbourg University, France
- Franco Giustozzi, INSA Strasbourg -ICube laborator, France

The conference organisers wish to thank them for their highly appreciated effort and contribution.

---

[7] https://www.nlm.nih.gov/research/umls/index.html.
[8] https://uts-ws.nlm.nih.gov/rest/content/current/CUI/code/relations?includeAdditionalRelationLabels=may_be_treated_by&apiKey.

References

1. Alsentzer, E., et al.: Publicly available clinical BERT embeddings. In: Proceedings of the 2nd Clinical Natural Language Processing Workshop, pp. 72–78. Association for Computational Linguistics, Minneapolis, Minnesota, USA (2019)
2. Ayalew, M.B., Tegegn, H.G., Abdela, O.A.: Drug related hospital admissions; a systematic review of the recent literatures. Bull. Emerg. Trauma **7**(4), 339 (2019)
3. Beltagy, I., Lo, K., Cohan, A.: SciBERT: a pretrained language model for scientific text. In: Proceedings of the 2019 Conference on Empirical Methods in Natural Language Processing and the 9th International Joint Conference on Natural Language Processing (EMNLP-IJCNLP), pp. 3615–3620 (2019)
4. Chicco, D.: Siamese neural networks: an overview. In: Artificial Neural Networks, pp. 73–94 (2021)
5. Chua, W.W.K., Jae Kim, J.: BOAT: automatic alignment of biomedical ontologies using term informativeness and candidate selection. J. Biomed. Inform. **45**(2), 337–349 (2012)
6. Cohan, A., Feldman, S., Beltagy, I., Downey, D., Weld, D.S.: Specter: Document-level representation learning using citation-informed transformers. In: Proceedings of the 58th Annual Meeting of the Association for Computational Linguistics, pp. 2270–2282 (2020)
7. Devlin, J., Chang, M.W., Lee, K., Toutanova, K.: BERT: pre-training of deep bidirectional transformers for language understanding. In: Proceedings of NAACL-HLT, pp. 4171–4186 (2019)
8. Euzenat, J., Shvaiko, P.: Ontology Matching. Springer, Heidelberg (2013). https://doi.org/10.1007/978-3-642-38721-0
9. Gao, T., Yao, X., Chen, D.: Simcse: simple contrastive learning of sentence embeddings. In: Proceedings of the 2021 Conference on Empirical Methods in Natural Language Processing, pp. 6894–6910 (2021)
10. Gu, Y., et al.: Domain-specific language model pretraining for biomedical natural language processing. ACM Trans. Comput. Healthc. **3**(1), 1–23 (2022)
11. Hanahan, D., Weinberg, R.A.: The hallmarks of cancer. Cell **100**(1), 57–70 (2000)
12. Hertling, S., Portisch, J., Paulheim, H.: Matching with transformers in melt (2021)
13. Jin, Q., Dhingra, B., Liu, Z., Cohen, W., Lu, X.: PubMedQA: a dataset for biomedical research question answering. In: Proceedings of (EMNLP-IJCNLP), pp. 2567–2577 (2019)
14. Johnson, A.E., et al.: MIMIC-III, a freely accessible critical care database. Sci. Data **3**(1), 1–9 (2016)
15. Kanakarajan, K.r., Kundumani, B., Sankarasubbu, M.: BioELECTRA: pretrained biomedical text encoder using discriminators. In: Proceedings of the 20th Workshop on Biomedical Language Processing, pp. 143–154. Association for Computational Linguistics, Online (2021)
16. Kolyvakis, P., Kalousis, A., Kiritsis, D.: DeepAlignment: unsupervised ontology matching with refined word vectors. In: Proceedings of NAACL-HLT, 787–798, pp. 787–798 (2018)
17. Lee, J., et al.: BioBERT: a pre-trained biomedical language representation model for biomedical text mining. Bioinformatics **36**(4), 1234–1240 (2020)
18. Liu, F., Shareghi, E., Meng, Z., Basaldella, M., Collier, N.: Self-alignment pre-training for biomedical entity representations. In: Proceedings of NAACL-HLT, pp. 4228–4238 (2021)

19. Mary, M., Soualmia, L., Gansel, X., Darmoni, S., Karlsson, D., Schulz, S.: Onto-logical representation of laboratory test observables: challenges and perspectives in the snomed CT observable entity model adoption, pp. 14–23 (2017)
20. Muennighoff, N., Tazi, N., Magne, L., Reimers, N.: MTEB: massive text embedding benchmark. arXiv preprint arXiv:2210.07316 (2022)
21. Nentidis, A., Bougiatiotis, K., Krithara, A., Paliouras, G.: Results of the seventh edition of the BioASQ challenge. In: Cellier, P., Driessens, K. (eds.) ECML PKDD 2019. CCIS, vol. 1168, pp. 553–568. Springer, Cham (2020). https://doi.org/10.1007/978-3-030-43887-6_51
22. Ormerod, M., Martínez del Rincón, J., Devereux, B.: Predicting semantic sim-ilarity between clinical sentence pairs using transformer models: evaluation and representational analysis. JMIR Med. Inform. 9(5), e23099 (2021)
23. Osman, I., Ben Yahia, S., Diallo, G.: Ontology integration: approaches and chal-lenging issues. Inf. Fusion 71, 38–63 (2021)
24. Peng, Y., Yan, S., Lu, Z.: Transfer learning in biomedical natural language pro-cessing: an evaluation of BERT and ELMo on ten benchmarking datasets. In: Proceedings of the 18th BioNLP Workshop and Shared Task, pp. 58–65 (2019)
25. Peng, Y., Yan, S., Lu, Z.: Transfer learning in biomedical natural language pro-cessing: an evaluation of BERT and ELMo on ten benchmarking datasets. In: Pro-ceedings of the 18th BioNLP Workshop and Shared Task, pp. 58–65. Association for Computational Linguistics, Florence, Italy (2019)
26. Portisch, J., Hladik, M., Paulheim, H.: Background knowledge in ontology match-ing: a survey. Semantic Web, pp. 1–55 (2022)
27. Reimers, N., Gurevych, I.: Sentence-BERT: sentence embeddings using Siamese BERT-networks. In: Proceedings of (EMNLP-IJCNLP), pp. 3982–3992. Associa-tion for Computational Linguistics, Hong Kong, China (2019)
28. Shvaiko, P., Euzenat, J.: Ontology matching: state of the art and future challenges. IEEE Trans. Knowl. Data Eng. 25, 158–176 (2013)
29. Vela, J., Gracia, J.: Cross-lingual ontology matching with CIDER-LM: results for OAEI 2022 (2022)
30. Wang, K., Reimers, N., Gurevych, I.: TSDAE: using transformer-based sequential denoising auto-encoderfor unsupervised sentence embedding learning. In: Find-ings of the Association for Computational Linguistics: EMNLP 2021, pp. 671–688 (2021)
31. Wang, W., Wei, F., Dong, L., Bao, H., Yang, N., Zhou, M.: MiniLM: deep self-attention distillation for task-agnostic compression of pre-trained transformers. Adv. Neural. Inf. Process. Syst. 33, 5776–5788 (2020)
32. Wu, J., Lv, J., Guo, H., Ma, S.: DAEOM: a deep attentional embedding approach for biomedical ontology matching. Appl. Sci. 10(21) (2020)
33. Zimmermann, A., Euzenat, J.: Three semantics for distributed systems and their relations with alignment composition. In: Cruz, I., et al. (eds.) ISWC 2006. LNCS, vol. 4273, pp. 16–29. Springer, Heidelberg (2006). https://doi.org/10.1007/11926078_2

Theorizing, Modeling and Visualizing Business Ecosystems. What Should Be Done?

Eddie Soulier[1]([⊠]), Didier Calcei[2], Maxime Guery[3,4],
and Tzolkin Garduno-Alvarado[1]

[1] Computer Science and Digital Society (LIST3N) laboratory, Université de
Technologie de Troyes, Troyes, France
{eddie.soulier,tzolkin.garduno_alvarado}@utt.fr
[2] ISG International Business School, Paris, France
didier.calcei@isg.fr
[3] CReSTIC, Reims, France
[4] R&D, Data Nostra, Paris, France
mguery@datanostra.ai

Abstract. Ecosystems are nowadays a dominant organizational form in
the digital age. But this construct lacks consensus on its empirical scope,
its key theoretical features and its theoretical roots. The paper proposes
an integrative framework as well as a method and a tool for calculating
an ecosystem based on simplicial complexes and the HYPE platform.
It concludes that a data-driven and visualization approach is needed to
the study of the dynamic, emergent and adaptive dimensions of today's
platform-based ecosystems.

Keywords: Business ecosystems · Simplicial complex · Q-Analysis ·
Modularity · Complementarity · Platforms

1 Introduction

Ecosystems are nowadays considered in economics, management sciences or computer science disciplines as a dominant organizational form in the digital age. The number of conferences and articles devoted to them is considerable and growing. The concept of ecosystem in these fields originated in the mid-1990s with Moore, around the notion of "business ecosystems" [1].

Many researchers have noted that the main epistemological problem with the business ecosystem concept is its controversial reference to biology and ultimately its metaphorical nature. Yet work on ecosystem definitions and typology has led to a "conceptual proliferation" of the notion and a lack of consensus on the scope of the concept [2–5]. Among many others [5] states that "This

---

D. Calcei, M. Guery and T. Garduno-Alvarado—These authors contributed equally to this work.

© The Author(s), under exclusive license to Springer Nature Switzerland AG 2023
P. Collet et al. (Eds.): CCE 2023, LNCS 13927, pp. 30–46, 2023.
https://doi.org/10.1007/978-3-031-44355-8_3

conceptual and application heterogeneity has contributed to conceptual and terminological confusion, which threatens to undermine the utility of the concept in supporting cumulative insight." (p. 2).

2   Related Work

The study on business ecosystems can be represented from two main perspectives. The first is essentially the theory of business ecosystems in the fields of economics, management sciences or organizational theories, as illustrated in the recent reference article [7]. The article by [8] can be seen as a milestone in clarifying approaches to conceptualizing the ecosystem construct. It too notes the plethora of conceptions that hinders good scientific progress. To clarify the notion of ecosystem he contrasts two conceptions: "the ecosystem-as-affiliation" and "the ecosystem-as-structure". The former is mainly underpinned by explanations of the emergence, maintenance and evolution of ecosystems in terms of links, with the risk of confusing this construct with other related concepts (platforms, multi-sided markets, networks, supply chains, value networks, etc.) and above all of limiting the analysis of ecosystems to their relational and/or intentional aspect. On the other hand, conceptions of "ecosystems-as-structure" are underpinned by explanations in terms of activities (notably around the co-construction of value propositions between the actors in the ecosystem studied) rather than links, which imply much stronger structural constraints than affiliations.

Our work clearly falls within the second alternative. This is why we have mobilized work on complex systems, dependency matrices, production systems or capabilities. The second perspective is opposed to traditional management science approaches based on primary data collection methods, such as case studies or interviews, which have difficulty adapting and reframing their assumptions when it comes to understanding large, complex, dynamic and multifaceted ecosystems. A growing number of researchers have instead begun to use secondary data sources (and unstructured data) that are increasingly openly available in digital form such as press release, annual reports, news, blogs and webpages, public filings, and social media [9–12]. We are also part of this second alternative. While the first perspective refers to the conceptualization of what a business ecosystem is (links or activities), the second perspective refers to methodology (based on primary sources or real-time and data-oriented).

Our diagnosis is as follows: while the data-driven approach to ecosystems seems more relevant today than more traditional approaches based on the exploitation of primary data, the former will naturally tend to rely on a conception of the ecosystem as an affiliation (or network) rather than as a structure. Thus, placing the primitives of the ecosystem on nodes and links without intermediate constructs tends to favor the multiplication of analysis of mainly binary relationships between actors (or some of their attributes, such as products and services) and connections (licencing, joint ventures, patents, etc.) to the detriment of taking into account n-ary relationships that are more characteristic of the structure of an ecosystem.

The difficulty is then transferred to the analyst who must himself triangulate the insights obtained from the multiple data sources. This is particularly evident in the approach of [11]. In contrast, a data-driven approach to ecosystems, but from a perspective of ecosystems-as-structure, remains to be explored. This is precisely the objective of our paper.

3   Towards a Theory of Ecosystems

An approach to "ecosystems-as-structure" does not preclude the choice of particular primitives. Thus [8] proposes the following structural definition, where we can note the occurrence of notions whose properties are obviously difficult to qualify: "The alignment structure of the multilateral set of partners that need to interact in order for a focal value proposition to materialize" (p. 40). The structural properties here are alignment structure, multilateral (which means that ecosystem is a set of relationships that are not decomposable to an aggregation of bilateral interactions.), being a set (i.e., it is not open-ended) or the fact that the productive level of analysis of ecosystems is in the value proposition as it materializes (or more broadly the product and that the concern is with bringing about the activities required for its instantiation). Our own state of the art has convinced us that the most frequently cited analytical elements of focus in today's authoritative definitions, including [8], are modularity and complementarity. For example [7] defines the ecosystem as "A set of actors with varying degrees of multilateral, nongeneric complementarities that are not fully hierarchically controlled" (p. 2264) while [13] proposes the following definition: "A network of autonomous firms and individuals whose products or actions are complementary" (p. 7).

In the following subsections we propose to characterize more precisely the properties of modularity and complementarity. We will show that these two properties also allow us to establish a structural link between ecosystems and another very important distributed form of organization today, platforms.

3.1   Modularity

On the one hand, the theory of complex systems assimilates any system to a system whose hierarchical structure is quasi-decomposable, and endowed with specific properties and behavior. This opens up important possibilities for describing and understanding complexity and, more generally, for studying complex systems [14].

This theoretical basis has been widely taken up in the pioneering work of [15], as well as in Langlois' theory of modularity [16]. This conception of modularity takes up Simon's idea of loosely-coupling and the idea of decomposing the increasing complexity of a system (a product or an organization for example) in order to better control it [14]. A modular system includes explicit design rules (module architecture, interfaces between modules and interoperability standards) and hidden design parameters related to the tacit character of the design.

The development and partial generalization of the modular approach partly explains the development of new distributed forms of organizations including ecosystems (Sect. 1).

Modularity is not limited to the structure of the system (technological modularity) but also impacts the organization (organizational modularity) as well as the value (economic modularity).

[17] suggest that modularity can be in design, in product, in production, in organization and also in use. In more general terms, the potential for correspondence between product systems and organizational systems has come to be known as the 'mirroring hypothesis' [18]. The idea of "mirroring" suppose that organizational ties correspond to technical dependencies. And more broadly, alignment (or lack thereof) can be examined at two levels of analysis: intrafirm (technologies) and interfirm (boundaries choices) as well as the broader industry structure [19].

3.2 Complementarity

Another source of explanation for the development of ecosystems is the emergence of an economy of inter-firm co-operation, which can be found in particular in [20]. In accordance with Richardson, our general hypothesis concerning ecosystems is that every economic system implies a division of labor, which in turn implies coordination. The principle of the division of labor is not limited to coordination through the hierarchy (firm) or through the market, but relies as much on the dense network of cooperation and affiliation through which firms are interrelated. Business ecosystems are one form, among others, of this last coordination modality. It is also convenient to think of industry as carrying out a large number of activities (research, development, marketing, operation, etc.). And finally, it is stated that these activities have to be carried out by organizations with appropriate capabilities (knowledge, experience and skills).

[20] assumes that activities which require the same capability for their undertaking can be called similar activities. But the organization of industry has also to adapt itself to the fact that activities may be complementary. In particular, activities are complementary when they represent different phases of a process of production and require in some way to be coordinated. This coordination can be effected in three ways: by direction, by cooperation or through market transactions. And when the need to coordinate the production through particular activities, one can speak of closely complementary activities. It is then possible to summarize Richardson's model as follows (Fig. 1):

Nature of the capabilities	Complementary	Closely complementary
Similar	Undetermined	Direction
Dissimilar	Market transactions	Cooperation

Fig. 1. Toward a capabilities approach to economic organization (elaborated from [20]).

The conclusion to be drawn from the model for our purposes is that the prime reason for the existence of the complex networks of cooperation is based on the need to coordinate closely complementary but dissimilar activities. This coordination cannot be left entirely to direction (firm) because the activities are dissimilar, and cannot be left to market, because the activities concerned are closely complementary although distributed among several independent actors involved in different phases of a production process, and therefore require to be coordinated by different coordination mechanisms than the hierarchy or the market.

A considerable body of research has adopted this approach to coordination through capability, and in particular in relation to the ecosystem concept. Special mention should be made of the work of [21, 22].

Thus, many definitions of business ecosystems identify complementarities as the main mechanism explaining dependence between actors and as a source of ecosystem emergence.

3.3 Ecosystem Definitions and Relation to Platforms

Modularity and complementarity usually work together and contribute to increasing the mutual dependence between the actors, to the point where ecosystems emerge. But the action of these two forces is not limited to ecosystems. Business platforms also seem to be dependent on the mechanisms of modularity and complementarity. Whereas until now the two constructs have been the domain of separate research streams, it can be said that a growing number of researchers are articulating the two concepts. As [22] notes "Complementarity is the handmaiden of platforms, and platforms feed ecosystems". Put differently, an ecosystem without a platform is small, weak and fragmented. Conversely, a platform-based ecosystem is likely to be dominant [23]. Thus, platforms and ecosystems have emerged as new constructs to describe how economic actors interact as they seek to create and capture value [7].

Researchers in this field now tend to refer to a "platform-based ecosystem" to highlight the convergence of the two notions, around the generic mechanism of dependency. But the question remains: how to model the dependency generated by modularity strategies and the exploitation of complementarities within platform-based ecosystem?

4   Modeling and Analysis of Dependencies: Dependency Matrix, Simplicial Complexes and Hypergraphs

It is fortunate that some researchers specializing in design theory and the study of industrial evolution are also convinced that technology and products in industrial design can be assimilated to a complex system (and even as a complex adaptive system, with properties of aggregation, non-linearity, flows and diversity) [24], and therefore studied from this perspective. The concept of a system has thus become the cornerstone of the study of industrial organization and inter-firm cooperation. One way of studying these complex systems (not exclusive) is based, as we have seen, on the principle of decomposing a structure and analyzing the properties of dependence at several scales of organization. In this article, we propose to start from a tool dedicated to the analysis of the structure and interactions of the elements of a system, the Design Structure Matrix (DSM), also known as The Dependency Structure Matrix: it enables the user to model, visualize, and analyze the dependencies among the entities of any system [25]. We will then proceed with the method of simplicial complexes, which we will generalize to hypergraphs. Indeed, the matrix and the graph (or network) are the two main methods of representing a relational structure.

4.1 Dependency Matrix

The DSM is represented as a square N × N matrix (or N-Square or N2 diagram), mapping the interactions among the set of system elements. Generally, DSM convention start with inputs in rows and outputs in columns. Basic DSM can be extended including many attributes of the interactions like number or importance, impact, or strength, and using more numerical values, symbols or colors. Interactions between elements may be of various types depending on the nature of the system (spatial proximity, information flow, energy transfer, material flow and so on). DSM has been used to model many types of systems (product, process...).

DSM models can also be partitioned or rearranged using various analytical methods such as clustering and sequencing. Clustering algorithms aim to minimize the number or strength of interactions outside clusters, and to minimize the size of the clusters [26]. In doing so, they help to improve the modularity of systems. Baldwin and Clark used DSM to illustrate the nature of modularity in the design of complex engineering systems product architecture and discussed the benefit of modular architectures [15].

In summary a dependency matrix is used to model the dependencies between the elements of a system, i.e. its structure, and that structure (or architecture, in a design context) drives or causes the emergence of system attributes, functions, and behavior. Dependency matrix tools draws heavily on the thinking of Herbert Simons about the architecture of complexity and nearly-decomposable system [14].

4.2 Simplicial Complexes

However, as has been well demonstrated in great detail [10], if the identification of the presence/absence of a link and of sets and regions in the data is faster with a matrix due to its ordered structure compared to network representations using clustering algorithms, networks offer a better ability to traverse chains of links (i.e. connectivity/paths) as paths are naturally evident in networks, but not in matrices. The other strong argument is that according to usability tests with users [10], network representations are a better visualization method than matrices whatever the criterion considered (usefulness, usability, quickness, etc.).

Therefore, we propose a topological approach based on simplicial complexes, able to consider the multidimensionality of relations between the elements usually identified in a DSM: tasks, organizations, components or more abstracts parameters (see Sect. 6 below). It is completed with HYPE, a tool developed for the modeling of hypergraphs (a generalization of a graph, in which edges can connect any number of vertices) and the implementation of a Q-analysis algorithm, which allows to find links between elements and to analyze the structure of these links. Simplicial complexes allow studying n-ary relations among sets.

Specifically with regard to business ecosystems, the relationships could be, for example, between organizations (companies, partners, startups, venture capital firms, etc.) and capabilities (including knowledge, skills, and technologies) or between companies and products, projects, markets or competitors, or between companies and patents. Simplicial complexes allow studying n-ary relations among sets. For example, all members of a family share the same relationship that could BELONGS_TO. They enable the multidimensionality of relations among entities to be calculated and are used in many areas, such as social systems modeling, urban planning or decision making [27] or more recently Smart City [28].

The simplicial complex come from the algebraic topology field. A simplicial complex is composed of two sets, a set of vertices1 (X) and a subset (Y) of (X) called simplices and therefore be approached as a bipartite graph. A simplex is determined by an ordered set of vertices $\sigma = <v_0, v_1, ..., v_p>$ and it owns a geometrical representation.

The dimension p of a simplex is given by its number of vertices minus one and is written p-simplex. The simplicial complex K is written KY(X, R) where R is the relation between the sets Y and X. The opposite relation can also be analyzed, namely KX(Y, R-1), called the conjugate complex.

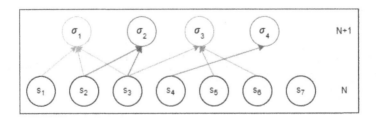

Fig. 2. A simplicial complex represented as a bipartite graph.

[27] developed a method to study the structural characteristics of simplicial complexes named Q-analysis. He also introduced the concepts of hierarchy and cover set. Hierarchy does not imply any meaning of superiority instead of levels of classification. Considering only two levels in the hierarchy, the (N+1)-level set acts as a cover of the set at the N-level. Elements of the (N+1)-level set are subsets of the N-level set. The Q-analysis consists in analyzing the structural connectivity of simplicial complexes for each dimension of the simplicial

complex (from zero to the highest dimension in the complex). This structural connectivity introduces the notion of q-nearness: two simplices are q-near if they share p vertices, with $q = p - 1$. For example, on Fig. 2, the simplices σ_1 and σ_2 shared two vertices (s_1 and s_2) so there are 1-near. Finally, one important measure that will be used is the structure vector Q which represents the number of components for each q-dimension of analysis. The simplicial complexes and q-analysis developed by Atkin were generalized by [29] and its hypernetwork object. A clarification of the hypernetwork term in the literature is given in [30].

4.3 Hypergraphs

The simplicial complexes and q-analysis developed by Atkin were generalized by [29] through the concept of hypernetwork. As [29] said: "A set of relational simplices is called a hypernetwork. When all the simplices have dimensions zero or one, a hypernetwork is a network. Thus hypernetworks are natural generalizations of networks. Hypernetworks are particularly useful for representing multilevel structure because n-ary relations provide a way of assembling a set of parts at one level into a whole at a higher level." A hypernetwork is defined as a hypergraph that is augmented by a weight for each hyper-relation. A hypernetwork H is then defined as a weighted hypergraph consisting of a set X of vertices, a set E of hyperrelations and a set W of weights such that H = (X; E; W) The weights represent the strength of the attachment of vertices within each hyperrelationship and allow the hyperlattice to represent a probabilistic model.

However, as we do not use this concept here for ecosystem modelling, but rather the concepts of simplicial complex, we propose not to retain the concept of hypernetwork but that of hypergraph.

In fact, a simplicial complex is already a hypergraph, but it has the specificity of favoring a geometrical or topological representation, whereas this is not the case for a hypergraph. Hence, the concept of hypergraph is more generic and common than those of simplicial complexes or hypernetworks. To conclude on this point, graphs (or networks), simplicial complexes, hypernetworks and hypergraphs, as long as they are considered within the framework of the analysis of complex socio-technical systems and its general relational formalism developed by [27,28] are equivalent, and their choice depends on the task at hand. To go further, you may wish to refer to [31] and the recent reference book on simplicial complexes [32]. We now hold several models for computing the dependency structure of any complex system, including the ecosystem as we have defined it.

5 HYPE, a Tool to Compute Simplicial Complexes and Hypergraphs

To perform calculations on simplices, an application named HYPE was co-conceived by the UTT LIST3N laboratory and ENGIE Lab CRIGEN CSAI (the Computer Science and Artificial Intelligence Laboratory) and developed by Data Nostra (https://datanostra.ai/). The main objective of Hype is to provide a model of the simplicial complexes and hypergraphs and analyze their structures and dynamics. The simplicial complexes are represented as a directed graph, where vertices and simplices are distinguished according to the direction of the arcs. Three versions were developed. The new version provides more structural metrics and introduces the notion of traffic that will not be developed here.

HYPE is composed of three parts: one giving an overview of the data and the possibility to edit it; one for structural analysis ("backcloth"); and one for the dynamic analysis ("traffic"). The fact of having a tool for calculating simplicial complexes (and/or hypergraphs, which is roughly the same) and for Q-Analysis is a major contribution. Indeed, our observation was precisely that to our knowledge there was no tool for computing this type of structure and dynamics. This is the reason why a 5-year development was funded to develop HYPE (For a fully developed use case application of HYPE on Smart City Strategy analysis, see [28]) (Fig. 3).

Fig. 3. Hype tool interface.

The first step consists in choosing the direction of the relationship we want to analyze before performing a Q-analysis. The algorithm used consists of three steps: (1) the dimensions are computed for each simplex; (2) the q-near relationships are computed for each simplex by counting the number of vertices in common; (3) for each q dimension and each simplex, the algorithm determines which simplices can be reached. Thus, each simplex has a set with its associated simplices, allowing the components (that is, groups of connected simplices at dimension q) to be found if there are disjoint sets.

The pseudo-code in HYPE for performing a Q-analysis on a graph is as follows:

```
ComputeDimension ( simplexes );
ComputeQnear ( simplexes );
dim_max = GetMaxDimension ( simplexes );
for d:=0 to dim_max do
begin
     Retrieve the q–graph where the simplexes have a
     dimension greater than or equal to i as well as
     the q–near relations having a q greater than or
     equal to i.

     Run the Weakly Connected Components (WCC)
     algorithm to retrieve the components at dimension i.
end;
```

The results of the Q-analysis are provided through a visualization of the components, the list of the components for a given q-dimension, and the structure vector—also represented with a chart line. The visualization is called a q-complex [29]. It shows the simplices existing at a given dimension q. There is a link between simplices if they are at least q-near. Vertices can be accessed by clicking on a simplex. This visualization allows a representation of the q-nearness of the simplicial complex and makes a graph easier to interpret. However, vertices are not visually represented, thus we miss some information-for example, if a simplex is a face of another or if there are holes in the structure.

6   Application: From Dependence Matrices to Hypergraphs

This section presents an example of the computation principles for a creation of synthetic business ecosystem using the tool HYPE.

The DSM (DSM), also known as the Dependency Structure Matrix, provides a representation of a complex system and a capture method for the interactions/interdependencies/interfaces between system elements (i.e. sub-systems and modules). Initially, because of the complexity of data collection and calculations of the dependency between the elements of a system, a dependency matrix was able to model and analyze dependencies of only one single type within one single domain. As an example, for a product, e.g. the domain "components" can be regarded. Dependency matrices were later extended to domain mapping matrices. The goal was to enable matrix methodology to include not just one domain at a time but to allow for the mapping between two domains. For example to shows how persons (domain one) can be mapped to the tasks (domain two) in a process. And finally, the matrices can then be used to model whole systems consisting of multiple domains, each having multiple elements, connected by various relationship types, called Multiple Domain Matrix (MDM). The types of dependencies most frequently identified in single or dual domain matrices can be classified according to whether the entity considered is rather static (such as organizations or components of a system) or dynamic (such as tasks or parameters, e.g. temporal).

However, the aim is to align these usual entities with those considered more suitable for the study of business ecosystems. As an example, [11] recommends very conveniently that at a high-level, ecosystem research is interested in the configuration of different types of entities (i.e., "nodes") and their connections (i.e., "links"). At the node level, the most common examples include companies, people, products and services, patents, and technologies. At the link level, researchers have examined a wide range of direct connections between entities, including interfirm (e.g., R&D, supply chain, marketing, licensing, technology transfer, joint ventures, and alliances), investments, acquisitions, or mergers.

In contrast, in a multi-domain dependency model these static and dynamic entities are considered to be related to each other. This is expressed in the notion of "relational multidimensionality", which HYPE seeks to simulate for the ecosystems use case (Fig. 4).

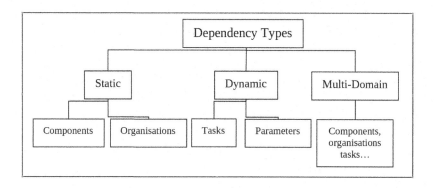

Fig. 4. Types of dependence matrix models (adapted from [26]).

These matrices are relevant for two main reasons: on the one hand they are used by certain researchers to characterize ecosystems, as in 's case for example; on the other hand the notion of "multi-domains" is very close in spirit to Atkin's work on the idea of levels of "entangled hierarchies", where at each level we have a mathematical set which acts as cover of a set below it, in the sense that this cover is not a partition in which the elements are disjoined. It is therefore possible to transform these dependency matrices into simplicial complexes and, by generalizing, into hypergraphs. The Q-analysis technique then allows us to analyze the different relationships between different elements between different successive levels (in the sense of cover and not of a partition). This overlap is expressed mathematically as a q-connectivity. The property of overlap (of organizations, activities, artefacts and so on) is then considered as an important structural property of any ecosystem.

In our project, we assume that an ecosystem links several types of inter-actions, which creates many areas of overlap (in activities, roles, resources, concepts, etc.) between the connected entities, as outlined in the multi-domain models. Tools such as DSMs can then be usefully complemented by methodologies more suited to exploring the combinatorics of large socio-technical systems, defined by a multi-dimensional geometry, in order to understand their behavior. This is where the simplicial complexes and Q-Analysis come in.

Simplicial complexes have been used to model n-ary relationships. In our case, we have several types of n-ary relations. For each type of interaction, a simplicial complex can therefore be created, as in the example below (Fig. 5).

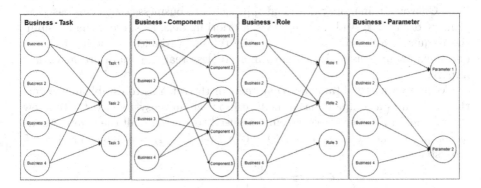

Fig. 5. The Multi-domain abstract simplicial complexes for ecosystem modeling.

However, we want to use all the interactions in the same simplicial complex to explore the combinatorics of any ecosystem. It is then necessary to adapt the way the simplicial complex is constructed to ensure that the simplexes of the simplicial complex represent the business ecosystems. The HYPE tool, which calculates a q-analysis from a simplicial complex, makes use of the fact that one can move from a simplicial complex to a bipartite graph in order to model n-ary relationships in a graph-oriented database. The advantage of considering a bipartite graph rather than a simplicial complex is mainly "technical": to the best of our knowledge there is no database system that allows to store n-ary relations, and therefore the use of a bipartite graph solves this specific but quite essential problem.

Our contribution is therefore to transform our simplicial complex into a bipartite graph. We then need three distinct sets: X, R and Y.

- The set X is composed of the firms.
- The set Y is composed of the elements necessary for the calculation of the objective function, in our case the targeted business ecosystems.
- The set R is composed of the different n-ary relations between the firms: TASK_1, TASK_2, TASK_3, COMPONENT_1, COMPONENT_2, COMPONENT_3, ROLE_1, ROLE_2, ROLE_3, PARAMETER_1, PARAMETER_2, PARAMETER_3, etc.

The fact that a company participates in TASK_1 in the simplicial starting complex will become a full-fledged relationship in our model with several interactions. According to this hypothesis, the simplicial complex will be able to represent ecosystems that are sets of several firms. Technically, it is an n-ary relationship between several firms. In addition, the simplicial complex will be able to keep the n-ary relations between companies (business-task, business-component, business-role and business-parameter) by transforming the simplexes of our original simplicial complexes into relation types. In a computational modeling approach to ecosystem structure and dynamics, and in particular in a data-driven approach, we have the possibility to create or generate synthetic business ecosystems from secondary data mined from open datasets and semi- or unstructured data. Conversely, in more traditional approaches to business ecosystems based on primary data (case studies, interviews, a priori models, lists, etc.), the possibilities to quickly add new sources, to modify rules or variables, to modify research questions or analysis tasks, to have more or less real time data are much less important.

A simple way to obtain the ecosystems of the set Y is to establish as a rule that as soon as a company has a relationship then an ecosystem exists. To know the maximum number of ecosystems, we need to calculate all the combinations of companies, i.e.: $C(4,1) + C(4,2) + C(4,3) + C(4,4) = 4 + 6 + 4 + 1 = 15$ ecosystems.

$$C(4,1)=\frac{4!}{(1!(4-1)!)}=\frac{4!}{1! * 3!}=4$$

$$C(4,2)=\frac{4!}{(2!(4-2)!)}=\frac{4!}{2! * 2!}=6$$

$$C(4,3)=\frac{4!}{(3!(4-3)!)}=\frac{4!}{3! * 1!}=4$$

$$C(4,4)=\frac{4!}{(4!(4-4)!)}=\frac{4!}{4! * 0!}=1$$

From the four simplicial complexes, we obtain the "merged" simplicial complex represented by the following matrix, for better readability (Table 1).

Table 1. Representation of the "merged" simplicial complex from four simplicial complexes.

Combinations	Business/Ecosystem	Business 1	Business 2	Business 3	Business 4
Business 1	Ecosystem 1	COMPONENT_2 COMPONENT_5			
Business 2	Ecosystem 2				
Business 3	Ecosystem 3				
Business 4	Ecosystem 4				ROLE_3
Business 1 / Business 2	Ecosystem 5	COMPONENT_1 PARAMETER_1	COMPONENT_1 PARAMETER_1		
Business 1 / Business 3	Ecosystem 6				
Business 2 / Business 3	Ecosystem 7				
Business 1 / Business 4	Ecosystem 8	TASK_1 ROLE_1			TASK_1 ROLE_1
Business 2 / Business 4	Ecosystem 9				
Business 3 / Business 4	Ecosystem 10			TASK_3 COMPONENT_4	TASK_3 COMPONENT_4
Business 1 / Business 2 / Business 3	Ecosystem 11	TASK_2 ROLE_2	TASK_2 ROLE_2	TASK_2 ROLE_2	
Business 1 / Business 2 / Business 4	Ecosystem 12				
Business 1 / Business 3 / Business 4	Ecosystem 13				
Business 2 / Business 3 / Business 4	Ecosystem 14		COMPONENT_3 PARAMETER_2	COMPONENT_3 PARAMETER_2	COMPONENT_3 PARAMETER_2
Business 1 / Business 2 / Business 3 / Business 4	Ecosystem 15				

7   Perspectives: Computational Modeling of Business Ecosystem Dynamics

This article lays the groundwork in terms of theory, modelling and tools to better understand and analyze business ecosystems. However, is not intended to be an applied approach in the first instance. The first aim is to reconstruct a robust theory of business ecosystems, which does not currently exist, according to the researchers working in this field, in order to develop a conceptual ecosystem data framework. This second field of research, that of the analysis and visualization of ecosystems from data, is still emerging, but promising [11]. The main issue is that current data-driven approaches aim to provide ecosystem intelligence for decision support, offering generic analytical services that are often insufficiently informed by theories of business strategy, organizational ecology, inter-firm networks or economic. In our paper, we have tried to preserve this top-down and bottom-up articulation by showing the generic character of modularity and similarity which both express a form of "combinatorial dependency between entangled autonomous entities". It was therefore necessary to find a mathematical form expressing this main property, according to us, of business ecosystems (this is the pivotal role of matrices, already used to represent the dependencies of the elements of a complex system and how they are linked) generalized by complexes and then finally by hypergraphs. Finally, we had to check the feasibility of creating a synthetic but sufficiently realistic ecosystem and with our HYPE tool, capable of triangulating different types of data in the same way as multi-domain matrices do in the DSM research field and the like, including organizations (companies, startups, etc.), components (products and services, technologies, etc.), activities (processes, projects, tasks, etc.) and even more abstract parameters. It is this whole chain that we wanted to demonstrate the feasibility and the coherence. However, two perspectives need to be further developed. On the one hand, the complexity and dynamicity of concrete ecosystems require a data-driven approach, as recommended by [11]. The main methodological steps of such an approach are: identification of business ecosystem analysis tasks (visualize, analyze, and interpret); identification of objects (industry, companies, etc.), characteristics and objective function; identification of data sets and semantics for nodes and dependencies (whether graph theory is involved); creation of synthetic business ecosystems; design and development of experimental visualizations. On the other hand, more recently, there has been a call to adopt a complex adaptive systems lens to the study of ecosystems [24]. It has been argued that phenomena like dynamism, emergence, or adaptability are often missed in studies with a predominantly static snapshot investigations of ecosystems. Ecosystem orchestrators are also seeking to better understand how the trajectory of ecosystems can be increasingly more predictable over time. These are two examples of closely related perspectives that will certainly guide future research on ecosystem modelling, simulation and visualization.

Scientific Validation

This paper has benefited from the remarks of the following reviewers:

- Ali Ayadi, Strasbourg University, France
- Samer El Zant, Strasbourg University, France
- Franco Giustozzi, INSA Strasbourg - ICube laborator, France

The conference organisers wish to thank them for their highly appreciated effort and contribution.

References

1. Moore, J.F.: Predators and prey: a new ecology of competition. Harvard Bus. Rev. 75–86 (1993)
2. Shipilov, A., Gawer, A.: Integrating research on interorganizational networks and ecosystems. Acad. Manag. Ann. **14**(1), 92–121 (2020). https://doi.org/10.5465/annals.2018.0121
3. Suominen, A., Seppänen, M., Dedehayir, O.: A bibliometric review on innovation systems and ecosystems: a research agenda. Eur. J. Innov. Manag. **22**(2), 335–360 (2019). https://doi.org/10.1108/EJIM-12-2017-0188
4. Thomas, L.D.W., Autio, E.: Innovation ecosystems (2019). SSRN: https://ssrn.com/abstract=3476925 or https://doi.org/10.2139/ssrn.3476925

5. Thomas, L.D.W., Autio, E.: Innovation Ecosystems in Management: An Organizing Typology, Oxford Encyclopedia of Business and Management. Oxford University Press, Oxford (2020)
6. Baldwin, C.Y.: Design rules: past and future. Ind. Corporate Change **32**(1), 11–27 (2023). https://doi.org/10.1093/icc/dtac055
7. Jacobides, M.G., Cennamo, C., Gawer, A.: Towards a theory of ecosystems. Strateg. Manag. J. **39**(8), 2255–2276 (2018). https://doi.org/10.1002/smj.2904
8. Adner, R.: Ecosystem as structure: an actionable construct for strategy. J. Manag. **43**(1), 39–58 (2017). https://doi.org/10.1177/0149206316678451
9. Basole, R.C., Clear, T., Hu, M., Mehrotra, H., Stasko, J.T.: Understanding interfirm relationships in business ecosystems with interactive visualization. IEEE Trans. Visual Comput. Graph. **19**(12), 2526–2535 (2013)
10. Basole, R.C., Huhtamäki, J., Still, K., Russell, M.G.: Visual decision support for business ecosystem analysis. Expert Syst. Appl. **65**, 271–282 (2016). ISSN 0957-4174. https://doi.org/10.1016/j.eswa.2016.08.041
11. Basole, R.C.: Understanding ecosystem data. In: Proceedings of the 53rd Hawaii International Conference on System Sciences (2020)
12. Basole, R.C., Armbruster, D., Cortez, N., Barnett, B., Guilak, F.G., Kempf, K.G.: Computational modeling of business ecosystem dynamics. In: HICSS 2023, pp. 1334–1338 (2023)
13. Baldwin, C.Y.: Design Rules, Volume 2: How Technologies Shape Organizations, chapter 14, Introducing Open Platforms and Ecosystems. Working Paper 19-035. Harvard Business School
14. Simon, H.A.: The architecture of complexity. In: Simon, H.A. (ed.) Facets of Systems Science. International Federation for Systems Research International Series on Systems Science and Engineering, vol. 7. Springer, Boston (1962). https://doi.org/10.1007/978-1-4899-0718-9_31
15. Baldwin, C.Y., Clark, K.B.: Design Rules: The Power of Modularity, vol. 1. MIT Press, Cambridge (2000)
16. Langlois, R.: Modularity in technology and organization. J. Econ. Behav. Organ. **49**, 19–37 (2002)
17. Gavras, K., Kostakis, V.: Mapping the types of modularity in open-source hardware. Des. Sci. **7**, E13 (2021). https://doi.org/10.1017/dsj.2021.11
18. Sanchez, R., Mahoney, J.T.: Modularity, flexibility, and knowledge management in product and organization design. Strateg. Manag. J. **17**(S2), 63–76 (1996)
19. Schilling, M.A., Steensma, H.K.: The use of modular organizational forms: an industry-level analysis. Acad. Manag. J. **44**(6), 1149–1168 (2001)
20. Richardson, B.: The organisation of industry. Econ. J. **82**, 883–896 (1972). https://doi.org/10.2307/2230256
21. Teece, D.J.: Profiting from technological innovation. Res. Policy **15**(6), 285–305 (1986)
22. Teece, D.J.: Profiting from innovation in the digital economy: enabling technologies, standards, and licensing models in the wireless world. Res. Policy **47**(8), 1367–1387 (2018). https://doi.org/10.1016/j.respol.2017.01.015
23. Gawer, A.: Digital platforms and ecosystems: remarks on the dominant organizational forms of the digital age. Organ. Manag. Innov. (2021). https://doi.org/10.1080/14479338.2021.1965888
24. Phillips, M., Ritala, P.: A complex adaptive systems agenda for ecosystem research methodology. Technol. Forecast. Soc. Chang. (2019). https://doi.org/10.1016/j.techfore.2019.119739

25. Steward, D.: The design structure system: a method for managing the design of complex systems. IEEE Trans. Eng. Manag. **EM-28**, 71–74 (1981)
26. Eppinger, S.D., Browning, T.R.: Design Structure Matrix Methods and Applications. MIT Press, Cambridge (2012). https://doi.org/10.7551/mitpress/8896.001.0001
27. Atkin, R.: Combinatorial Connectivities in Social Systems: An Application of Simplicial Complex Structures to the Study of Large Organizations. Birkhäuser Verlag, Basel (1977)
28. Berrou, Y., Soulier, E., Calvez, P., Birregah, B., Rousseaux, F.: Hype: a data-driven tool for smart city profile (SCP) discrimination. In: Kayakutlu, G., Kayalica, Ö. (eds.) Decision Making Using AI in Energy and Sustainability. Springer, Cham (2023)
29. Johnson, J.: Hypernetworks in the Science of Complex Systems. Imperial College Press, London (2014)
30. Guery, M., Blot, M., Rousseaux, F., Soulier, E., Cormier, S.: Je relie système complexe, combinatoire, biologie des systèmes et apprentissage profond, qui suis-je ? Hyper-réseau, définitions et cas d'usage. Rencontres des Jeunes Chercheurs en Intelligence Artificielle (RJCIA), Plate-Forme Intelligence Artificielle (PFIA) ⟨hal-03294974⟩ (2021)
31. Berrou, Y., Guery, M., Soulier, E.: Limits and potential solutions to represent and analyze multidimensional and heterogeneous situations. In: 2022 International Joint Conference on Information and Communication Engineering (JCICE), Seoul, Republic of Korea, pp. 46–52 (2022). https://doi.org/10.1109/JCICE56791.2022.00021
32. Bianconi, G.: Higher-Order Networks (Elements in the Structure and Dynamics of Complex Networks). Cambridge University Press, Cambridge (2021). https://doi.org/10.1017/9781108770996

Machine Learning, Artificial Evolution and Genetic Programming

A Comparative Study of YOLO V4 and V5 Architectures on Pavement Cracks Using Region-Based Detection

Rauf Fatali[1,2,3(✉)], Gulzar Safarli[2], Samer El Zant[1,2], and Rabih Amhaz[1,3]

[1] ICUBE Laboratory, UMR CNRS 7357, University of Strasbourg, Strasbourg, France
[2] French-Azerbaijani University (UFAZ), Azerbaijan State Oil and Industry University, Baku, Azerbaijan
[3] Icam, site de Strasbourg-Europe, Strasbourg, France
`rauf.fatali@etu.unistra.fr`

Abstract. The frequent utilization of land transportation systems has led to the further deterioration of roads and caused traffic hazards. Early detection of asphalt pavement distresses has a necessary role in eliminating these hazards. Implementing an efficient automated method for detecting, locating, and classifying pavement distresses could help to address this problem in its early phase. This automated system has the potential to assist governments in maintaining road conditions effectively, especially those that aim to build smart cities. Furthermore, smart cars equipped with sensors and cameras can further contribute to road conditions and pavement distress inspection. The YOLO algorithm has demonstrated its potential to automate the detection process with real-time object detection and has shown promising results to be integrated into smart cars. The primary focus of this paper was to compare the performance of YOLOv4 and YOLOv5 in detecting thin and small crack objects using two publicly available image datasets, EdmCrack600 and RDD2022. Our comparisons were based not only on the architectures themselves but also on the number of classes in datasets that represent various types of pavement cracks. Additionally, we introduced an augmentation technique that is specific to crack objects in order to address the imbalanced class representation in the EdmCrack600 dataset. This technique improved final results by 11.2%. Overall, our comparisons indicated that YOLOv5 demonstrated better accuracy by achieving a mean average precision (mAP) of 65.6% on the RDD2022 dataset, and a mAP of 42.3% on the EdmCrack600 dataset.

Keywords: Crack Detection · Pattern Recognition · Computer Vision · Deep learning · YOLO · Architecture comparison · Smart cities · Smart cars

1   Introduction

Frequent utilization of land transportation [1] causes road-pavement surfaces to deteriorate and unstable climate events [2], such as heavy rainfall, flooding, and temperature fluctuations, can contribute to further deterioration of the roads if left unrepaired. Delaying attention to road maintenance poses potential safety hazards that can lead to road accidents, which will be the 5th leading cause of death in 2030 [3]. Therefore, governments have started to give more attention to road conditions and their maintenance.

Road conditions can be inspected manually or automatically. Manual inspection is time-consuming and labor-intensive particularly for large road networks [4,30], and requires a high level of domain expertise while being prone to human error. Due to its less efficiency, there is a significant demand for an automated inspection system.

The implementation of an effective automated method to detect, locate, and classify pavement cracks is vital in addressing these problems at an early phase. This early taken action has the potential to save significant amount of maintenance costs for the country's economic system, with potential savings of 20% [5,25]. Furthermore, using an automated system allows for a more efficient and accurate assessment of the road-pavement surface condition, reducing the margin for error and improving the overall safety of the transportation system.

On the other hand, smart cars [6,7] are supposed to be autonomous vehicles that understand the surrounding environment. The integration of an automated pavement crack detection system into smart cars will make it even easier to share information about road conditions with relevant organizations. We consider that smart cars equipped with sensors, cameras, and these automated systems will further contribute to the inspection of road conditions and pavement distresses.

In order to use these systems effectively by integrating them into smart cars, an efficient amount of data and algorithms must be employed that can provide precise detection at high speed. Recent progress in deep learning algorithms has enabled automation of complicated tasks. This progress demonstrates increased generalization capability and detection accuracy compared to traditional image processing techniques [8]. These algorithms use artificial neural networks trained on large datasets to identify specific patterns and anomalies from visual data by enabling fast and precise detection.

In the following sections, we will present an overview of the deep learning algorithms and their implementation in this particular application. Subsequently, we will explain the methodology for comparing algorithms and crack datasets, introduce our augmentation technique that is specific to crack objects, present the findings, and conclude on the results.

2   Related Works

Computer vision is one of the widely used fields of artificial intelligence in various disciplines that involves several tasks with different strategies, such as object classification, detection, and segmentation [9]. Object detection and segmentation involve two main phases: pattern recognition to recognize features from image data, and classification to classify each object into the appropriate class. While segmentation task uses pixel-wise detection to replace each pixel with the appropriate class, object detection task localizes objects and draws bounding boxes around them.

2.1 Region-Based Computer Vision Algorithms

Object detection has been widely used and many different approaches have been proposed to solve different types of problems in recent years [9]. There are two main types of object detectors, which are known as two-stage and one-stage detectors. As shown in Fig. 1, two-stage object detectors implement a whole process in two different stages, where they first generate a set of region proposals and then classify the objects within these regions. However, they are less efficient for real-time applications because they lack end-to-end implementation [17]. Examples of two-stage object detectors are Region-based Convolutional Networks (R-CNN) [10], Fast R-CNN [11], and Faster R-CNN [12]. On the other hand, there are one-stage detectors that are faster than two-stage detectors, where they directly locate and predict class probabilities in a single forward pass of the network. Single Shot MultiBox Detector (SSD) [13], and You Only Look Once (YOLO) [14–18] are examples of one-stage object detectors.

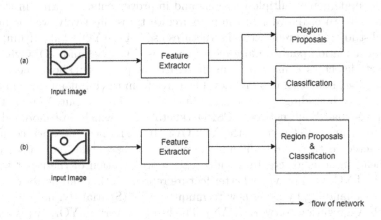

Fig. 1. Network flow of two-stage (a) and one-stage (b) detectors.

One of the early object detection algorithms, R-CNN, implements deep learning architecture in two stages: first, the selective search algorithm extracts region proposals for regions of interest (RoI), then a convolutional neural network extracts feature from each RoI and classify the object. Fast R-CNN improved the algorithm to run faster by extracting features in a single forward pass, instead of feeding each RoI separately. Faster R-CNN further improved the algorithm by using a Region Proposal Network which enables end-to-end training and faster processing times. Hacıefendioğlu, K., and Başağa, H. B. [19] used a pre-trained Faster R-CNN model to detect concrete road-pavement cracks under different weather conditions. According to their findings, the Faster R-CNN model struggles to detect cracks during fog, cloud, and nighttime. They demonstrated that Faster R-CNN is noise sensitive which has a significant effect on the decrease of overall accuracy by half. Xu, Xiangyang, et al. [20] compared R-CNN architecture with YOLOv3 considering both region-based and pixel-wise implementation. R-CNN performed well on the detection of deep and shallow crack types by combining two different approaches, while YOLOv3 with an object detection idea achieved lower confidence scores on these crack types. In contrast to R-CNN, the YOLO algorithm performs detection tasks on a dense set of predefined anchor boxes in a single forward pass of the network which makes the algorithm run much faster and compatible with real-time detection.

2.2   Evolution of YOLO Algorithm

Significant improvements for each new YOLO version have increasingly permeated investigations in terms of both architectural-wise and comparative studies. One of the key differences in YOLO [14] is the use of a regression-based method, which enables the direct prediction of bounding boxes and class probabilities for each object in a single pass through the network. Although YOLOv1 was fast, it had lower accuracy than other state-of-the-art algorithms due to its inability to detect small groups of objects [14]. Since its initial release, the YOLO algorithm has undergone multiple revisions and improvements, resulting in a more robust architecture. In order to compare architectures effectively, we conducted an initial study of the architectural structures used in the YOLO algorithm, with particular attention paid to more recent versions, YOLOv4 and YOLOv5.

Object detectors consist of 3 main structural parts: backbone, neck, and head. The backbone extracts high-level features from the input image, while the head produces bounding boxes and the final object class output. YOLOv4 uses an improved backbone network, CSPDarknet53 [21], which is a modified version of the DarkNet53 used in the YOLOv3 [16]. The neck network combines the extracted features from different levels of the backbone and passes them to the head in order to create a multi-scale representation of the input image. The neck of YOLOv4 provides better feature representation and better different object sizes handling by using new techniques, SPP (Spatial Pyramid Pooling), and Path Aggregation Network (PAN). The head network in YOLOv4 is almost the same as its predecessors, with the only difference being the use of a new Mish activation function that improved accuracy. Additionally, a mosaic data augmentation technique is introduced in YOLOv4 that selects four random images from a batch to generate a new image by combining them as illustrated in Fig. 2. In general, YOLOv4 uses a more complex network which provides significant improvements in object detection accuracy, speed, and robustness compared to its predecessors.

YOLOv5 [18] provides a lighter network that is more real-time applicable and also outperforms YOLOv4 in terms of speed. It uses a modified version of the

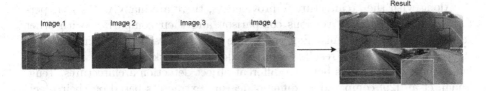

Fig. 2. Mosaic data augmentation.

YOLO head layer that is composed of three output blocks to predict bounding boxes, objectness scores, and class probabilities for a set of predefined anchor boxes. Additionally, compared to YOLOv4, YOLOv5 uses a new smooth and non-monotonic Swish activation function [22]. This activation function has been demonstrated to improve the efficiency of deep neural networks. Table 1 shows the difference between the structural parts of YOLOv4 and YOLOv5. Although YOLOv5 is an improved version of YOLOv4, there are some cases where it may underperform YOLOv4 in terms of accuracy due to the accuracy-speed trade-off inherent in the architecture.

Table 1. Architectural parts of YOLOv4 and YOLOv5.

	YOLOv4	YOLOv5
Neural Network Type	Fully convolutional	Fully convolutional
Backbone	CSPDarknet53	CSPDarknet53
Neck	SSP and PANet	PANet
Head	YOLO layer	YOLO layer

2.3   Implementation of YOLO Algorithm on Crack Detection

Many works have implemented YOLO architecture on crack detection across different types of surfaces in order to evaluate its architectural performance. Zhang, Yuexin, et al. [23] redesigned the general architecture of YOLOv3 by introducing the architectural change in MobileNetV2 which reduces the bounding box detection number in the region proposal network and avoids the model from overfitting. Additionally, they improved the speed of detection by integrating the attention mechanism into the architecture which mainly focuses on the useful information in the bridge crack images. Li, Li, et al. [24] also implemented the attention mechanism for YOLOv4 architecture which improved the performance in terms of accuracy by 2.96% mAP. Liu, Zhen, et al. [25] proposed a different detection idea by combining the YOLOv5 architecture with 3D ground-penetrating radar images to recognize internal asphalt pavement defects. This idea reduced road maintenance costs by $49,398/km, energy consumption by 16.94%, and carbon emission by 16.91%. Other improvements on the YOLOv4 and YOLOv5 [26–28] architectures have reduced inference time and increased sensitivity to noise for real-time surface crack detection.

Along with the architecture improvements, there are many works that performed different YOLO versions comparison and their comparison with other state-of-the-art algorithms. Especially, the YOLO version 2 [15] has demonstrated state-of-the-art results in object detection tasks and as a result, has led to more comparisons between different object detection architectures. Teng, Shuai, et al. [29] compared 11 different feature extractors based on their precision and computational cost for YOLOv2. ResNet18 architecture performed the best in response to the comparison by achieving an average precision of 89% while requiring a less computational cost for concrete crack detection. Mandal, Vishal, et al. [30] made a comparison of three different one-stage object detectors, YOLO, CenterNet, and EfficientDet. The YOLO algorithm outperformed others in detecting various crack types by achieving an F1 score of 58.14%, whereas the CenterNet and EfficientDet object detectors achieved 48.23% and 43.62%, respectively. Qiu, Qiwen, and Denvid Lau [31] compared different YOLO architectures on cracked tiled sidewalk images to find the best-performing architecture to integrate into the unmanned aerial vehicle for real-time inspection. According to their findings, ResNet50-based YOLOv2 and YOLOv4-tiny architectures outperformed others by getting high accuracy and fast inference speeds.

It appears that many works in the literature tend to emphasize the architectural aspects and put most of their effort into improving that point. We believe that it is crucial to not only select the most suitable architecture for fast crack detection but also to choose the appropriate data. Therefore, in this paper, we have mainly focused to evaluate the performance of both, architectures and datasets, while improving the datasets by implementing a specific augmentation strategy.

3 Comparison Methodology

Building an automated crack detection system is challenging due to the selection of appropriate architecture which should be capable of detecting almost all thin and small crack objects from each frame with high speed. In this paper, we have focused on comparing the performance of two architectures, YOLOv4 and YOLOv5. The selection of these architectures is warranted due to architectural improvements at a large scale in YOLOv4 providing better results in terms of accuracy, whereas YOLOv5 achieves similar results with faster inference time.

In this comparison, we used two publicly available image datasets, Edm-Crack600 and RDD2022, to train and test YOLO architectures. Each dataset represents diverse types of road-pavement cracks that can potentially impact the future condition of the road in a distinct manner. Therefore, comparisons are conducted not only by architectural evaluation but also by taking into account the number of classes within datasets.

3.1 Pavement Crack Datasets

EdmCrack600 dataset [32–34] contains 600 images with pixel-wise annotations taken from the roads in Edmonton, Canada. In order to perform object detection, we re-annotated this data using the open-source LabelImg tool [35] to draw a bounding box for each object in the image. During the annotation process, 8 different crack types are considered: block, longitudinal, transverse, reflective, edge, diagonal, alligator, and potholes.

Images in the dataset include several noises, such as shadow, low contrast, texture differences, various illumination conditions, etc. which makes it challenging for the crack detection task. Another advantage is including different types of cracks which are rarely found in the literature. Despite its advantages, this dataset has less amount of samples to train deep learning algorithms, and an imbalanced representation of crack types causes the model solely learn overrepresented classes well which affects overall accuracy.

The smaller number of samples in EdmCrack600 required us to train YOLO architectures on another dataset, RDD2022, to realize a comparison. RDD2022 dataset [36] has 47,420 samples from 6 different countries, China, the Czech Republic, Japan, India, the United States, and Norway. Its samples mainly contain 4 types of cracks: longitudinal, transverse, alligator, and potholes.

In this dataset, we observed that samples of each country include some types of cracks that are not included in the EdmCrack600. In order to compare the number of class types within both datasets, we removed these crack types from the RDD2022 dataset. After performing the processing, the total number of samples decreased to 23,767.

The key advantage of the RDD2022 dataset is its high capability of being trained on deep learning models through the large number of samples. However, we can observe some necessary crack types in EdmCrack600 that are not included in RDD2022. Although EdmCrack600 has some limitations, we kept it to compare with RDD2022, because it demonstrates a wider range of crack types. Additionally, in the next section, we will try to solve an imbalanced representation of crack types in EdmCrack600 by implementing our augmentation idea which is specific to crack images.

Overall, these datasets were divided into the train, validation, and test sets in the proportion of 80:10:10. Due to the less number of samples in the dataset, particularly the EdmCrack600, a significant proportion of the samples, specifically

Fig. 3. Data samples from EdmCrack600 (a) and RDD2022 (b) datasets.

80% of the data, has been used for the training, with the remaining 10% each used for validation and testing purposes. Figure 3 shows some training samples from each dataset which are taken from the cameras mounted to the car.

3.2   Image Augmentation

Taking all possible crack types into account is crucial for their future impact on the road as it is mentioned before. EdmCrack600 dataset provides almost all possible crack types from literature but in an imbalanced form. Removing the imbalanced representation of classes has the capability of improving overall accuracy while detecting all classes effectively. The general idea of the proposed image augmentation technique is encompassed in Algorithm 1.

Algorithm 1. Image Augmentation Algorithm

Require: under_classes
1: **Initialize** min_size = 640
2: **Initialize** coefs = initUnderClassCoefs(classes)
3: **for each** img_path, annot_path **in** images, annotations **do**
4:      img = read(img_path)
5:      annots = read(annot_path)
6:      **for each** annot **in** annotations **do**
7:          class = annot[0]
8:          bbox = annot[1:]
9:          **if** class in under_classes **then**
10:             cropped_img = crop(img, bbox, min_size)
11:             **for each** n in {1, ... , $coefs[class]$} **do**
12:                 transform = augmentation_pipeline(cropped_img, bbox)
13:                 transformed_img = transform['image']
14:                 transformed_bbox = transform['bbox']
15:                 save(transformed_img)
16:                 save(transformed_bbox)
17:             **end for**
18:         **end if**
19:     **end for**
20: **end for**

This algorithm can be divided into three main parts. The first part involves identifying the under-represented classes from the whole dataset. This is done by eliminating classes with high percentage representation within a dataset.

In the second part, we crop the identified under-represented classes from the original images by checking whether each image is contained by the under-represented class. The cropping is performed to ensure that the only region of interest is preserved and not consists of over-represented crack types. Since each image consists of several crack types, cropping is used in this step to avoid increasing the number of other types and to achieve a more balanced representation. Lastly, the size of cropped image is set to a minimum size of 640 pixels to meet the requirement of YOLO architecture.

The third and last part contains the application of the augmentation pipeline to cropped images until a balanced representation is achieved. The augmentation process involves applying a series of transformations to the cropped image. Applying appropriate transformations to datasets that exhibit variability based on the characteristics can significantly impact the final results. For instance, in the context of a crack, rotating a transverse crack by 90°C can result in transforming it into a longitudinal crack.

In this last part, several transformations are used to augment cropped images. Initially, a set of color transformations is applied that includes converting the image to grayscale, adjusting brightness or contrast, and slightly shifting RGB values in order to increase the variety of images. A subsequent set of transformations adds random noise to the images, such as rain, fog, snow, and blur to make it challenging to detect cracks. Additionally, some image transformations such as random flipping and rotating with low values are applied to the cropped images, and save the resulting augmented images to their corresponding directory.

Implementing this proposed image augmentation technique has the potential to solve class imbalance and increase the overall accuracy of the object detection algorithm. To be able to compare and evaluate the impact of the number of crack types, this augmentation technique is applied to the EdmCrack600 dataset which contains the most types of cracks.

3.3 Configuration of YOLOv4 and YOLOv5 Architectures

The YOLO architecture provides different sizes of networks to train object detection tasks. For comparisons, we selected the YOLOv4, YOLOv5-large, and YOLOv4-tiny, YOLOv5-small, accordingly large and small-sized networks.

Training of these architectures differs from each other according to their configuration file. The recommendation of the authors was highly considered in finding the optimal parameters of each architecture. In the YOLOv4 architecture, its parameters have a dependence on class number according to the equations[1]:

$$max\_batches = nb\_classes * 2000 \tag{1}$$

$$steps = (80\% of max\_batches), (90\% of max\_batches) \tag{2}$$

$$filters = (nb\_classes + 5) * 3 \tag{3}$$

From the above Eqs. (1–3), max_batches represents the total number of batches, steps reduces the learning rate at defined steps, filters controls the number of filters used in each convolutional layer. Additionally, the YOLOv4 model has to learn at most 2000 iterations per class [17].

The crack types within datasets are divided into 1, 4, and 8 classes to make comparisons. The single crack type dataset combines all types of cracks into a single category 'crack', whereas the 4 crack type dataset includes the common crack types from both datasets. Since the datasets are divided into 3 different representations of classes, we have modified the YOLOv4 config file as the result of the calculations. The almost same parameters, the total number of epochs, batch size, and image size, were used for each model in YOLOv5. All parameters for each model are shown in Table 2.

---

[1] https://github.com/kiyoshiiriemon/yolov4_darknet#how-to-train-to-detect-your-custom-objects.

Table 2. Network configuration of YOLO architectures.

YOLOv4 Network Configuration					
no. of classes	image size	iterations	max batches	steps	filters
1	640	2000	2000	1600, 1800	18
4	640	8000	8000	6400, 7200	27
8	640	16000	16000	12800, 14400	39

YOLOv5 Network Configuration			
network	image size	epochs	batch size
YOLOv5s	640	200	16
YOLOv5l	640	200	16

4   Experimental Results

4.1   Experimental Conditions

We used a workstation equipped with 64 GB RAM, Intel® Core™ i9-10900X CPU @ 3.70 GHz, and 2x NVIDIA GeForce RTX 2080 Ti 12 GB GPU, which provided fast and efficient computation. The 2×12 GB memory size allowed us to use optimal batch sizes during training and perform more complex computations. The implementation of these architectures in the PyTorch deep learning framework made GPU training even easier by offering a high-level interface. Python 3.10, Nvidia driver version 522.06, and CUDA version 11.8 is used for the PyTorch environment.

4.2   Scoring Methods

In the testing phase, the evaluation metrics, like precision, recall, and mean average precision (mAP) [37], are used to compare the performance of architectures. While precision (4) measures the percentage of correctly detected cracks from all detections, recall (5) measures the percentage of correctly detected objects from all ground truths. The average precision (AP) (6) is calculated for each class using precision and recall values and mAP (7) evaluates the overall performance by computing the mean value of APs. High results mean that the architecture is capable to detect objects as accurately as possible.

$$precision(p) = \frac{TP}{TP + FP} \tag{4}$$

$$recall(r) = \frac{TP}{TP + FN} \tag{5}$$

$$AP = \int_0^1 p(r)\, dr \tag{6}$$

$$mAP = \frac{1}{n} \sum_{i=1}^{n} AP_i \quad \text{for n classes} \tag{7}$$

TP (True Positive) - Correctly detected object
FP (False Positive) - Incorrectly detected object
FN (False Negative) - Not detected ground truth

4.3 Results and Interpretation

Before conducting any comparisons, it is necessary to acknowledge that the way of crack representations within the data can directly affect the overall results. These representations can be the perspective from which angle the images were taken, how much annotation an average each image contains, and a balanced representation of crack types. EdmCrack600 and RDD2022 datasets mainly consist of images captured from the perspective of a sensor mounted on a car, which poses a significant challenge in detecting small thin crack objects.

Table 3. Performance comparison of 4 different versions of YOLO on EdmCrack600 and RDD2022 datasets.

#Classes	Metrics	v4	v4-tiny	v5l	v5s
		EdmCrack600			
1	Precision	0.52	0.49	0.626	0.641
	Recall	0.34	0.12	0.386	0.272
	mAP@0.5	0.335	0.137	**0.423**	0.297
	Time(ms)	747.38	863.41	10.1	**5.4**
4	Precision	0.57	0.51	0.469	0.41
	Recall	0.34	0.17	0.263	0.193
	mAP@0.5	0.245	0.128	0.296	0.224
	Time(ms)	745.63	655.26	10.6	7.0
8	Precision	0.35	0.37	0.246	0.452
	Recall	0.25	0.15	0.23	0.209
	mAP@0.5	0.226	0.142	0.207	0.205
	Time(ms)	823.04	667.29	10.8	8.0

#Classes	Metrics	v4	v4-tiny	v5l	v5s
		RDD2022			
1	Precision	0.5	0.21	0.691	0.666
	Recall	0.44	0.02	0.613	0.593
	mAP@0.5	0.387	0.0596	**0.656**	0.63
	Time(ms)	697.84	720.08	15.4	**1.7**
4	Precision	0.46	0.15	0.674	0.652
	Recall	0.3	0.02	0.597	0.576
	mAP@0.5	0.462	0.102	0.632	0.606
	Time(ms)	724.16	669.45	20.0	1.8

Table 4. Performance comparison of YOLOv5l on non-augmented and augmented EdmCrack600 dataset.

#Classes	Metrics	original	augmented
		EdmCrack600	
8	Precision	0.246	0.453
	Recall	0.23	0.37
	mAP@0.5	0.207	0.319
	Time(ms)	10.8	10.1

The increased number of classes can affect the balanced class representation, which is noticeable in the EdmCrack600 dataset. While a model is trained using an imbalanced dataset, it will struggle to learn less-represented classes. Moreover, having a large number of annotations per image that indicates multiple crack samples in a single image, can pose a significant challenge during detection and may lead to reduced model precision and recall.

In order to perform comparisons, the original datasets were first trained on YOLO architectures using their built-in augmentation mechanism. Afterward, the augmented Edmcrack600 dataset, which includes all possible crack types, was trained by disabling the internal augmentations in the best-performed YOLO architecture.

Table 3 shows results on original datasets where YOLOv5l outperformed other architectures in terms of mAP, achieving a score of 0.656 and 0.408 on the RDD2022 and EdmCrack600 dataset with a single crack type, respectively. The overall results are not robust due to the mentioned complexity of both datasets. We can easily infer that the imbalanced class representation in the EdmCrack600 dataset has huge effects on its final results. The more balanced RDD2022 dataset with a less number of crack types performed better in this perspective. Additionally, increasing the size of the network resulted in longer inference times, potentially leading to underwhelming real-time detection results.

The augmented EdmCrack600 dataset was trained and validated on the best-performed architecture, YOLOv5l, which resulted in increasing mAP from 0.207 to 0.319, as shown in Table 4. It is observable that using augmentation techniques has the potential to improve overall results. The proposed augmentation strategy contributed to achieving a more balanced result by increasing the overall precision and recall of under-represented crack types.

In addition to comparisons, hyperparameter tuning and removing the mosaic augmentation from YOLO architecture were tested to see how they affect results. The results were affected by the mosaic augmentation removal, whereas tuned hyperparameters did not have much effect. The mosaic augmentation technique assists to represent more crack types in a single image by combining four different ones. Removing this technique resulted in a performance decrease by 8–9% mAP, particularly for datasets containing more crack types.

In general, YOLOv5 architecture outperformed YOLOv4 in terms of both accuracy and speed. Due to the large number of samples in RDD2022, YOLOv5 achieved higher precision, recall, and mAP values. Moreover, the implementation of the augmentation technique significantly increased the results of the EdmCrack600 dataset with 8 different crack types.

5   Conclusion

Automating crack detection problems using smart cars can help us to detect road-pavement distresses in the early phase. This paper represents a part of our state-of-the-art by comparing object detectors that can be implemented in real-time applications. The comparisons have been done by using two different featured publicly available datasets, EdmCrack600 and RDD2022, and trained them on the best-performed YOLO architectures, YOLOv4 and YOLOv5.

Detecting all possible cracks is crucial as different crack types affect the pavement surfaces differently. Therefore, our comparison methodology examined models based on both the number of crack types and the architectures themselves. Additionally, we proposed an augmentation strategy that augments under-represented crack objects to handle an imbalanced class representation.

The comparisons showed that YOLOv5 outperformed YOLOv4 in terms of accuracy and speed. Specifically, the large-sized version of YOLOv5 achieved an mAP of 65.6% on RDD2022 with a single crack type and an almost similar mAP of 63.2% on the same dataset with four different crack types. Augmenting the EdmCrack600 dataset, which is represented by almost all crack types, partially removed the imbalanced class representation, while improving the overall results from 20.7% to 31.9%. These results highlight the importance of having a well-balanced and well-annotated dataset with a sufficient amount of data that can help us to implement real-time detection using these state-of-the-art architectures.

As future work, we aim to investigate pixel-based algorithms that can improve precision while considerably increasing inference time. We also plan to improve the introduced augmentation algorithm to make it applicable in both techniques, object detection and segmentation. Afterward, we are looking forward to build a hybrid model that collaborates between the region and pixel-based models. This fast and precise final model can serve as an additional brick to be added to smart systems in future cars and contribute to the development of smart cities.

Scientific Validation

This paper has benefited from the remarks of the following reviewers:

- Darian Reyes, University of Limerick, Ireland
- Ernesto Tarantino, ICAR-CNR, Italy
- Karim Tout, Uqudo, UAE

The conference organisers wish to thank them for their highly appreciated effort and contribution.

References

1. Pais, J.C., Amorim, S.I.R., Minhoto, M.J.C.: Impact of traffic overload on road pavement performance. J. Transport. Eng. **139**, 9 (2013)
2. Qiao, Y., Flintsch, G.W., Dawson, A.R., Parry, T.: Examining effects of climatic factors on flexible pavement performance and service life. Transp. Res. Rec. **2349**, 100–107 (2013)
3. World Health Organization. Global status report on road safety: time for action. In: Violence, Injury Prevention, and World Health Organization. World Health Organization (2009)

4. Varadharajan, S., Jose, S., Sharma, K., Wander, L., Mertz, C.: Vision for road inspection. In: IEEE winter conference on applications of computer vision, pp. 115–122. IEEE (2014)
5. Yu, J.-M., Lee, C., Chen, L.-L.: Survival model-based economic evaluation of preventive maintenance practice on asphalt pavement. J. South China Univ. Technol. **40**(11), 133–137 (2012)
6. Arena, F., Pau, G., Severino, A.: An overview on the current status and future perspectives of smart cars. Infrastructures **5**(7), 53 (2020)
7. Huval, B., et al.: An empirical evaluation of deep learning on highway driving. arXiv preprint arXiv:1504.01716 (2015)
8. Sattar, D., Thomas, R.J., Maguire, M.: Comparison of deep convolutional neural networks and edge detectors for image-based crack detection in concrete. Constr. Build. Mater. **186**, 1031–1045 (2018)
9. Klette, R.: Concise Computer Vision: An Introduction into Theory and Algorithms, vol. 233. Springer, London (2014)
10. Girshick, R., Donahue, J., Darrell, T., Malik, J.: Rich feature hierarchies for accurate object detection and semantic segmentation. In: Proceedings of the IEEE Conference on Computer Vision and Pattern Recognition (2014)
11. Girshick, R.: Fast r-cnn. In: Proceedings of the IEEE International Conference on Computer Vision, pp. 1440–1448 (2015)
12. Ren, S., He, K., Girshick, R., Sun, J.: Faster r-cnn: towards real-time object detection with region proposal networks. Adv. Neural Inf. Process. Syst. **28** (2015)
13. Liu, W., et al.: SSD: single shot multiBox detector. In: Leibe, B., Matas, J., Sebe, N., Welling, M. (eds.) ECCV 2016. LNCS, vol. 9905, pp. 21–37. Springer, Cham (2016). https://doi.org/10.1007/978-3-319-46448-0_2
14. Redmon, J., Divvala, S., Girshick, R., Farhadi, A.: You only look once: unified, real-time object detection. In: Proceedings of the IEEE Conference on Computer Vision and Pattern Recognition, pp. 779–788 (2016)
15. Redmon, J., Farhadi, A.: YOLO9000: better, faster, stronger. In: Proceedings of the IEEE Conference on Computer Vision and Pattern Recognition, pp. 7263–7271 (2017)
16. Redmon, J., Farhadi, A.: Yolov3: an incremental improvement. arXiv preprint arXiv:1804.02767 (2018)
17. Alexey, B., Wang, C.-Y., Mark Liao, H.-Y.: Yolov4: optimal speed and accuracy of object detection. arXiv preprint arXiv:2004.10934 (2020)
18. Jocher, G., Chaurasia, A., Stoken, A., Borovec, J.: NanoCode012. In: Kwon, Y., et al. ultralytics/yolov5: v7.0 - YOLOv5 SOTA Realtime Instance Segmentation (v7.0). Zenodo (2022). https://doi.org/10.5281/zenodo.7347926
19. Hacıefendioğlu, K., Basri Başağa, H.: Concrete road crack detection using deep learning-based faster R-CNN method. Iranian J. Sci. Technol. Trans. Civil Eng. 1–13 (2022)
20. Xu, X., et al.: Crack detection and comparison study based on faster R-CNN and mask R-CNN. Sensors **22**(3), 1215 (2022)
21. Wang, C., Mark Liao, H., Wu, Y., Chen, P., Hsieh, J., Yeh, I.: Cspnet: a new backbone that can enhance learning capability of CNN. In: 2020 IEEE/CVF Conference on Computer Vision and Pattern Recognition Workshops (CVPRW), pp. 1571–1580 (2020)
22. Ramachandran, P., Zoph, B., Le, Q.V.: Searching for activation functions. arXiv preprint arXiv:1710.05941 (2017)
23. Zhang, Y., Huang, J., Cai, F.: On bridge surface crack detection based on an improved YOLO v3 algorithm. IFAC-PapersOnLine **53**(2) (2020)

24. Li, L., Fang, B., Zhu, J.: Performance analysis of the YOLOv4 algorithm for pavement damage image detection with different embedding positions of CBAM modules. Appl. Sci. **12**(19), 10180 (2022)

25. Liu, Z., Wu, W., Gu, X., Li, S., Wang, L., Zhang, T.: Application of combining YOLO models and 3D GPR images in road detection and maintenance. Remote Sens. **13**(6), 1081 (2021)

26. Yao, G., Sun, Y., Wong, M., Lv, X.: A real-time detection method for concrete surface cracks based on improved YOLOv4. Symmetry **13**(9), 1716 (2021)

27. Yao, G., Sun, Y., Yang, Y., Liao, G.: Lightweight neural network for real-time crack detection on concrete surface in fog. Front. Mater. **8** (2021)

28. Wan, F., Sun, C., He, H., Lei, G., Xu, L., Xiao, T.: YOLO-LRDD: a lightweight method for road damage detection based on improved YOLOv5s. EURASIP J. Adv. Signal Process. **2022**(1) (2022)

29. Teng, S., Liu, Z., Chen, G., Cheng, L.: Concrete crack detection based on well-known feature extractor model and the YOLO_v2 network. Appl. Sci. **11**(2) (2021)

30. Mandal, V., Mussah, A.R., Adu-Gyamfi, Y.: Deep learning frameworks for pavement distress classification: a comparative analysis. In: 2020 IEEE International Conference on Big Data (Big Data), pp. 5577–5583. IEEE (2020)

31. Qiu, Q., Lau, D.: Real-time detection of cracks in tiled sidewalks using YOLO-based method applied to unmanned aerial vehicle (UAV) images. Autom. Constr. **147**, 104745 (2023)

32. Mei, Q., Gül, M., Azim, M.R.: Densely connected deep neural network considering connectivity of pixels for automatic crack detection. Autom. Constr. **110**, 103018 (2020)

33. Mei, Q., Gül, M.: A cost effective solution for pavement crack inspection using cameras and deep neural networks. Constr. Build. Mater. **256**, 119397 (2020)

34. Mei, Q., Gül, M., Shirzad-Ghaleroudkhani, N.: Towards smart cities: crowdsensing-based monitoring of transportation infrastructure using moving vehicles. J. Civil Struct. Health Monitor. (2020)

35. Tzutalin. LabelImg (2015). https://github.com/tzutalin/labelImg. Accessed 15 Dec 2022

36. Deeksha, A., Maeda, H., Ghosh, S.K., Toshniwal, D., Sekimoto, Y.: RDD2022: a multi-national image dataset for automatic road damage detection. arXiv preprint arXiv:2209.08538 (2022)

37. Zhu, H., Wei, H., Li, B., Yuan, X., Kehtarnavaz, N.: A review of video object detection: datasets, metrics and methods. Appl. Sci. **10**(21), 7834 (2020)

Evolutionary Reduction of the Laser Noise Impact on Quantum Gates

Tam'si Ley[1,3]($\boxtimes$) (iD), Anna Ouskova Leonteva[1], Johannes Schachenmayer[2], and Pierre Collet[1]

[1] ICUBE, Université de Strasbourg, Strasbourg, France
[2] ISIS, Université de Strasbourg, Strasbourg, France
[3] QuantFi, Paris, France
`tamsi.ley2@gmail.com`

Abstract. As the size of quantum hardware progressively increases, the conjectured computational advantages of quantum technologies tend to be threatened by noise, which randomly corrupts the design of quantum logical gates. Several methods already exist to reduce the impacts of noise on that matter. However, a reliable and user-friendly one to reduce the noise impact has not been presented yet. Addressing this issue, this paper proposes a relevant method based on evolutionary optimisation and modulation of the gate design. This method consists of two parts: a model of quantum gate design with time-dependent noise terms, parameterised by a vector of laser phases, and an evolutionary optimisation platform aimed at satisfying a trade-off between the gate fidelity and a pulse duration-related metric of the time consuming simulation model. This feature is the main novelty of this work. Another advantage is the ability to treat any noise spectrum, regardless of its characteristics (e.g., variance, frequency range, etc). A thorough validation of the method is presented, which is based on empirical averaging of random gate trajectories. It is shown that evolutionary based method is successfully applied for noise mitigation. It is expected that the proposed method will help designing more and more noise-resisting quantum gates.

Keywords: Quantum computing · Noise resilience · Optimisation

1 Introduction

Quantum computing uses the laws of quantum physics to perform logical operations inaccessible to classical means: e.g., superposition and entanglement. In theory, an ideal quantum computer would solve some mathematical problems with exponentially fewer computing resources than any classical counterpart [1]. It applies to practical fields such as quantum chemistry [2], materials science [3], and cryptography [4].

However, quantum systems are highly prone to a noise, coming from interactions with the environment, or from imperfections in the control apparatus (e.g.,

P. Collet et al. (Eds.): CCE 2023, LNCS 13927, pp. 64–76, 2023.
https://doi.org/10.1007/978-3-031-44355-8_5

laser, electronic devices). Due to analog nature of those quantum systems, the noise critically affects the performance of quantum computers. Moreover, the noise also dramatically reduces the quantum computational power, and would prevent quantum computers from reaching any advantage on practical problems with regard to the classical counterparts. This can be seen by the following result: assuming a constant error rate and without any effective correction strategy, a large variety of random quantum circuits (i.e. programs) are efficiently simulated by classical computers [5–7], which would be far more difficult without noise. The ability to overcome noise is the central question raised by quantum computing skeptics [17]. Indeed, quantum circuits (programs) solving relevant problems, require millions of elementary quantum gates (logical operators). Thus, even with small noise rates, they need efficient strategies to suppress errors. The latter exist in theory, but they require average gate infidelity much lower than what current noise levels impose. Reducing the impact of noise on the gate design is a highly non-trivial challenge, for which several solutions have been proposed: e.g., [14–16]. Generally, these methods model the gate infidelity (inaccuracy) with equations that require long simulations, and do not cope well with a high standard deviation or high frequency fluctuations in the noise.

Addressing these issues, in this work, we focus on adapting a flat laser pulse suffering amplitude and dephasing noises, in order to implement a Rydberg blockade two-qubit gate, which is specific to the cold-atoms hardware. The theoretical information about that hardware is largely presented in the literature: e.g., [20]. In order to reduce the noise and simultaneously, to reduce the time spent in the Rydberg state, we formulate a quantum gate design as a continuous non-constrained bi-objective problem based on a time-expensive computer simulation. Taking into account the number of objectives (2) and the large number of decision variables (51), we set 100 candidate solutions in the population, where a computation time of around 1 min per each solution. In order to reduce the computational complexity, we use the CPU-parallel celebrated multi-objective algorithm Non-dominated Sorting Genetic Algorithm III (NSGA-III) provided by the EASEA (*EAsy Specification of Evolutionary Algorithms*) platform described in [19].

To our best knowledge, this work is the first attempt to present a quantum gate design task as a continuous large-scale multi-objective problem, solved by parallel optimisation algorithm. Our method is not limited by any characteristic of the noise, and allows us to select a pulse sequence (laser phases) and duration to implement the target gate. Moreover, EASEA provides different single and multi-objective optimisation algorithms, which can be easily applied for the problem of laser noise reducing in the further researches in order to investigate an impact of different optimisation techniques on the performance in terms of the accuracy and speed up.

This paper is organized as follows. Section 2 briefly outlines the related works. Section 3 describes the problem definition. Section 4 presents the proposed method based on the evolutionary optimisation. The experiments and results are shown in Sect. 5. Section 6 concludes this article.

2   Related Works

In this section, we briefly present the related works addressing the problem of laser noise impact reduction for quantum gate design presented in the literature. They can be broadly divided in four categories.

The first one is called noise mitigation, and consists of repeating some gates throughout the circuit, in order to reduce the influence of noise on the computation result [8]. This technique generally assumes that the gate noise is uncorrelated in time. However, correlated noise has been shown to bypass the current noise mitigation strategies, as experimentally proved in [9]. Thus, non-trivial correlations in time must be accounted for, when analysing noise impact on quantum computation.

The second category is robust optimal control, as was outlined in [10]. It converts noise impact minimisation, into an optimal control problem in an extended space with appropriate boundary conditions, and derives semi-analytical solutions to that problem. However, it only treats time-independent noise in a single direction (e.g amplitude or dephasing). Adapting that technique to time-dependent noise would increase the problem dimension exponentially in the number of harmonics, when considering all the cross products between operators. A slight variation of this approach is "inverse geometric optimisation", as introduced in [11]. The idea is to convert noise impact reduction into a Euler-Lagrange problem, leading to a second order non-linear differential equation. This approach allows to directly track the trajectory of the quantum state in a semi-analytical formulation. However, this method cannot be currently be adapted to either dephasing and/or time-dependent noise, due do its mathematical formulation [11].

The third category is the filter function formalism, as outlined in [14–16]. The idea is to formulate the average gate infidelity as a function of both the laser controls and the noise power spectral density. Then, it is optimised with differentiable methods such as gradient descent. However, that method fails when the noise intensity is of order 10% of the laser pulse intensity, such that the implicit first-order truncation does not ensure a low enough infidelity.

The fourth category·consists of estimating the noise impact with Monte Carlo summation of random gate trajectories; and to optimise the laser pulse with a separate algorithm. In [13], the laser control is decomposed in Fourier series, and the Fourier coefficients are optimized through the Nelder-Mead algorithm. In their work, dephasing noise is considered relative, like amplitude noise. This stands in contradiction to the convention in the literature. Our present work follows a similar path, but characterises the laser control with flat pulses, whose phases are optimised by a multi-objective algorithm.

3   Problem Definition

3.1   Context

Optically-trapped cold atoms constitute a promising hardware architecture for long term quantum computing due to long qubit life time, maturity of laser technology and flexibility of two-qubit interactions [20]. The idea of this technology is to encode bits as two specific orbitals, called "0" and "1", populated by the valence electron of some chosen special atomic species [20].

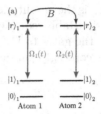

Fig. 1. Atomic transitions and Rydberg interaction. Illustration adapted from [21].

Upon interaction with a nearby electromagnetic field, electrons switch between orbitals. This is usually done with laser tuned in resonance with the atomic transition frequency between the said orbitals. In the literature, a π-pulse refers to a complete transfer between two orbitals, with a multiplication by the imaginary unit of the relevant orbital coordinate in the quantum state vector. Rydberg states refer to orbitals far away from the nucleus, exhibiting high electric dipole moments. When the resulting electric potential is much larger than the power of the electromagnetic field, the Rydberg blockade prevents two electrons to be simultaneously in a Rydberg state. This happens when atoms are closed to each other. The protocol outlined in [18] allows to design a universal two-qubit gate, using only the Rydberg blockade and four π-pulses between the "1" and a Rydberg orbitals. Thus, as we focus on laser noise, we only have to optimise the π-pulse. Figure 1 shows a simplified view of the atomic transition described above, where r is a Rydberg state, B is the Rydberg blockade strength and Ω_j is a function characterising the laser pulse.

3.2   Mathematical Model

Due to the mathematical description of quantum mechanics, the electron's quantum state is represented as a complex unit vector, whose dimension is the number of considered orbitals. In our case, there are 2: the 1 and r orbitals, as 0 is excluded from the transitions. Since the evolution of the vector is linear and norm-preserving, it is represented as a 2×2 complex unitary matrix $U(t)$, with $U(0)$ being the identity matrix. The interaction between the atom and an electromagnetic field, inducing the orbital transition, is mathematically represented as the following differential equation:

$$\dot{U}(t) = \imath \hat{H}(t) U(t) \qquad (1)$$

where $\hat{H}(t)$ is the hamiltonian matrix, which corresponds to the energy configuration of the system. The transition between two atomic orbitals is characterised by the complex Rabi frequency Ω, as shown in the equation below:

$$\hat{H}(t) = \begin{pmatrix} \varepsilon_d(t) & (1 + \varepsilon_a(t))\Omega^*(t) \\ (1 + \varepsilon_a(t))\Omega(t) & -\varepsilon_d(t) \end{pmatrix} \qquad (2)$$

where ε_d is the dephasing noise, ε_a is the amplitude noise. In the absence of noise, the pulse will be the fastest, if the Rabi frequency has a constant modulus, as explained in [21]. Since we want the gates to be fastest as possible, in order to avoid other types of noises, we accordingly parameterise the Rabi frequency:

$$\Omega = 2\pi f_{\max} e^{\imath\varphi} \qquad (3)$$

where $f_{\max}$ is the maximal frequency of the laser pulses and φ is the phases of the laser pulses. In the noiseless case, the phase is constant $\varphi = 0$. Here, we set it as a piece-wise constant function, with a fixed number of slices (N): $\varphi(t) = \varphi_i$ for $t \in [\frac{iT}{N}, \frac{(i+1)T}{N}]$. The solution of the differential Eq. 1 is a random matrix written as $U(\varphi, t)$. For the sake of clarity, the list of all the mathematical symbols used in this work is summarised in Table 1.

Table 1. List of symbols used in the problem definition.

Symbol	Significance (unit)
$\lvert 0 \rangle$	Ground orbital (–)
$\lvert 1 \rangle$	Excited orbital (–)
$\lvert r \rangle$	Rydberg orbital (–)
$\imath$	Complex imaginary unit (–)
t	Running time ($1/f_{\max}$)
T	Pulse duration ($1/f_{\max}$)
U	Pulse matrix (–)
$\dot{U}$	Derivative of pulse matrix (–)
Ω	Rabi frequency (rad $f_{\max}$)
Ω^*	Complex conjugate thereof (rad $f_{\max}$)
$\hat{H}$	Hamiltonian matrix (rad $f_{\max}$)
U_0	Target pulse matrix (–)
$f_{\max}$	Maximal Rabi frequency (1)
ν_0	Maximal noise frequency ($f_{\max}$)
φ	Vector of laser phases (rad)
N	Number of time slices/laser phases
F	Pulse infidelity (-)
G	Time in Rydberg state ($1/f_{\max}$)
ε_a	Amplitude noise (rad $f_{\max}$)
ε_d	Detuning noise (rad $f_{\max}$)

This model can be transformed to an optimisation problem. From an optimization point of view, the real-world quantum gate design problem, presented above, is a typical expensive continuous bi-objective optimization problem without constraints. A bi-objective problem aims at optimizing two values of interest (objectives), which are antagonist. The answer is a set of trade-offs solutions (a vector with the input parameters) between the defined objectives. In Sect. 3.3, we present its inputs and objectives.

3.3   Values of Interest and Input Parameters

In this study, we consider 2 values of interests (objective functions) and 51 input parameters.

Input Parameters. The parameters and their ranges of variations are summed up in Table 2, where the following notation is used:

- φ is a vector of N elements, which refers to the values of the laser phase in the orbital transitions. In the current model $N = 50$ as a reasonable number required for both processes: simulation and optimisation.
- T is the duration of the model simulation, which has an impact on the time spent by the electron in the Rydberg state (G);
- f_{max} is the maximal frequency the laser emits to. In our problem definition, we normalise all units with $f_{max} = 1$, which means that the model can be applied to any value of that frequency. In recent experiments, typically $f_{max} = 1$ GHz.

Table 2. List of all inputs.

Input	Min	Max	Unit
Phases: $\varphi[0 - 50]$	0	2π	rad
Time: T	1	5	$1/f_{max}$

Objective Functions. We seek to make $U(\varphi, T)$ (see Eq. 1) as close as possible to $U_0 := \begin{pmatrix} 0 & i \\ i & 0 \end{pmatrix}$, because this matrix represents the π-pulse that we look for, since we base our work on the protocol of [18], which features only π-pulses. This motivates us to define the gate infidelity as follows:

$$F(\varphi, T) := \mathbb{E}(1 - \text{Tr}(U(\varphi, T)U_0^\dagger)/4) \tag{4}$$

A important source of errors in quantum computation, is spontaneous photon emission. In this random process, super excited states like the Rydberg ones, tend to spontaneously revert to a lower-energy state, releasing a photon. This cannot be prevented, so the only way to minimise the risk of occurrence is to minimise the time spent by the electron in the Rydberg orbital. Assuming the electron starts in the 1 orbital, this quantity is given by:

$$G(\varphi, T) := \mathbb{E}\left(\int_0^T |\langle r|U(\varphi, t)|1\rangle|^2 dt\right) \tag{5}$$

Let's briefly show that these two quality criteria are antagonistic. Simulating flat pulses leads to the appearance of noise terms of the form $\varepsilon(\frac{jT}{N})$ in the computations. Since the number N of slices is fixed, these terms tend to vanish as T grows to infinity. Thus, the impact of noise can be mitigated by extending the pulse duration, and choosing a trivial φ. In other words, increasing T tends to reduce F, as well as simplifying the choice of φ, but it would potentially imply a larger value of G and thus a higher risk of Rydberg state decay. On the other hand, $0 \leq G \leq T$ (because the integrand is lower than 1), so an optimal G would rather be found by decreasing T, but in turn this complexifies the search for optimal phases. Consequently, to find the trade-off between these objectives is required.

4   Proposed Method

The goal of this study is to reduce the gate infidelity (i.e. the impact of laser noise) by finding the optimal laser phases φ, without increasing the time spent in the Rydberg state, in order to minimise the risk of Rydberg state decay. Consequently, it will improve the global gate quality. To achieve this goal, we propose a CPU-parallel multi-objective optimisation-based method, since the quantum gate design can be formulated as a continuous bi-objective computationally expensive problem (as was shown above). Indeed, a multi-objective

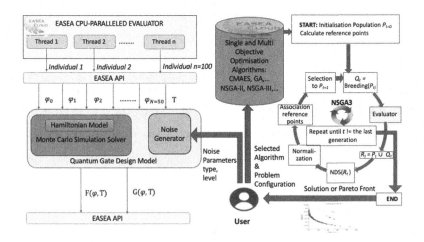

Fig. 2. Simplified scheme of the proposed method.

optimization process allows us to find: (i) all possible non dominated solutions – combinations of φ and T, which is called the Pareto set; (ii) its image in the objective space, which presents the Pareto front. Thus, we consider to define a set of optimal parameters of the model (i.e., the phases vector of the laser pulses and the duration of the model simulation), by minimizing the objective functions (i.e., overall infidelity and time spent in the Rydberg state), calculated by simulation. The proposed method consists of two following parts:

- A Quantum gate design presented in Sect. 3.2, which consists of simulating the laser pulse hamiltonian, on noisy trajectories; and computing the objective functions with Monte Carlo average. For the sake of completeness, the noise generation details are provided in online supplementary materials: https://git.unistra.fr/tsley/thesis.
- The EASEA platform, an open-source compiler, which supports single and multi-objective optimization thanks to its own base of the templates of different state-of-the-art algorithms [19]. The main advantage of EASEA is that it allows scientists to apply evolutionary algorithms to solve their real-world problems through a user-friendly interface with CPU and/or GPU parallelisation. More precisely, this compiler automatically couples one of the algorithm template files and a problem to be optimised, and provides the C++ based code of the selected algorithm with the integrated problem in it and the compiling file. Consequently, it suits perfectly as a software support for our study. Notably, the quantum gate design model can be modified without changing other parties of the code, due to the very flexible structure of EASEA.

By this concept, we had to select an optimisation algorithm template (*.tpl file), define the problem in terms of the pseudo-code (*.ez file) and define the noise parameters, such as the spectrum (white, pink, etc.) and its level w.r.t. maximal intensity of the laser pulse. The simplified scheme of the considered method is schematically depicted in Fig. 2. It details the programming relation between: (i) the EASEA CPU-parallel evaluator with our quantum gate design model presented on the left and (ii) the selected multi-objective algorithm: Non-dominated Sorting Genetic Algorithm (NSGA-III), shown on the right in Fig. 2. NSGA-III originally presented in [22], is based on the non-dominated sorting selection mechanism and uses a predefined set of reference points to ensure diversity in the solutions [22]. NSGA-III was selected in this work between other templates, because of the following reasons: (i) it is efficient on several multi- and many-objective problems [23] (in future, the current problem can be extended to a many-objective version); (ii) it does not require any additional hyper-parameters; (iii) it introduces a computationally fast approach, by which the reference point set is adaptively updated on the fly based on the association status of each reference point over a number of generations [22,23]; (iv) it can handle constraints without introducing any new parameter, which can be useful in our next research, where some constraints will be taken into account; (v) it can easily be scaled for solving single-objective problems [23]. The following steps explain how this method performs:

1. The selected optimization algorithm, e.g., NSGA-III, starts by randomly generating the initial set of solutions, where each solution consists of the parameters presented in Table 2;
2. Its main cycle is repeatedly executed until the last generation (see the right part of Fig. 2);
3. NSGA-III creates the new child population Q_t from the parent population P_t by the classical breeding operators used in NSGA-III [22]: Simulated Binary crossover (SBX) crossover and Polynomial mutation operator.
4. The *EASEA Evaluator* executes 100 threads to compute F and G in parallel (see the left part of Fig. 2). Each executed thread works out the model code with its own combination of input parameters and generated noise.
5. Each thread returns the output values (the overall infidelity (F) and the time spent in the Rydberg state (G)) back to the NSGA-III.
6. NSGA-III performs according to its description presented in [22] and goes to the next generation.

Also, important to emphasise that NSGA-III of EASEA is designed for CPU parallel use (several hundred computing threads), which allows us to reduce the runtime.

5 Experimental Analysis

5.1 Experimental Design

All values of the setting parameters (both for the simulation model and for the optimisation algorithm) presented below, are the same during all provided experiments. For all experiments we use the problem definition presented in Sect. 3.3. The decision variables are defined as the presented input parameters. For single-objective study, we use only F as a single optimisation function and applied the well-known Covariance Matrix Adaptation Evolution Strategy (CMA-ES) algorithm [25] from the EASEA plateform. For multi-objective study, as it was presented above, the NSGA-III algorithm is applied.

Model Settings. In this paper, we chose to work with $1/f$ noise, also known as pink or flicker noise, since it is widely present in electronic devices, and thus in the quantum hardware that they control. So, we generate 10^6 samples thereof, each time as a sum of sines and cosines with 25 uniformly log-spaced harmonics, in the interval $[f_{max}, 100f_{max}]$, thereby approximating a high-frequency noise. Remind that f_{max} is the characteristic unit of the problem, and is set to 1. Remind that the optimisation target is a π-pulse to implement a Rydberg blockade two-qubit CZ gate. We effectuate three tests with respective noise levels of 10%, 20% and 30% of the maximal laser pulse intensity.

Optimisation Settings. For all experiments, the number of decision variables equals 51, according to the problem definition. The parameter settings of CMA-ES is limited by the number of generations = 300, the population size = 100 and the number of threads = 100. The parameter settings of NSGA-III are presented in Table 3, where p_c is Simulated Binary (SBX) crossover probability, η_c is crossover distribution index, p_m is polynomial mutation probability, η_m is polynomial distribution index, M is the number of objectives, P is a given integer value, which refers to the number of divisions considered along of each objective axis, H is the number of reference points, N is the population size, G is the number of generation and Th is the number of threads. The selection of P, H and N was made according to the rules defined in [22]: (i) if a problem has less number of objectives, a larger number of P is required (100 is recommended value in bi-objective case); (ii) H is calculated by the approach´of Das and Dennis [24]; (iii) the population size is set as the smallest multiple of four higher than the number of reference points (in our case $N=H$).

Table 3. Parameter settings of NSGA-III.

Parameter	p_c	η_c	p_m	η_m	M	P	H	N	G	Th
Value	1.0	30	1/51	20	2	99	100	100	200	100

5.2 Result Analysis

The obtained results are shown in Fig. 3 and described below.

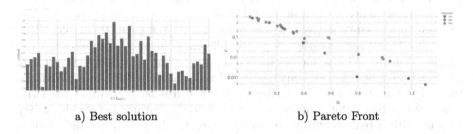

a) Best solution   b) Pareto Front

Fig. 3. Obtained results.

Single-Objective. This study started with a single-objective optimisation of F, with a fixed $T = 1$ and a noise intensity of 10%. After 136 generations of 100 candidates, the algorithm CMA-ES found an optimal solution $F = 0.005052$.

This solution in terms of the coordinates of φ is presented in log scale in Fig. 3 (a). This result is better than the gate infidelity $F = 0.0055$ obtained with the naive choice of setting all the 50 phase to be zero: $\varphi = \mathbf{0}$. This result confirmed us that artificial evolution can bring some improvements in robust gate designs, and motivated us to explore multi-criteria optimisation for simultaneous antagonistic problems.

Multi-objective. The Pareto fronts obtained for three selected noise levels (%10, %20 and %30 of $2\pi f_{\max}$) are presented in Fig. 3(b), where the axe F is presented in log scale. As it seen from Fig. 3(b), the lowest minimum of F was obtained in the case of 10% noise level (presented in blue).

For the rightmost element of the Pareto front, the pulses we find result in a compromise between an infidelity slightly higher than the naive case, and a shorter time spent in the Rydberg state, signalling a preference in reducing Rydberg decay risk. For elements of the leftmost Pareto front, the situation is reversed. This shows that NSGA-III drives the solutions to satisfactory compromises, which should be investigated w.r.t. possible values of the Rydberg decay rate. For all cases, the shape of the Pareto Front is slightly discontinuous, however the solutions are not irregularly distributed in the objective space. It shows that for all selected noise levels, NSGA-III is able to find solutions in the different regions of the objective space, providing the possible variations of trade-off between the overall infidelity and the time spent in the Rydberg state. We assume that these results can be improved by increasing the population size and the number of generations.

6   Conclusion

The multi-objective based method we propose aims at introducing a reliable gate design, which allows us to reduce both the laser noise impact and the risk of Rydberg state decay. As a result, this method provides a variety of trade-offs between these two objectives, within a reasonable run-time, thanks to CPU-parallelization. It can be easily applied to different noise and laser pulses models. The problem studied here focuses on decomposing a flat pulse affected with pink noise on both amplitude and phase with different noise intensity levels. With the trust of the multi-objective optimization method, thanks to EASEA platform, it is now possible to look for interesting gate design features for a wide variety of noise with a reduced run-time. Moreover, as the EASEA platform provides different single and multi-objective optimisation algorithms, which can be easily coupled with the problem of laser noise reduction, we prospect to investigate the impact of different optimisation techniques on the performance in terms of the accuracy and speed up in further works. Also, further research with different noise types would be considered. However, our work inherited the drawbacks of the protocol outlined in [18], in the sense that its setup would require an individual laser for each atom, which is difficult to attain. Therefore, beyond simply noise-corrected π-pulses, future works will involve a global pulse model with higher degrees of freedom, similarly to [21]. This would correspond to a single laser for all the atoms, able to design multi-qubit Rydberg blockade gates. It is expected that this method can help to make a qualitative step toward developing robust quantum gates.

Scientific Validation

This paper has benefited from the remarks of the following reviewers:

- Smita Kasar, Maharashtra Institute of Technology, India
- Ayman Youssef, Electronics research institute, Egypt
- Douglas Motadias, State University of Rio de Janeiro, Brazil

The conference organisers wish to thank them for their highly appreciated effort and contribution.

References

1. Aaronson, S., Arkhipov, A.: The computational complexity of linear optics. In: Proceedings of the Forty-Third Annual ACM Symposium on Theory of Computing, pp. 333–342 (2011)
2. Cao, Y., et al.: Quantum chemistry in the age of quantum computing. Chem. Rev. **119**(19), 10856–10915 (2019)
3. Kairys, P., et al.: Simulating the Shastry-Sutherland Ising model using quantum annealing. Prx Quantum **1**(2), 020320 (2020)
4. Shor, P.W.: Polynomial-time algorithms for prime factorization and discrete logarithms on a quantum computer. SIAM Rev. **41**(2), 303–332 (1999)
5. Zhou, Y., Stoudenmire, E.M., Waintal, X.: What limits the simulation of quantum computers? Phys. Rev. X **10**(4), 041038 (2020)
6. Noh, K., Jiang, L., Fefferman, B.: Efficient classical simulation of noisy random quantum circuits in one dimension. Quantum **4**, 318 (2020)
7. Napp, J.C., La Placa, R.L., Dalzell, A.M., Brandao, F.G., Harrow, A.W.: Efficient classical simulation of random shallow 2D quantum circuits. Phys. Rev. X **12**(2), 021021 (2022)
8. Urbanek, M., Nachman, B., Pascuzzi, V.R., He, A., Bauer, C.W., de Jong, W.A.: Mitigating depolarizing noise on quantum computers with noise-estimation circuits. Phys. Rev. Lett. **127**(27), 270502 (2021)
9. Schultz, K., et al.: Impact of time-correlated noise on zero-noise extrapolation. Phys. Rev. A **106**(5), 052406 (2022)
10. Van Damme, L., Ansel, Q., Glaser, S.J., Sugny, D.: Robust optimal control of two-level quantum systems. Phys. Rev. A **95**(6), 063403 (2017)
11. Dridi, G., Liu, K., Guérin, S.: Optimal robust quantum control by inverse geometric optimization. Phys. Rev. Lett. **125**(25), 250403 (2020)
12. Dawson, C.M., Nielsen, M.A.: The Solovay-kitaev algorithm. arXiv preprint arXiv:quant-ph/0505030 (2005)
13. Huang, C.H., Goan, H.S.: Robust quantum gates for stochastic time-varying noise. Phys. Rev. A **95**(6), 062325 (2017)

14. Le, I.N.M., Teske, J.D., Hangleiter, T., Cerfontaine, P., Bluhm, H.: Analytic filter-function derivatives for quantum optimal control. Phys. Rev. Appl. **17**(2), 024006 (2022)
15. Hangleiter, T., Cerfontaine, P., Bluhm, H.: Filter-function formalism and software package to compute quantum processes of gate sequences for classical non-Markovian noise. Phys. Rev. Res. **3**(4), 043047 (2021)
16. Kang, M., et al.: Designing filter functions of frequency-modulated pulses for high-fidelity two-qubit gates in ion chains. Phys. Rev. Appl. **19**(1), 014014 (2023)
17. Vardi, M.Y.: Quantum hype and quantum skepticism. Commun. ACM **62**(5), 7–7 (2019)
18. Jaksch, D., Cirac, J.I., Zoller, P.: SL Rolston, R. Côté and MD Lukin. Phys. Rev. Lett. **85**, 2208 (2000)
19. Collet, P., Lutton, E., Schoenauer, M., Louchet, J.: Take it EASEA. In: PPSN VI (2000)
20. Morgado, M., Whitlock, S.: Quantum simulation and computing with Rydberg-interacting qubits. AVS Quant. Sci. **3**(2), 023501 (2021)
21. Jandura, S., Pupillo, G.: Time-optimal two-and three-qubit gates for Rydberg atoms. Quantum **6**, 712 (2022)
22. Deb, K., Jain, H.: An evolutionary many-objective optimization algorithm using reference-point-based non dominated sorting approach, part I: solving problems with box constraints. IEEE Trans. Evol. Comput. **18**(4), 577–601 (2013)
23. Seada, H., Deb, K.: U-NSGA-III: a unified evolutionary optimization procedure for single, multiple, and many objectives: proof-of-principle results. In: Proceedings of the Evolutionary Multi-criterion Optimization: 8th International Conference (EMO 2015), Guimarães, 29 March–1 April 2015, Part II, pp. 34–49 (2015)
24. Das, I., Dennis, J.E.: Normal-boundary intersection: a new method for generating the Pareto surface in nonlinear multicriteria optimization problems. SIAM J. Optim. **8**(3), 631–657 (1998)
25. Hansen, N., Auger, A.: CMA-ES: evolution strategies and covariance matrix adaptation. In: Proceedings of the 13th Annual Conference Companion on Genetic and Evolutionary Computation, pp. 991–1010 (2011)

Short Time Series Forecasting Method Based on Genetic Programming and Kalman Filter

Lalla Aicha Kone[1,2]([✉]) [ID], Anna Ouskova Leonteva[1], Mamadou Tourad Diallo[2], Ahmedou Haouba[2], and Pierre Collet[1] [ID]

[1] ICUBE Laboratory, Strasbourg University, Strasbourg, France
[2] Reasearch Unit of Scientific Computing, Computer Science and Data Science, University of Nouakchott, Nouakchott, Mauritania
lallaaicha.k@gmail.com

Abstract. Accurate forecasting of the baccalaureate admission statistics is a crucial step towards an improvement of the educational system in Mauritania and its responsiveness to the economical needs. Since an available historical information is collected only over last ten years, an accurate forecasting technique for short time series is required. Addressing this issue, the presented paper proposes a tool based on the genetic programming and Kalman filter. This tool allows to make accurate short term prediction for short time series and easily set up experiments. A tool validation on different data sets is presented, where the provided tool provides more robust forecasting results comparatively with the state-of-the-art techniques. It is expected that this tool can help to make a qualitative jump in the improvement of Mauritanian education system.

Keywords: Short time series forecasting · Genetic programming · Kalman filter

1 Introduction

As a good education system is a prerequisite for successful economic growth, Mauritania has engaged in a significant effort to increase the quality of national education since 1992[1]. Despite the progress made in recent years in terms of the global access to education, there are still many shortcomings in the education system, which is also being impacted by the SARS-CoV-2 pandemic crisis (COVID-19)[2]. To address these challenges, the Mauritanian government requires a short-term recommendation system to meet the country's economical needs

---

[1] https://documents1.worldbank.org/curated/en/982661583533195267/pdf/
Mauritania-Enhanced-Heavily-Indebted-Poor-Countries-HIPC-Initiative.pdf.
[2] https://documents.worldbank.org/en/publication/documents-reports/
documentdetail/819601592919148037.

P. Collet et al. (Eds.): CCE 2023, LNCS 13927, pp. 77–89, 2023.
https://doi.org/10.1007/978-3-031-44355-8_6

in terms of financing and developing new education programs and infrastructures. In this context, a reliable forecasting approach to predict the baccalaureate admission statistics is needed in order to provide such kind of recommendations.

Despite numerous forecasting techniques proposed during recent years, a choice of the most suitable forecasting method is not obvious, due to a credibility of their results is greatly affected by the quality and quantity of the available historical data [11]. The data of Mauritanian baccalaureate admission statistics has been collected since 2013 and is presented in the form of 22 time series of only 10 points (one point for one year). Each time series is associated with an indicator of Baccalaureate Admission Rate (BAR): e.g., the baccalaureate types, subject areas, genders, etc. Consequently, the problem we address can be classified as a short-term forecasting for very short time series.

The short time series forecasting is seldom considered in the literature, even though the capability to produce accurate forecasts with few past data points can be useful in many research cases, where no historical data is available [7]. There are three common ways to deal with a small dataset in order to avoid overfitting effect: (i) to choose simple models; (ii) to combine several models; (ii) extend the dataset by using synthetic samples.

In this paper, we focus on a combined model and provide a comfortable GPU-paralleled forecasting tool based on coupling Genetic Programming (GP) [13] with Kalman Filter (KF) [9] for short time series predictions. The idea to implement KF on the basis of GP model is not new: the coupling extended KF with GP has already been introduced for forecasting monthly water demand in [17]. However, it has never been applied for short time series. Our choice of this method is explained by the properties of its components. GP is an evolutionary inspired tree-structured technique [13], whose main advantages are as follows: (i) it does not require any prior specific knowledge about a functional form of the final solution, (e.g., linear or nonlinear, etc.); (ii) it has small number of hyper-parameters; (iii) it provides an interpretable model. However, a GP-based model can be overfitted due to the lack of training data. As every GP model can be represented in the form of the state space model, KF seems to be a good candidate to improve the accuracy of GP forecasting results. Indeed, KF works in the context of a state space model to compute the sequence of filtering current state of a dynamic system that is excited by a stochastic noise. Thus, the use of KF with GP could provide better forecasts. Compiling all together, we contribute by two inputs: (i) a new insight about a coupling method of GP and KF for the short time series forecasting; (ii) a new forecasting tool based on this method for making a step forward the further improvement of the educational system in Mauritania. The applicability of the presented tool is validated by the experiments conducted on the four short time series *versus* the classical state-of-the-art-techniques.

This paper is structured as follows. Section 2 outlines the state-of-the-art relevant methods. Section 3 presents the proposed forecasting tool with used materials. We report the experiments and evaluation results on four data sets of the baccalaureate admission in Sect. 4. Section 5 concludes this article.

2   Related Work

As we focus on the short time series forecasting, in this section, we briefly review
the state-of-the-art methods aimed at this issue.

Random Walk, Mean Method: Random Walk (RW) and Mean method are the
simplest forecasting methods: in the RW, the forecast for the next period is equal
to the last observed value plus a random noise; in the Mean method, the future
predictions are equal to the arithmetic average of the observed values. However,
they are generally recommended to use for the short time series case[3],[4]. Indeed,
in the short yearly series of M3 competition, RW was among the methods which
give the best results [8]. Among their limitation, the problem in using the RW
method for the time series with trend and the sensitivity of the Mean method
to extreme values, so the predictions can be biased.

AutoRegressive Integrated Moving Average (ARIMA): ARIMA forecasting
model aims at describing the autocorrelations in the stationary data (i.e., when
the mean and variance doesn't change over time). Its acronym describes the
component as follows: (i) AR – AutoRegression models calculate a forecast by
regressing on an observation and its prior values; (ii) I – Integrated models
(used for non-stationary data), in which, the actual values of the data have been
replaced with the differences between each value and its prior value, in order to
make the time series stationary; (iii) MA – Moving Average models calculate a
forecast by regressing on the past prediction errors instead of the actual past
values. ARIMA was not developed for short time series, but it is one of the
most widely used approaches for time series forecasting and it has already been
applied for this issue [14].

The Simple Exponential Smoothing Method (SES): SES is another popular
time series forecasting method for univariate data without trend or seasonality.
It requires a single parameter, so called smoothing factor α. This factor controls
the rate at which the influence of the observations at prior time steps decay
exponentially and usually has the range of possible values between 0 and 1.
Large value of α makes the model to pay attention mainly to the most recent
past observations, whereas its smaller value takes more of the prior observations
into account. Addressing to short time series forecasting, in [18], the authors
applied this method for short yearly series. They conclude that SES model is
suitable only for short-term forecasts.

The Grey Model: The grey model is an approach that was build for short time
series [3]. Using the differential equations to exploit the data, this model requires
less information to predict future observations with good accuracy. However, it
can lead to unacceptable prediction errors in some cases, as it was shown in [3].
Thus, a new algorithm based on the standard rolling grey model optimized by
a meta-heuristic optimization algorithm (RGMMOA) has been proposed [5]. It
demonstrates a higher accuracy comparatively with the standard grey models.

---

[3] https://robjhyndman.com/hyndsight/short-time-series/.
[4] https://otexts.com/fpp2/long-short-ts.html.

Other Methods: Many related works concerning a combination of KF with different forecasting models have been proposed in literature. Mainly, KF has been used for modeling predictive systems as a hybrid method together with a ARIMA model [1,2], demonstrating very good results. In [17], the extended KF is combined with GP for forecasting of water monthly demand. However, these combined method has never been applied for short time series forecasting.

We borrow this idea to combine GP with KF for short time series forecasting because of the following reasons:

1. The GP-based model has several important features: (i) it does not need any kind of assumptions: e.g., stationarity, invertibility, etc.; (ii) GP provides a possible nonlinear and deterministic mathematical equation to fit data, consequently, its evolved model can be interpretable in the future works, especially when the number of observation points will be larger; (iii) it has not any strong limitations for a minimum number of training points.
2. GP-based model can be not accurate, due to the lack of data. Since KF uses a series of measurements observed over time, containing noise and other inaccuracies, and produces an estimate of unknown variables, this estimate tends to be more accurate than a single measurement alone. Consequently, KF can improve the forecasting results.

3   Materials and Method

We adapt the method presented in [17] though the following modifications: (i) the discrete KF is applied instead of the extended KF as the most simple and convenient version of KF for the described problem; (ii) we do not use the previous lags as decision variables (input data); (iii) GP algorithm uses an interval arithmetic approach (presented in [6]) for protection of mathematics operators; (iv) GPU-paralleled version of GP is applied for having ability to work with a large-sized population in small number of generations that allows us to reduce the runtime and accelerate the convergence rate.

3.1   Used Techniques in the Proposed Method

Genetic Programming: GP is an evolutionary inspired and population based modeling technique, which can be used to explain nonlinear relationships between some input and output of the observed data [12,17]. Indeed, GP creates a mathematical equation that would fit the observed data via some features (i.e., inputs or so called decision variables) and target value (i.e., output) from this data [13]. The main evolutionary steps are shown in Fig. 1. As it seen from Fig. 1, potential solutions (i.e., individuals) in GP are the expressions represented using a tree data structure. Thus, an individual contains operators as nodes of the tree (that can be arithmetical, trigonometric, logarithmic and logical functions) and variables as the leaves.

For sake of brevity, we do not provide the detailed description of the classical GP algorithm largely presented in the literature (e.g., in [13]). Instead, we directly outline the configuration steps of GP algorithm used in this work:

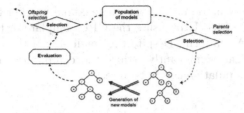

Fig. 1. Flowchart of GP. The illustration is adapted from [12].

1. specifying a terminal set for each time series, which consists of (i) only one decision variable - a timestamp (x); (ii) an ephemeral random constant (ERC), which selects a random number that is uniformly distributed in the interval $[0, 1]$;
2. specifying a target variable for each time series: $\tilde{y} = f(x)$, where x is a timestamp and f - is the obtained equation by the GP algorithm;
3. specifying the set of primitive functions for representing an individual f (the same for all time series): Add (ADD), Subtract (SUB), Multiply (MUL), Divide (DIV), square root (SQRT), exponential (EXP) and trigonometric functions (SIN, COS). In order to protect operators against the cases, when the function can produce the value like Nan (not a number) and Inf (infinity) and at the same time to avoid the known negative effects from protected operators [6], we implemented the interval concept (presented in [6]) in the regression template of the EASEA (*EAsy Specification of Evolutionary Algorithms*) platform (described in [4]). By integrating an interval information into the operator process, the number of invalid solution (which can be produced during the search) are significantly reduced, which is especially important, when the model was trained on small-sized data.
4. choosing the fitness function (for all time series): to evaluate a tree-based individual (the accuracy of obtained equation), Root Mean Square Error (RMSE) is selected:

$$RMSE = \sqrt{(\frac{1}{n}) \sum_{i=1}^{n} (\tilde{y}_i - y_i)^2} \tag{1}$$

where $\tilde{y}$ - the computed data from the obtained equation $f(x)$, y is observed data and n is the number of observed samples.
5. choosing the selection operator for sampling individuals: in this work, the individuals (equations) with better target values are picked using a tournament selection method with non-generational replacement [15]. The weak elitism with an elite number of 1 is used: (i) to avoid premature convergence of the GP algorithm; (ii) to not lose the best individual.
6. Setting the GP parameters: (i) maximal tree depth: 5; (ii) evaluator goal: minimise; (iii) other hyperparameters (i.e., population size, probabilities of performing the crossover and mutation, number of generation, etc.) were defined empirically and their values are presented in the experimental settings;

7. Specifying the termination criterion: the maximal number of generations;
8. Parallelizing GP on GPU by using the GPU template of the GP algorithm from the EASEA platform. Despite the small size of the dataset, the GPU implementation can significantly reduce the computational cost, especially when the large population size is required.

Kalman Filter: KF is a powerful method for estimating the state vector of a linear dynamic system described in the state space from noisy observations using the previous state and weighting [9,16,19]. The KF algorithm was originally presented in [9] and described in the details in many papers: e.g., in [19]. It has been widely used in a lot of real-world applications (e.g., NASA's Apollo 11 mission)[5], including forecasting (e.g., [16,17]).

Before we discuss application of KF for short time series forecasting in the domain of baccalaureate admission statistics, first, we briefly discuss a few key working principles of the discrete KF algorithm (used in this work) The discrete KF algorithm is schematically shown in Fig. 2, where its ongoing cycle is presented: (i) the predict step projects the current state estimate ahead in time; (ii) the correct step adjusts the projected estimate by an actual measurement at that time [19]. In order to make Fig. 2 clearer, the comments with the used notations are briefly presented below. During the predict step, the state error covariance matrix (P) is calculated from its previous value, the dynamic system matrix (A) and the noise covariance matrix (Q). Then, during the correct step, the matrix P is calculated from the Kalman gain (K), the observation matrix (H) and predicted P. The matrix A and Q are constant and have to be known for each instant of time, so the only variable that affects P is the Kalman gain. As it seen from the first equation of the correct step at Fig. 2, K is calculated from predicted P, H and the matrix of observation noise (R) that are either constants. Thus, the Kalman gain is an important element of KF, which is the regulator between the estimate and the measurement. As it seen in the equation of the gain in Fig. 2, K decides (based on error from previous estimations), which of either the estimate or measurement to give more weight. More precisely, if a

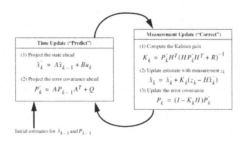

Fig. 2. Kalman filter equations and instruction. The illustration is adapted from [19].

---

[5] https://www.cs.unc.edu/~welch/kalman/siam_cipra.html.

prediction (an estimate) is good, then the Kalman gain works to cancel out the effect of new measurements, in other case it gives weight to the new measurements to make subsequent predictions. Important to notice that A, Q and R are generally used as tuning parameters which the user can adjust to attain the desired performance [10].

Now, we explain the application of KF in this work. In order to implement KF on the basis of the mathematical equation obtained by the GP process, the latter has to be defined as a dynamical system in the state space form [17]. We define the following dynamical system (using the same notations that in Fig. 2):

1. Let the predicted state x in time k be composed of position and velocity: $x_k = x_{k-1} + T\dot{x}_{k-1}$, where T is the sampling period;
2. The optional control input (u) is defined as an acceleration term $u_k = \frac{\ddot{x}_{k-1}T^2}{2}$ (see the first equation in predict step in Fig. 2);
3. The output is position measurement (z_k), calculated from the mathematical equation of GP.

3.2 Method Description

Once the techniques (GP and KF) used as a basis of the proposed method have been described and the integrated modifications to match our research case are detailed, we compile all together to provide a comfortable and robust forecasting tool with required predictive reliability for short time series. To make the presented method more general, user-friendly, and to simplify a code-coupling process between GP, KF and a historical data, the open-source EASEA platform is used as a software basis. The EASEA is a compiler, to automatically merge a scientific problem (specified in problem description file *.ez)[6] with an algorithm template (in this case, the GP algorithm template) into a CPU or GPU parallel C++ code [4]. It significantly simplifies a forecasting process, because the EASEA application does not require special knowledge about GP algorithms from users.

The presented tool based on the EASEA platform is schematically depicted in Fig. 3. As explained, KF uses a series of measurements observed over time from GP model (containing inaccuracies due to a lack of data for GP modeling) and produces estimates of unknown variables, which tend to be more accurate than those based on a single measurement of GP alone. Thus, the predictions produced by the equation of the GP model is considered as a new measurement for being filtered.

The considered tool is assumed as an ongoing process, where the GP model will be updated with each new data points.

---

[6] http://easea.unistra.fr.

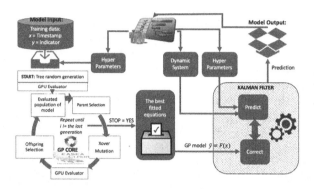

Fig. 3. The simplified structure of the proposed tool.

4   Experiments and Results

The objective of the presented below experiments is to study the forecasting capacities of the proposed algorithm and to make a statistical analysis of its performance w.r.t. the state-of-the-art algorithms on different datasets. We do not provide a cross-validation (leave-one-out) tests of our algorithm in this work, because of the following reasons: (i) we can not use several time series for training and one for test, because all short time series contain completely different information, and the individual model is made for each time series; (ii) if we will use the same set for a leave-one-out test - in many cases we will predict the past based on the future.

4.1   Experiments Settings

Data Sources (9 Different Time Series Are Used in Total): Four short time series from the real dataset provided by the Department of Orientation and Scholarships of the Ministry of Higher Education and Scientific Research in Mauritania, associated with the following indicators of the baccalaureate admission: (i) the total rate of baccalaureate admission (total BAR); (ii) the rate of baccalaureate admission in the first session (BAR in 1st session); (iii) the rate of baccalaureate admission in mathematics (BAR in M); (iv) the rate of girls baccalaureate admission in literature (BAR (girls) in L). Each time series contains only 10 observations collected from 2013 to 2022, where the train/test ratio is 6/4. Figure 4 shows these time series (in %) divided on training and test sets by red line. The shapes of these curves are different and challenging to forecast, due to a few number of training points.

Three different short time series selected from World Bank Open Data[7]: (i) Primary Completion Rate (PCR) female (% of relevant age group) in Bulgaria : 36 observations, where the train/test ratio is 31/5; (ii) Literacy Rate (LR), adult

---

[7] https://data.worldbank.org/.

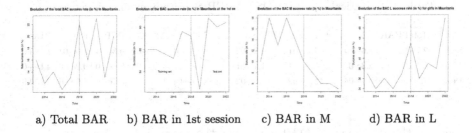

| a) Total BAR | b) BAR in 1st session | c) BAR in M | d) BAR in L |

Fig. 4. Evolution of the indicators.

total (% of people ages 15 and above) in Sub-Saharan Africa: 35 observations, where the train/test ratio is 30/5; (iii) Renewable Electricity Output (REO) (% of total electricity output) in Indonesia: 30 observations, where the train/test ratio is 25/5.

Two following short time series (20 observations) from the M3 forecasting competition[8] for yearly interval are selected: №10 and №120, where the train/test ratio is 14/6.

GP Parameter Settings: (i) population size = 15000; (ii) number of Generations = 500; (iii) crossover probability = 90%; (iv) mutation probability = 10%. We use the large population size in order to: (i) accelerate the convergence; (ii) load the GPU card with enough threads to keep it busy.

KF Parameter Settings: The values of measurement and process noise were selected empirically for each dataset.

State-of-the-Art Models: (i) Five methods from R package FMA (Forecasting Methods and Applications)[9]: Random walk, Mean Method; SES, ARIMA (in mode auto) and Neural Network based forecast method; (ii) Grey model: the MATLAB source code is borrowed from [5].

Metrics of Performance: (i) RMSE is the Root Mean Squared Error between the predicted and actual values (returns the value in the same scale as a target); (ii) MAPE Mean Absolute Percentage Error between the predicted and actual values (returns the value in %).

4.2   Results and Analysis

In order to define the GP-based models for the proposed method, the GP algorithm was run 30 times on training set for each time series, and the best model (equation) was selected by the smallest value of RMSE between 30 obtained solutions. Table 1 summarises the statistical results of these runs on the selected training sets: RMSE value of the best obtained equation, the mean RMSE value and the standard deviation (STD).

As seen from Table 1, the most inaccurate models are for M3-competition data series. However, their large value of RMSE can be explained by the different

---

[8] https://forecasters.org/resources/time-series-data/m3-competition/.
[9] https://github.com/robjhyndman/fma.

86   L. A. Kone et al.

Table 1. Statistical reports (RMSE) of GP algorithm on all training sets.

Metric	Total BAR	BAR in 1st	BAR in M	BAR L in L	M3-10	M3-120	PCR	LR	REO
STD	2.7e-02	1.0e-04	1.0e-01	4.2e-02	2.4e+01	5.2e+01	9.3e-01	9.0e-01	1.7e+0
Mean	6.1e-02	2.3e-04	2.5e-01	1.1e-01	8.2e+01	3.0e+02	5.5e+0	3.2e+0	4.5e+0
Best	7.5e-03	1.1e-04	8.1e-02	7.3e-02	2.5e+01	9.1e+01	3.1e+0	1.9e+0	2.0e+0

scales in the data: in the M3 time series, the target values are much larger comparatively with the others, where the data presented in %. Probably, this results can be improved by an additional tuning of hyper parameters of the GP algorithms (e.g., by increasing the population size) and should be investigated in the future works. The very small values of RMSE for the baccalaureate admission data can be explained by a few number of observations in the training set (only 6 points).

The comparative results of the proposed method (the best equation integrated in KF) *versus* the obtained GP-models (the best equation) and the selected state-of-the-arts algorithms are presented in Table 2 and Table 3. As seen from Table 2, KF+GP shows the best performance in terms of RMSE in 5 test cases from 9. In the other cases, the delta between KF+GP and the best performed methods are very small (around 0.5–2.5 %). In terms of MAPE metric, KF+GP provides the best performance in 3 test cases. Moreover, in the other cases, this metrics is very close to the best one (1–5 %). Figure 5 summarises the MAPE values obtained by the models for all test cases in the violin plot. From Fig. 5, Table 2 and Table 3, we can conclude that, in general, the proposed method shows more robust and stable results comparatively to the others.

Table 2. Forecasting errors (RMSE).

Algorithm	Total BAR	BAR in 1st	BAR in M	BAR in L	M3-10	M3-120	PCR	LR	REO
RW	05.52	**6.57**	**03.90**	**05.36**	4488.55	1970.13	08.21	2.59	3.34
Mean	05.06	6.91	07.66	05.732	3298.74	6129.48	09.68	9.75	2.83
Ses	04.30	6.91	05.70	05.634	4488.53	1970.28	08.21	2.59	3.18
Arima	05.06	6.72	07.66	05.732	6572.42	4810.95	09.11	**1.01**	3.34
Net	04.66	7.12	09.27	15.105	4682.02	**0890.64**	10.58	2.04	2.97
GP	07.22	7.09	04.63	07.523	3861.33	9873.90	08.18	4.50	3.69
GP+KF	**03.68**	8.94	**03.91**	06.04	**2243.66**	5311.63	**03.26**	2.70	**2.81**
GM	10.53	6.77	04.57	06.99	9697.06	4899.21	15.51	1.77	4.27

Table 3. Forecasting errors (MAPE).

Algorithm	Total BAR	BAR in 1st	BAR in M	BAR L in L	M3-10	M3-120	PCR	LR	REO
RW	30.26	10.19	064.58	13.31	101.20	20.16	08.98	03.45	16.65
Mean	21.01	11.79	127.67	08.55	060.03	72.24	10.72	14.66	21.03
Ses	**18.37**	12.25	111.68	**08.36**	101.20	20.16	08.98	03.45	**15.75**
Arima	21.01	11.79	127.67	08.55	147.96	48.28	09.91	**01.26**	16.65
Net	22.87	12.54	145.27	37.36	105.35	**09.03**	11.75	02.68	16.54
GP	37.85	12.54	059.89	12.02	087.01	88.69	07.68	05.92	20.54
GP+KF	19.95	10.55	**050.39**	09.61	**050.81**	41.94	**03.21**	03.13	20.60
GM	57.91	**09.26**	065.49	16.85	244.97	46.36	16.29	02.53	21.79

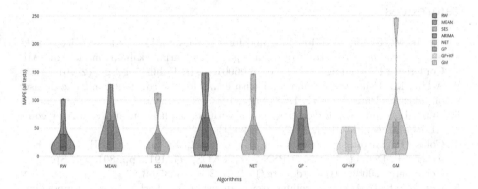

Fig. 5. Violin plot of mean absolute percentage error (MAPE) for all test cases.

5   Conclusion

The continually changing statistics of Baccalaureate admission rate in Mauritania requires a flexible short time series forecasting instrument to predict and control the education reality. This works lays out a method aims at being efficient for this issue, which is based on the integration of GP-based model in the KF algorithm. We also propose a software tool based on the presented method. Thanks to the EASEA platform, this tool is a GPU-paralleled user-friendly instrument, which helps to reduce the time for setting up different experiments. It is validated that the proposed method is useful when the number of observations are limited and provides the stable and robust results (in terms of RMSE and MAPE) relatively with classical state-of-the-art methods. Thanks to the presented tool, it is convenient to launch the proposed method to predict the short-time series of Baccalaureate admission in short-term horizon. Finally, the presented method can be generalized to time series of a different length and nature in different domains.

Scientific Validation

This paper has benefited from the remarks of the following reviewers:

- Mario Giacobini, University of Torino, Italy
- Meghana Kshirsagar, University of Limerick, Ireland
- Ulviya Abdulkarimova, French Azerbaijani University, France

The conference organisers wish to thank them for their highly appreciated effort and contribution.

References

1. Aamir, M., Shabri, A.: Modelling and forecasting monthly crude oil price of pakistan: a comparative study of arima, garch and arima kalman model. In: AIP Conference Proceedings, vol. 1750, p. 060015. AIP Publishing LLC (2016)
2. Aslam, M.: Using the kalman filter with arima for the covid-19 pandemic dataset of pakistan. Data Brief **31**, 105854 (2020)
3. Bilgil, H.: New grey forecasting model with its application and computer code. AIMS Mathematics **6**(2), 1497–1514 (2021)
4. Collet, P., Lutton, E., Schoenauer, M., Louchet, J.: Take it EASEA. In: Schoenauer, M., Deb, et al. (eds.) PPSN 2000. LNCS, vol. 1917, pp. 891–901. Springer, Heidelberg (2000). https://doi.org/10.1007/3-540-45356-3_87
5. Cui, Z., et al.: A hybrid rolling grey framework for short time series modelling. Neural Comput. Appl. **33**(17), 11339–11353 (2021)
6. Dick, G.: Interval arithmetic and interval-aware operators for genetic programming. arXiv preprint arXiv:1704.04998 (2017)
7. Fong, S.J., Li, G., Dey, N., Crespo, R.G., Herrera-Viedma, E.: Finding an accurate early forecasting model from small dataset: a case of 2019-ncov novel coronavirus outbreak. arXiv preprint arXiv:2003.10776 (2020)
8. Hibon, M., Makridakis, S.G.: M3-Competition. INSEAD (1999)
9. Kalman, R.: A new approach to liner filtering and prediction problems, transaction of asme. J. Basic Eng. **83**(1), 95–108 (1961)
10. Kim, Y., Bang, H.: Introduct. Kalman Filter Appl. Introduction and implementations of the Kalman filter **1**, 1–16 (2018)
11. Kirshners, A., Borisov, A.: A comparative analysis of short time series processing methods. Inf. Technol. Manag. Sci. **15**(1), 65–69 (2012)
12. Kommenda, M., et al.: Application of genetic programming on temper mill datasets. In: 2009 2nd International Symposium on Logistics and Industrial Informatics, pp. 1–5. IEEE (2009)
13. Koza, J.R.: Genetic programming as a means for programming computers by natural selection. Stat. Comput. **4**, 87–112 (1994)
14. Lusk, E.J., Neves, J.S.: A comparative arima analysis of the 111 series of the makridakis competition. J. Forecast. **3**(3), 329–332 (1984)
15. Maitre, O., Sharma, D., Lachiche, N., Collet, P.: DISPAR-tournament: a parallel population reduction operator that behaves like a tournament. In: Di Chio, C., et al. (eds.) EvoApplications 2011. LNCS, vol. 6624, pp. 284–293. Springer, Heidelberg (2011). https://doi.org/10.1007/978-3-642-20525-5_29

16. Morrison, G.W., Pike, D.H.: Kalman filtering applied to statistical forecasting. Manage. Sci. **23**(7), 768–774 (1977)
17. Nasseri, M., Moeini, A., Tabesh, M.: Forecasting monthly urban water demand using extended Kalman filter and genetic programming. Expert Syst. Appl. **38**(6), 7387–7395 (2011)
18. Ostertagová, E., Ostertag, O.: The simple exponential smoothing model. In: The 4th International Conference on Modelling of Mechanical and Mechatronic Systems, pp. 380–384. Technical University of Košice, Slovak Republic (2011)
19. Welch, G., et al.: An introduction to the Kalman filter (1995)

Performance Upgrade of Sequence Detector Evolution Using Grammatical Evolution and Lexicase Parent Selection Method

Bilal Majeed[1]([✉])(ORCID), Samuel Carvalho[2](ORCID), Douglas Mota Dias[1,3](ORCID),
Ayman Youssef[4](ORCID), Aidan Murphy[5](ORCID), and Conor Ryan[1](ORCID)

[1] University of Limerick, Limerick, Ireland
bilal.majeed@ul.ie
[2] Technological University of the Shannon: Midlands Midwest, Limerick, Ireland
[3] Rio de Janeiro State University, Rio de Janeiro, Brazil
[4] Electronics Research Institute, Cairo, Egypt
[5] Trinity College Dublin, Dublin, Ireland

Abstract. Quickly designing correct and efficient digital circuits is a crucial need for the electronics industry. Several Electronic Design Automation tools are used for this task. Still, they often lack the diversity of designs that search-based techniques can offer, such as our system producing three different designs for a 5-bit '11011' Sequence Detector. Sequence Detectors are some of the most crucial digital sequential circuits evolved in this work using Grammatical Evolution, a Machine Learning technique based on Evolutionary Computation. Compared to the literature, a reasonably small training data set is used to generate diverse solutions/circuits. A comparison is delivered of the results of the evolved circuits using two different parent selection techniques, tournament selection and lexicase selection. It is shown that the evolved circuits using a small training data set have shown a hundred percent test accuracy on a vast amount of test data sets, and the performance of lexicase selection is much better than tournament selection while evolving these circuits.

Keywords: Electronic Design Automation · Evolvable Hardware · Grammatical Evolution · Sequence Detector · Lexicase Selection

1 Introduction

Designing digital circuits is a time-consuming and complex task for designers, which involves passing crucial tests to the system to validate the circuit. It can also involve rigorous verification in the environment in which the circuit will perform. Today, Hardware Description Languages (HDLs) are used throughout the industry to aid in designing circuits [3]. Electronic Design Automation (EDA) tools are used by designers to efficiently use their time and resources to design digital circuits correctly [5]. Some industrial tools use machine learning, such as [24], while some others are based on synthetic intelligence, such as [7] and [4]. Despite having such tools available, digital circuit design involves a lot of human effort. Intelligent and smart EDA tools can make it easier and quicker for the designers to test the circuit on Field-Programmable Gate Arrays (FPGA) before implementing the Application-Specific Integrated Circuit (ASIC). None of the available EDA tools currently use Evolutionary Computation (EC), a search-based technique inspired by the Darwinian theory of evolution. EC had its roots in 1948 when Alan Turing proposed the genetic search method for the first time in history. Since its introduction, the EC research field has expanded significantly and has shown consistent results in different application areas. There are various types of EC methods nowadays, including Genetic Algorithms (GA) [15], Genetic Programming (GP) [8], Evolutionary Strategies (ES) [21], etc. The field of study dedicated to the evolution of circuits or electronic hardware is called Evolvable Hardware (EH). EH is divided into two major categories: intrinsic evolution [34] and extrinsic evolution [6]. In intrinsic evolution, the circuit is evolved and tested on hardware such as an FPGA, while in extrinsic evolution, it is evolved and tested through simulations. This work uses Grammatical Evolution (GE) to create sequential circuits. GE is a GP technique using context-free Backus-Naur Form (BNF) grammars for genotype-to-phenotype mapping. This allows the designers to write the rules of the problem according to the circuit's structure and design requirement in grammar and let the system evolve the solutions from there.

Very High-Speed Integrated Circuit Hardware Description Language (VHDL) [18], and Verilog [3] are the most commonly used HDLs. System-Verilog (SV) [25], a superset of Verilog, is used in this work. SV has some significant advantages over Verilog; in addition to being an HDL, it is also Hardware Verification Language (HVL).

Digital circuits are typically divided into two types: combinational circuits and sequential circuits. Combinational circuits are not time-dependent and provide the output solely based on the current input of the system. They give the output as soon as the input changes. In contrast, a sequential circuit's output is dependent not only on the current input but the previous inputs of the system as well. Unlike combinational circuits, a sequential circuit follows a pattern of inputs to reach a specific output. This pattern is shown in terms of the states of the system. The sequential circuits have a memory element attached to save these states.

A sequential circuit can be represented as a Finite State Machine (FSM) [16]. An FSM is a pictorial representation of the states of a sequential circuit (can be seen here) and shows the state transition based on the system's current state and/or input. It also shows the output of the system against each transition. There are two types of FSMs, Mealy and Moore. The output of the Mealy machine depends upon the current state and input of the system, while in the case of a Moore machine, the output solely depends upon the system's current state.

This paper proposes a single-stage automatic design of some hard-to-design sequential circuits named Sequence Detectors (SDs). SDs are specific kinds of sequential circuits that detect a binary input sequence (such as 3-bit '101') and give '1' at the output on the positive edge of the clock when the sequence is detected. SDs are used in many systems, particularly critical systems such as alarm generation on sensing a specific sequence of events. Throughout this paper, we refer to a human-made circuit which solves the problem as the *gold circuit*, and such a circuit does not involve any evolution or automation. For example, the comparison of the gold circuit vs evolved 6-bit '111000' is shown here. Overlapping means it can detect two consecutive sequences, such as '111000111000'.

2 Related Work on Digital Circuits Evolution

The first work ever presented on the evolution of SD was by Ali et al. in 2004 [1], where they evolved 4-bit ('1010') and 6-bit ('011011') SDs using GA and four different evolutionary stages. The proposed 6-bit SD differs from the 6-bit SD given in our work here as it combines two '011' 3-bit SDs, which is far easier to evolve than evolving the 6-bit SD. Another work, presented in 2005 by Popa et al., evolved the same hardware using GA [20]. It achieved much better and optimised solutions while using fewer computational resources.

Presented by Yao et al. in 2007, a 3-bit SD ('110') evolved using an incremental, evolutionary approach with GA at its base [32], which evolves the basic modules of the large circuits with a greedy search in a small search space. Due to the evolution of basic modules in a small search space, this system is too focused on the evolution of specific circuits and not generalized. Another system generated to evolve the overlapping 3-bit SD is presented by Xiong et al. [31], which could detect separate or overlapping '101' and '100' sequences. This is evolved intrinsically over hardware. The exact lead author presented an applicable version of this work to the cardiovascular system in [27], where they evolved the same SD using GA-based extrinsic and intrinsic evolution and showed their work's implementation on FPGA. In both works, for 3-bit (not complex at all to evolve), the computational resources used are massive compared to ours.

In another work presented by Tao et al. [28] in 2012, a 4-bit SD is evolved using a GA. They first evolved the basic circuits (small modules), which are then used to generate the whole circuit of SD. The proposed method comprises three evolutionary stages, which is a lot to evolve such a small SD. In our work, we evolved the 4-bit SD using far fewer computational resources and just one evolutionary stage.

In all the presented works above, SDs only evolved at the gate level. In our previous work [11], 3, 4, 5 and 6-bit SDs are evolved on the behavioural level using the tournament selection as the parent selection method. GE is used as the base for the evolution of SDs. 3, 4, and 5-bit SDs are successfully evolved using just one evolutionary stage, a performance upgrade compared to all previous works. However, 6-bit SD could not be evolved with the single-stage automated system. Hence, the grammar encapsulation was used, in which grammar is fed with the best individual achieved so far and given the system a chance to evolve from there (detail in the [11]) to evolve 6-bit SD. Following the scheme proposed in [12], 50-bits long 1,000 training sequences are used (500 with desired seq. + 500 without desired seq). However, in this work, we conjectured that fewer cases could be used and started with the minimum bits required in the training sequences for each SD.

The system presented here also evolves SDs on the behavioural level. Behavioural level designs are recommended for the complex circuits [13] since parts of gate level codes such as *transif0* and *rpmos* cannot be synthesised. Also, gate-level codes do not scale flexibly as behavioural-level codes. Although evolving circuits on the behavioural level are challenging as well [23] due to its usage of highly expressive statements such as *for* or *while* loops and conditional statements such as *if-else*, but they can be synthesised.

Another challenge in evolving sequential circuits such as SDs at the behavioural level is deciding the structure and amount of training and test data required for evolution. Compared to [11], in this work, we have used far fewer training sequences, and the length of each sequence is also less than that used in that work (see Sect. 5 for detail). When compared with [11], it can be seen that tournament selection has shown almost the same results using more extensive and minimum bit length training sequences. However, our significant progress in this work is that Lexicase selection has shown outstanding results using minimum bit length training sequences compared to Tournament selection with identical length sequences.

3   Grammatical Evolution

GE [22] is a grammar-based Genetic Programming (GP) technique which uses rules written in Backus-Naur form (BNF) grammars for genotype to pheno-type mapping. It typically uses context-free grammar and can evolve struc-tures/objects written in any language. It has shown success in combinational [33] as well as sequential circuit designing [11], symbolic regression [2], and classifi-cation [17]. GE can generate HDL codes for circuits which then can be analysed for their efficiency and power/hardware consumption. A sample of genotype to phenotype mapping on gate level for HDL circuit design is shown in Fig. 1 here. BNF grammars used in GE comprise a set of four tuples: Starting symbol (S), Production rule (P) Non-terminal (N) and Terminal (T). S is a part of the first P and is an N where the mapping starts. In the shown example, it is < var > where the first list of N starts on the Right Hand Side (RHS) of the first P. N are the parts of grammar which can be found on either the right or left side of equality such as < var > (found on the RHS of first P and is also found on the Left Hand Side (LHS) of third P in shown example) and are further mapped to T. In contrast, T can not be further mapped to anything and can only be found on the right side of the equation, such as '!' and '&', which can only be seen on the RHS of the second P.

It can be seen in Fig. 1 that each chunk of 8 bits is first converted into decimals, and then each decimal value is used to expand the P of grammar until we get to an expression having just T in them. This example shows the generation of logic gates between two variables x and y, which are the circuit's inputs and gives three gates in the options named AND, OR, and NOT. Please note that since the NOT gate can not be implied between two inputs (x and y) as it is an operation of inversion. It can only be used with one of the two variables, such as !x, using the second N of the first P. When the mapping finishes in the example given, the final expression implies the OR gate between the two input variables of the circuit, i.e., x and y. A detailed step-by-step explanation of this example can be seen in [11].

4   Tournament Selection vs Lexicase Selection

Parent selection is a significant part of the evolutionary cycle. It selects the individuals used before crossover and mutation to create offspring for the next generation. These parents are usually among the fittest individuals from the current generation, which can lay strong offspring for the next generation. The fitness score of each individual is assigned to it based on its performance on the training data set.

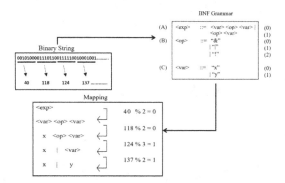

Fig. 1. Genotype to Phenotype Mapping in GE to Create SV Expression With Variables (x,y) And Logic Gates (& (AND), — (OR), and ! (NOT)).

Tournament Selection (TS) [14] runs a number of tournaments among n-individuals and selects the best based on its fitness value. In our case, the value of n is set to two. For example, two individuals are randomly selected with fitness scores of 320 and 321, and the TS method will choose the individual with a score of 321 as a parent. In our experiments, an individual's fitness value is its absolute fitness value computed after it is evaluated for all the test cases.

In contrast, Lexicase Selection (LS) [26] does not pick an individual based on its aggregated (across all test cases) fitness value. Instead, it picks individuals based on their performance on certain test cases, which means this method picks specialists rather than generalists. For example, only those individuals who solve a specific test case can be selected. If there is a tie between two individuals, they can be chosen.

LS has shown excellent results in solving problems related to different fields, such as regression problems [19] and evolutionary robotics [9]. It has especially shown outstanding performance in the evolution of digital circuits [23, 29, 30] as well.

5   Data Set Generation

The size of the training data set was seen to influence the system's performance significantly. Different schemes for selecting training data set size were devised and experimented with for both Tournament and Lexicase Selection. In contrast with the length of sequences as defined in [11] (can be seen here), where they followed the technique proposed in [12], we use training sequences with the minimum required bits to evolve the SDs to get a correct solution. The word 'correct' implies the performance of a circuit if it is evolved using the training data set with minimum bit sequences and gives a hundred per cent test accuracy on a more extensive test data set (50-bit 1,000 sequences) used in [11].

Table 1. Training Data Set Generation Scheme Using Minimum Number of TVs Required.

Sequences For Overlapping SDs Accordingly	Minimum Bits Required Per Sequence	Total Number of Sequences	Sequences With '1' in Their Output	Resulting Distributed TVs
3-bit '101' ==>'10101'	5	$2^5 = 32$	11/32	$32 \times 5 = 160$
4-bit '1101' ==>'1101101'	7	$2^7 = 128$	31/128	$128 \times 7 = 896$
5-bit '11011' ==>'11011011'	8	$2^8 = 256$	31/256	$256 \times 8 = 2048$
6-bit '111000' ==>'111000111000'	6	$2^6 = 64$	1/64	$64 \times 6 = 384$

In this work, Mealy machines are evolved, which respond quickly and use fewer hardware resources than Moore machines. We have evolved overlapping FSMs for these circuits to detect the desired sequences coming adjacent to each other at the input, resulting in a highly responsive and generic SD. It can be seen in Table 1 that the minimum bits required per sequence are higher than the bits of the sequence under detection, as it is an overlapping SD. However, this condition does not apply to the 6-bit '111000' SD since it does not matter if it uses overlapping sequence detection; the detection of the new incoming sequences will always start from the first state, i.e. $S0$, which is usually a case in human-made FSMs. So, in this case, the minimum length for each sequence for 6-bit '111000' SD is six.

As the SDs are designed to detect the binary sequences, the minimum number of producible sequences for any n-bits per sequence is 2^n. It can be seen in the third column of Table 1 that the total number of sequences required for training the system is far less than the 1,000 sequences (500 with desired seq. + 500 without desired seq) used in [11]. The number of n-bit sequences having the actual sequence required to be detected (such as 3-bit '101') out of a total of 2^n sequences can also be seen in the orange colour, far less than 500 used in [11]. However, it can be seen that for the 6-bit SD, we have one sequence out of 64 for the 6-bit '111000' sequence. We will discuss the effect of it later in Sect. 6. As discussed in [11], for n-bit SD, each 50-bit sequence is distributed in 50 TVs for each of the 1,000 sequences resulting in a total Test Vectors (TV) and overall fitness of 50,000. In the proposed method, total TVs and fitness are far less than 50,000, as shown in the last column of Table 1.

6   Experiments and Results

6.1   Experimental Setup, Tools and Evolutionary Parameters

BNF grammars used in this work are the same as those used in [11]. Figure 2 shows the 3-bit '101' SD sample grammar from [11]. The structure of this grammar creates the SV module for the circuit by combining the parameter list indicated by <parameters> with the sequential (always) block, which is comprised of conditional (if/else) statements. These (if/else) statements are used to determine the current state and input of the system, as well as to set the next state and output accordingly. In grammar, the current states are hard-coded, while the following states are evolved according to the current state and input. These evolvable states and outputs which belong to T come in the < states_ block > from the last two N, i.e., <state> and <out> respectively.

Table 2. Evolutionary Parameters.

Parameter	Value	Parameter	Value
No. Of Runs	30	Crossover Probability	0.9 (One Point)
Population Size	1,000		
No. Of Generations	30	Selection	Tournament
Initialisation	Sensible	Elitism	Yes
Mutation Probability	0.01	Test Vectors	1,000

To evolve the SD using this grammar, we used Grammatical Algorithms in Python for Evolution (GRAPE) [10], a Python-based implementation of GE. In this system, we also use Icarus Verilog, a Verilog/SystemVerilog simulator used here to evaluate individuals. All the experiments are run here on Dell OptiPlex 5070 desktop computer. This system comprises a single RAM of 16 GB, 1 TB HDD, 256 GB SSD, and a 64-bit quad-core 9th generation i7 processor with a 12 MB cache. The primary frequency of this used processor is 3.0 GHz, which can reach 4.7 GHz when required.

6.2 SD Evolution Using Minimum and Increased Length Sequences

Given the experimental setup, evolutionary parameters shown in Table 2 and minimum TVs taken from length sequences, 3-bit '101', 4-bit '1101', 5-bit '11011', and 6-bit '111000' SDs are evolved using Tournament and Lexicase parent selection methods. The results can be seen in Table 3. As one might expect, as we approach the more complex SDs, the success rates decrease. It can be seen in Table 3 that Lexicase performed better than Tournament for 4-bit '1101' and 5-bit '11011' SDs. Since lexicase apparently did not do better for 3-bit '101' and 6-bit '111000', Wilcoxon statistical significance tests were run on the values taken from these experiments. For 3-bit '101' and 6-bit '111000', using the fitness values of the best-resulting individual in each run, we find p-values above our threshold of 0.05, demonstrating no statistically significant difference between the two setups since the difference between the success rates and the achieved max fitness values (383/384 vs 384/384 for 6-bit SD) is extremely low. However, for the 4-bit '1101' SD, the p-value is 0.0256 which is less than 0.05 and indicates that there is a significant difference between the results of these two setups

```
<final>          ::= <parameters> \n <sequential>
<parameters>     ::= "reg [1:0]state = 2'b00;\n
                            parameter S0 = 2'b00;\n
                            parameter S1 = 2'b01;\n
                            parameter S2 = 2'b11;\n "
<sequential>     ::= "always @ (posedge clk) begin \n
                        if (rst == 1)begin \n
                            state <= S0; \n
                            out <= 0; \n end \n
                        else if (rst == 0) \n begin \n
                            if (state == S0) \n begin \n
                                "<states_block> \n" end \n
                            else if (state == S1) \n begin \n
                                "<states_block> \n" end \n
                            else if (state == S2) \n begin \n
                                "<states_block> \n" end \n
                        end \n end \n"
<states_block>   ::= "if (inp==1)\n begin \n
                        state <= " <state> ";\n
                        out <= "<out>"; end \n
                     else if(inp == 0) \n begin \n
                        state <= " <state> ";\n
                        out <= "<out>"; end"
<state>          ::= "S0"|"S1"|"S2"
<out>            ::= "0"|"1"
```

Fig. 2. BNF grammar to evolve SV if/else statements deciding next state and output of 3-bit '101' SD.

and the success rates (21/30 vs 04/30) backing this claim, tells that Lexicase is performing much better than Tournament here. The graph representing the mean of the best fitness across all thirty runs for thirty generations for 4-bit SD can be seen here.

Table 3. Comparison Of Success Rates Of Evolved SDs With Lexicase vs Tournament Selection Using Minimum Length Sequences.

Seq. Detector	Success Rate (Tournament)	Success Rate (Lexicase)	Wilcox Test Results Based On Max. Fitness (P-Value)	Wilcox Test Results Based On Mean Of Avg. Fitness (P-Value)
3-bits '101'	30/30	**28**/30	0.1607	≪0.001
4-bits '1101'	**04**/30	**21**/30	0.0256	≪0.001
5-bits '11011'	**01**/30	**03**/30	0.3784	≪0.001
6-bits '111000'	**01**/30	Zero/30	0.3337	≪0.001

Since these SDs are evolved using significantly less training data set compared to the previous work when we tested them against the generalised test data used in [11], i.e., 50-bits 1,000 sequences (500 with desired seq. + 500 without desired seq.), 3-bit '101' and 4-bit '1101', SDs gave us a hundred per cent success rate for both Tournament selection and Lexicase selection as shown in Table 4 and Table 5. We did not get such great results for 5-bit '11011' (02/03 for Lexicase and 01/01 for Tournament); however, we obtained the generalised solutions of 5-bit '11011' SD with both parent selection techniques.

Table 4. Performances Of Sequence Detectors Evolved Using Lexicase Selection On Generalised Test Data Set.

Seq Detector	Pop. Size Taken For Evol.	Success Rate (Lexicase)	Performance On Test Set (1,000 Sequences Each Of 50-bits)
3-bits '101'	1,000	**28**/30	28/28
4-bits '1101'	1,000	**21**/30	21/21
5-bits '11011'	1,000	**03**/30	**02**/03
6-bits '111000'	1,000	Zero/30	–
6-bits '111000'	2,000	Zero/30	–
6-bits '111000'	5,000	**01**/30	Zero/01

For the 6-bit '111000' SD, no success was achieved using Lexicase selection with the evolutionary parameters used in any experiments. We increased the population size from 1,000 to 2,000 and then 5,000. With 5,000, a single solution was found, which did not perform perfectly on the test data, as shown in Table 4.

For the same SD using Tournament selection, one success was achieved with a population size of 1,000. Still, the experiments were run with a population size of 2,000 and 5,000 to compare the results fairly, as shown in Table 5. One correct solution was discovered when using a population size of 2,000 but, when the population was increased to 5,000, no solutions were found. Such results are not to be unexpected when dealing with such small numbers of successes with stochastic systems, but we reran the 2,000 and 5,000 population sizes, this time with 100 repetitions. The results are in the bottom half of Table 5.

Table 5. Performances Of Sequence Detectors Evolved Using Tournament Selection On Generalised Test Data Set.

Seq Detector	Pop. Size Taken For Evol.	Success Rate (Tournament)	Performance On Test Set (1,000 Sequences Each Of 50-bits)
3-bits '101'	1,000	30/30	30/30
4-bits '1101'	1,000	04/30	04/04
5-bits '11011'	1,000	01/30	01/01
6-bits '111000'	1,000	01/30	Zero/01
6-bits '111000'	2,000	01/30	Zero/01
6-bits '111000'	5,000	Zero/30	–
6-bits '111000'	2,000	01/100	Zero/01
6-bits '111000'	5,000	05/100	Zero/05

Thus far, no successful candidate has evolved which could perform perfectly on the test data set for the 6-bit SD. We believe the key reason for this is that the training set is too biased, as it contains just a single positive case since just one out of 64 training sequences has 6-bit '111000' in them. Rather than doubling the number of bits for each sequence, we incrementally increased the length and selected an equal number of sequences with and without'111000'. For example, in 7-bit sequences, only four out of 128 sequences contained the key '111000' pattern. So, in addition to selecting these four sequences, four more sequences are randomly selected, which do not have 6-bit '111000' in them. From these, distributed TVs were generated using the same technique used for the minimum length sequences as shown in the last column of Table 3. Following this increase in the bits of each training sequence, only one successful generalized solution was found while evolving with 9-bit sequences and using the Lexicase selection method as shown in Table 6 while no generalized solution could be found with Tournament selection as seen in Table 6. Although for 7-bit training sequences, Tournament performed a little better than Lexicase selection (30/30 vs 29/30), the overall performance of Lexicase is much better than Tournament, which can be seen in Table 6. Following the P-value, it can be said that both selection methods' performance is the same for 7-bit training sequences since Lexicase is falling behind by just one run out of 30.

The evolved FSM of 6-bit '111000' SD can be seen in comparison with human-made gold FSM here which is entirely different from all the solutions evolved in [11].

Table 6. Performance Comparison Of 6-bit SD Evolved Using Equal And Lengthened Seqs. With Lexicase And Tournament Selection on Generalised Test Data Set.

Sequence Bits ==>Seqs.	Equal No. Of TVs (With Seq. + Without Seq.)	Success Rate (Lexicase)	Performance On Test Set (Lexicase)	Success Rate (Tournament)	Performance On Test Set (Tournament)
7 ==>128	4 + 4 = 8	**29**/30	Zero/29	30/30	Zero/30
8 ==>256	12 + 12 = 24	**07**/30	Zero/07	**01**/30	Zero/01
9 ==>512	32 + 32 = 64	**04**/30	01/04	Zero/30	–

7   Conclusion

This paper uses the Grammatical Evolution and Lexicase Parent Selection methods to present an enhanced performance in the successful evolution of 3-bit, 4-bit, 5-bit, and 6-bit Sequence Detectors. It is shown that Lexicase has performed much better than the Tournament Parent Selection method. Another achievement is the successful evolution of generalized solutions using a minimal number and length of training sequences compared to the literature for 3-bit, 4-bit and 5-bit Sequence Detectors. However, for 6-bit, we had to increase the size of the sequences. These generalized solutions have performed excellently on a vast amount of test data sets. Since the evolved circuits here are the single input and single output Sequence Detectors, it is planned to extend this work to evolve multi-input and/or multi-output Sequence Detectors. It is also planned to evolve the current states of the Finite State Machines in addition to the next states and outputs (evolved in this work) of the presented circuits.

Acknowledgments. This work is supported by the Science Foundation Ireland grant #16/IA/4605. The third author is also financed by the Coordenação de Aperfeiçoamento de Pessoal de Nível Superior - Brazil (CAPES), Finance Code 001, and the Fundação de Amparo à Pesquisa do Estado do Rio de Janeiro (FAPERJ).

Scientific Validation. This paper has benefited from the remarks of the following reviewers:
- Malcolm Heywood, Dalhousie University, Canada
- Ting Hu, Queen's University, Canada
- Karim Tout, Uqudo, UAE

The conference organisers wish to thank them for their highly appreciated effort and contribution.

References

1. Ali, B., Almaini, A.E.A., Kalganova, T.: Evolutionary algorithms and theirs use in the design of sequential logic circuits. Genet. Program. Evolvable Mach. **5**, 11–29 (2004)
2. Ali, M., Kshirsagar, M., Naredo, E., Ryan, C.: Towards automatic grammatical evolution for real-world symbolic regression. In: Proceedings of the 13th International Joint Conference on Computational Intelligence - Volume 1: ECTA, pp. 68–78. INSTICC (2021)
3. Ciletti, M.D.: Advanced Digital Design with the Verilog HDL, 2nd edn. Prentice Hall Press, Hoboken (2010)
4. Eagle: Eagle by autodesk (1988). https://www.autodesk.com/products/eagle/overview. Accessed 1 Nov 2022
5. Farrahi, A., Hathaway, D., Wang, M., Sarrafzadeh, M.: Quality of EDA CAD tools: definitions, metrics and directions. In: Proceedings IEEE 2000 First International Symposium on Quality Electronic Design (Cat. No. PR00525), pp. 395–405. IEEE, San Jose, CA, USA (2000)
6. Kalganova, T.: An extrinsic function-level evolvable hardware approach. In: Poli, R., Banzhaf, W., Langdon, W.B., Miller, J., Nordin, P., Fogarty, T.C. (eds.) Genetic Programming, pp. 60–75. Springer, Heidelberg (2000). https://doi.org/10.1007/978-3-540-46239-2_5
7. KiCad: KiCad electronic design automation (1992). https://www.kicad.org/. Accessed 1 Nov 2022
8. Koza, J.R.: Genetic Programming: On the Programming of Computers by Means of Natural Selection. MIT Press, Cambridge (1992)
9. La Cava, W., Moore, J.: Behavioral search drivers and the role of elitism in soft robotics. In: ALIFE 2018: The 2018 Conference on Artificial Life, pp. 206–213 (2018)
10. de Lima, A., Carvalho, S., Dias, D.M., Naredo, E., Sullivan, J.P., Ryan, C.: GRAPE: grammatical algorithms in Python for evolution. Signals **3**(3), 642–663 (2022)
11. Majeed., B., et al.: Evolving behavioural level sequence detectors in systemverilog using grammatical evolution. In: Proceedings of the 15th International Conference on Agents and Artificial Intelligence - Volume 3: ICAART, pp. 475–483 (2023)
12. Manovit, C., Aporntewan, C., Chongstitvatana, P.: Synthesis of synchronous sequential logic circuits from partial input/output sequences. In: Sipper, M., Mange, D., Pérez-Uribe, A. (eds.) ICES 1998. LNCS, vol. 1478, pp. 98–105. Springer, Heidelberg (1998). https://doi.org/10.1007/BFb0057611
13. Mealy, B., Tappero, F.: Free Range VHDL. Free Range Factory (2013); eBook (2018), USA (2018)
14. Miller, B.L., Goldberg, D.E.: Genetic algorithms, tournament selection, and the effects of noise. Complex Syst. **9**, 193–212 (1995)
15. Mirjalili, S.: Genetic Algorithm, pp. 43–55. Springer, Cham (2019). https://doi.org/10.1007/978-3-319-93025-1_4
16. Morris, M., Ciletti, M.D.: Digital Design. Pearson Prentice Hall, Upper Saddle River (2007)
17. Murphy, A., Murphy, G., Amaral, J., Mota Dias, D., Naredo, E., Ryan, C.: Towards incorporating human knowledge in fuzzy pattern tree evolution. In: Hu, T., Lourenco, N., Medvet, E. (eds.) European Conference on Genetic Programming (Part of EvoStar), vol. 12691, pp. 66–81. Springer, Cham (2021). https://doi.org/10.1007/978-3-030-72812-0_5

18. Navabi, Z.: VHDL: Modular Design and Synthesis of Cores and Systems. McGraw-Hill, New York (2007)
19. Orzechowski, P., La Cava, W., Moore, J.H.: Where are we now? A large benchmark study of recent symbolic regression methods. In: Proceedings of the Genetic and Evolutionary Computation Conference, pp. 1183–1190. Association for Computing Machinery (2018)
20. Popa, R., Aiordăchioaie, D., Sîrbu, G.: Evolvable hardware in Xilinx Spartan-3 FPGA. In: Proceedings of the 2005 WSEAS International Conference on Dynamical Systems and Control (ICDSC), pp. 66–71 (2005)
21. Rudolph, G.: Evolutionary Strategies, pp. 673–698. Springer, Heidelberg (2012). https://doi.org/10.1007/978-3-540-92910-9_22
22. Ryan, C., Collins, J.J., Neill, M.O.: Grammatical evolution: evolving programs for an arbitrary language. In: Banzhaf, W., Poli, R., Schoenauer, M., Fogarty, T.C. (eds.) EuroGP 1998. LNCS, vol. 1391, pp. 83–96. Springer, Heidelberg (1998). https://doi.org/10.1007/BFb0055930
23. Ryan., C., Tetteh., M.K., Dias., D.M.: Behavioural modelling of digital circuits in system verilog using grammatical evolution. In: Proceedings of the 12th International Joint Conference on Computational Intelligence - ECTA, pp. 28–39. INSTICC, SciTePress (2020)
24. Solido: Solido design solutions (2005). https://eda.sw.siemens.com/en-US/ic/solido/. Accessed 1 Nov 2022
25. Spear, C.: SystemVerilog for Verification. A Guide to Learning the Testbench Language Features, 2nd edn. Springer, New York (2008). https://doi.org/10.1007/978-1-4614-0715-7
26. Spector, L.: Assessment of problem modality by differential performance of lexicase selection in genetic programming: A preliminary report. In: Proceedings of the 14th Annual Conference Companion on Genetic and Evolutionary Computation. p. 401–408. GECCO '12, Association for Computing Machinery, New York, NY, USA (2012)
27. Tani, F.I.J.U., Tani, M.M.: An evolutionary circuit model for cardiovascular system: an FPGA approach. Int. J. Comput. Inf. Technol. Eng. (2011)
28. Tao, Y., Cao, J., Zhang, Y., Lin, J., Li, M.: Using module-level evolvable hardware approach in design of sequential logic circuits. In: 2012 IEEE Congress on Evolutionary Computation (CEC), pp. 1–8. IEEE, New York (2012)
29. Tetteh, M., Dias, D.M., Ryan, C.: Grammatical evolution of complex digital circuits in SystemVerilog. SN Comput. Sci. 3(3), 188 (2022)
30. Tetteh, M.K., Mota Dias, D., Ryan, C.: Evolution of complex combinational logic circuits using grammatical evolution with SystemVerilog. In: Hu, T., Lourenço, N., Medvet, E. (eds.) Genetic Programming, pp. 146–161. Springer, Cham (2021). https://doi.org/10.1007/978-3-030-72812-0_10
31. Xiong, F., Rafla, N.I.: On-chip intrinsic evolution methodology for sequential logic circuit design. In: 2009 52nd IEEE International Midwest Symposium on Circuits and Systems, pp. 200–203. IEEE, New York (2009)
32. Yao, R., Wang, Y., Yu, S., Gao, G.: Research on the online evaluation approach for the digital evolvable hardware. In: Kang, L., Liu, Y., Zeng, S. (eds.) ICES 2007. LNCS, vol. 4684, pp. 57–66. Springer, Heidelberg (2007). https://doi.org/10.1007/978-3-540-74626-3_6
33. Youssef, A., Majeed, B., Ryan, C.: Optimizing combinational logic circuits using grammatical evolution. In: 2021 3rd Novel Intelligent and Leading Emerging Sciences Conference (NILES), pp. 87–92. IEEE, New York (2021)

34. Zhang, Y., Smith, S., Tyrrell, A.: Digital circuit design using intrinsic evolvable hardware. In: Proceedings of 2004 NASA/DoD Conference on Evolvable Hardware, pp. 55–62. IEEE, New York (2004)

Fuzzy Pattern Trees
with Pre-classification

Aidan Murphy[1]($\boxtimes$)(iD), Anthony Ventresque[1](iD), and Conor Ryan[2](iD)

[1] Lero, Trinity College Dublin, Dublin, Ireland
murpha56@tcd.ie
[2] Lero, University of Limerick, Limerick, Ireland

Abstract. Fuzzy Pattern Trees evolved using Grammatical Evolution have been shown to be a robust Explainable Artificial Intelligence technique. We trained a black-box classifier, XGBoost, to identify and remove instances our evolved Fuzzy Pattern Tree model was seen to struggle to classify correctly. This framework mimics a human-computer interactive approach, where the removed instances would be classified by the human and not the Fuzzy Pattern Tree model. We investigated a range of fitness functions to ascertain which is most suitable for use with pre-classification by examining their accuracy, errors and how well they perform with the pre-classifier. We show that Fuzzy Pattern Tree classifiers, on each benchmark and using every fitness function, improved when used with a pre-classification method. Fuzzy Pattern Tree models with pre-classification found better performance than any other black-box classifier on all the benchmarks considered and routinely removed less than 10% of test data for human inspection.

Keywords: Grammatical Evolution · Fuzzy Logic · Explainable AI

1 Introduction

Machine Learning (ML) systems are ubiquitous today, infiltrating every facet of modern life. The cheap cost of hardware to train models, the availability of large amounts of free data online and powerful open-source software packages and tools, some of which require little or no experience in writing computer code, have led to a boom in the number of ML applications available today.

Deep learning's (DL) ability to continually scale sets it apart from other ML approaches [8]. This has meant that errors continue to decrease on historical benchmarks, and domains in which it was once deemed impossible to succeed are now being investigated.

These achievements, however, have not been without their critics [11]. DL requires more and more data to scale. This vast amount of data often goes unvalidated and may contain bias or other potentially harmful content which the ML application may perpetuate [2]. The larger these models grow, the deeper they go into the "black box". The model's common sense, or its potential harms,

P. Collet et al. (Eds.): CCE 2023, LNCS 13927, pp. 104–117, 2023.
https://doi.org/10.1007/978-3-031-44355-8_8

can only be judged by involving a proxy or post hoc, observing its outputs and inferring the model's logic from them. The nature of the systems under investigation cannot be investigated.

This is particularly important in safety-critical or high-impact areas, such as self-driving cars, loan approval systems or, rather infamously, prisoner recidivism rates [4]. The primary concern for building an ML systems for such problems, if appropriate, should not be how close to perfect a system scores on some arbitrary training data. Instead, it should focus on why the system made the mistakes in classification it did. Understanding how or why the system failed and not how often it did can be more important.

However, ML systems dealing in these areas, which have drastic effects on people's lives, often go into the "wild" without any sort of fail-safe. A human using these systems may not be able to discern when it is or is not appropriate to use them. To tackle these issues, a new area of research spawned, explainable artificial intelligence (XAI). XAI aims to create interpretable models and methods that can somehow explain themselves without, or with minimal, impact on performance. A successful example of XAI has been Fuzzy Pattern Trees (FPTs). Based on fuzzy set theory, an FPT is a hierarchical tree structure, not a rule list. As a fuzzy model, it uses linguistic labels and is thus more easily interpretable. It has been shown that this interpretability, naturally, is contingent on the trees not being excessively large [18].

FPTs evolved using grammatical evolution (GE) have been shown to produce more accurate and smaller models than those produced by any other method [14]. Crucially, GE also allows for human expertise to be incorporated into the search, both before and during evolution [19]. This makes FPTs very suitable for interactive evolution and for working with and augmenting a human user. However, their performance still lagged behind that of black-box classification methods [16].

This paper uses a pre-classification approach with FPTs, where FPTs are incorporated with a black-box classifier that can accurately predict the FPTs "blind spots". The ML system will not classify these instances, but instead could be given to a user to inspect and make the classification decision. By removing these "blind spots" we show the performance of FPTs will increase, but their interpretability remains high. XGBoost was used as the black-box pre-classifier, and the FPTs were evolved using Structured Grammatical Evolution (SGE).

Section 2 reviews the main background concepts GE, Fuzzy GE and Human-in-the-loop ML. Section 3 explains the pre-classification methods and describes the paper's contributions in more detail. Next, Sect. 4 presents the experimental set-up which was used, a summary of the data, and outlines the fitness measures which were investigated and the parameters used for each classifier. Section 5 presents the main results of the experiments described in 4. Finally, Sect. 6 summarises the research and discusses future work suitable for investigation.

2   Background

2.1   FPTs

An FPT is a hierarchical, tree-like structure. The internal nodes are fuzzy logical and fuzzy arithmetic operators, and the leaf nodes are the fuzzified input variables and constants. FPTs have independently been introduced by [7] and [25], who called this type of model Fuzzy Operator Trees. The FPT model class is related to several other model classes, including fuzzy rule-based systems (FRBS), and fuzzy decision trees (FDT).

FPTs which use GE as their search technique was recently introduced [15]. This approach, FGE, showed competitive performance against black box methods and was shown to outperform another GP variant, Cartesian GP, on a set of benchmark classification problems [23].

To perform classification using FGE a set of FPTs is needed, one for each class that exists in the problem. These FPTs serve as the logical description of the class. This sets FGE apart from traditional classification approaches in GE, which only require one expression to be evolved, regardless of the number of classes in the problem. To classify an individual, a boundary or boundaries are decided upon. The output of the tree is then compared against this boundary, and a decision is made about its classification. This approach has many downsides; much time, effort and expertise are required to optimise these boundaries [6].

FGE evolves one, large solution and treats the subtrees of this solution as its FPTs, as seen in Fig. 1. The FPT which yields the largest output for an individual, is declared the winner, and that individual is designated as belonging to that class. This is illustrated in Fig. 2. The root node of the tree is responsible for this process. Representing each FPT as subtrees of one large solution combined with GE's inbuilt separation between search space and program space leads to another major advantage FGE experiences. No special or protected operators are needed for crossover or mutation. A simple grammar augmentation is all that is needed to tackle different problem specifications.

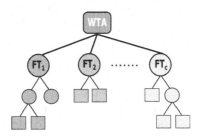

Fig. 1. Pictorial representation of a multi-classifier evolved by GE, where FT_c is the fuzzy tree for each available class, and at the root the winner take all (WTA).

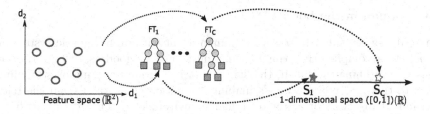

Fig. 2. Graphical depiction of the mapping process from the feature space to a 1-dimensional space [0,1] using a set of fuzzy trees FT_1 to FT_c.

2.2 GE

Grammatical Evolution (GE) [21] is an evolutionary computation search technique which uses a grammar, generally, a context-free grammar (CFG) written in Backus-Naur form (BNF), to find syntactically correct executable programs which solve a given problem. It is often thought of as a variant of genetic programming (GP) [9], due to the most common representation of GE programs as Koza LISP style trees [22]. As with many other evolutionary algorithms, GE's inspiration comes from observing nature, specifically genetics. GE creates programs by mapping an integer string using a grammar. The evolutionary operators do not occur on the actual computer program, but on the string that creates the program, combined with the grammar. This separation between the search space and the program space makes GE unique among EC techniques and have seen it achieve success in a wide variety of domains, including digital circuit design [24], automatic test case generation [17] and symbolic regression [1].

The separation between the search and program spaces is seen as one of GE's strengths. However, this separation leads to a disruptive effect known as *ripple*, also known as *ripple effects* [20]. Simply put, small changes to an individual, particularly in the first few codons of an individual, have drastic effects on the resulting phenotype. The phenotype of a child solution may be almost entirely different from its parent despite there being very little variation, perhaps only one codon difference, in their respective genotypes. This occurs with both crossover and mutation. As our approach evolves both FPTs simultaneously, these ripple effects will be particularly concerning.

To alleviate these concerns, the FPTs in this paper are evolved using Structured Grammatical Evolution (SGE) [10]. SGE overcomes the poor locality of GE and limits the ripple by altering the construction of the genome. In standard GE, the genome comprises a list of numbers which are used, left to right, to map to an individual. In SGE, the genome is a set of lists, each list corresponding to a non-terminal in the grammar. When that non-terminal is selected, the list corresponding to that non-terminal is used to complete the mapping and not the next number on the list, which is used in GE. This ensures that any change to a codon is confined to that non-terminal and that a crossover or mutation does not "ripple" throughout the solution.

2.3   Human in the Loop FPTs

Many ML systems aim to replace a human agent with an automatic system or model. To accomplish this, the machine must make as good as, or better, decisions than a human would in the same situation. However, a major stumbling block to this goal is a machine's inability to reason or abstract from the relationships it discovers or adapt to dynamic environments. The goal of artificial general intelligence (AGI) is to develop systems with this 'common sense'. However, recent criticism has suggested that this is a far away, possibly unobtainable, goal despite the immense sums of money already spent.

ML benchmarks often place machines and humans in direct opposition to each other, seeking to create AI which reaches human-level performance on a specific task. A more fruitful avenue may be to instead look at ways in which ML can augment human experts, through increasing their efficiency, optimising their expertise or otherwise. For example, self-driving cars have been shown to have difficulty and display dangerous behaviour in dense urban environments but can be quite safe on well-lit and maintained motorways or highways. Requiring a human driver to only navigate the vehicle in terrain the self-driving system finds difficult, with the self-driving system operating in the lower risk areas, would minimise the time needed for manual driving and maximise safety.

Using ML in conjunction with doctors has already shown success in the medical imaging domain [12]. Their system achieved better accuracy than a single human; however, it is standard practice in hospitals that at least two specialists examine the scans. Against such a "double reading" system, the ML failed to attain better results. Interestingly, in contrast to direct competition with humans, when the ML system is used in conjunction with specialists, they claim that the specialists' workload will be drastically reduced as the machine can act as the "second reader" in most cases.

3   Pre-classification

We wish to investigate the effect applying a pre-classification method has on the performance of FPTs. This framework would mimic a human-ML interaction system and provide two main benefits. Firstly, it would not force the FPT model to make predictions on instances it has previously struggled to classify and would likely make a mistake in classification. Secondly, it would allow the human interacting with the ML model to continually validate their previous interpretation. If the human is repeatedly given cases they believe the FPT systems should easily classify, it may mean their original interpretation of the model was incorrect, or the context of the model has changed. This will allow for early identification of such problems and build further trust in the system.

We first fit the FPT model and observe its accuracy. The worst 20% of misclassed training samples (or all missclassed training samples if accuracy was above 80%) are identified and a more robust black-box model is constructed to identify these. In our framework, these are the cases that the model will defer to the expert on, so it is not necessary that this classification procedure is transparent. The test data is first preprocessed through this model, and those cases the FPT model is deemed likely to struggle with are removed. The FPT model is then tested on the remaining data. An outline of this process is illustrated in Fig. 3.

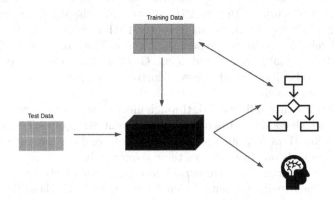

Fig. 3. Pictorial representation of a pre-classification framework. Our pre-classifier is denoted as the black-box.

3.1   Fitness Functions

The output of an FPT is bounded [0,1]. A perfect classifier would yield an output of 1 from the FPT which represents the class in question, and every other FPT would output 0 (for binary classification, in our case, this is just one other FPT). This would yield a score of +1. An exact imperfect classifier would yield a score of −1, i.e. give an output of 0 from the FPT of the class and 1 from the other FPT. This allows for the construction of an error interval, as the errors are bounded [−1, 1] for binary classification, and from this, we can assess which points an FPT classifier struggles to classify. Moreover, we can assess how confident the classifier was in making these predictions. An error of −1 means the FPT classifier was very confident in its prediction, despite being completely incorrect. A score of −0.1 would mean it was incorrect in classification but was not sure which class it belonged to, a score of +0.1 means it was correct but unsure, and so on.

In order to create a strong pre-classifier, these scores need to be as separable as possible. Previously, Root Mean Square Error (RMSE), more familiar in Symbolic regression, has been used as the fitness function in FPT evolution. RMSE measures how close the FPT representing the class is from 1 and how far the FPT representing the incorrect class is from 0. That is to say, how far from a perfect classifier this individual is. This allows for a more steady fitness ascent than a more coarse measure like accuracy. However, it is unclear which fitness function would work best with a pre-classifier.

Therefore, four other fitness metrics were investigated along with RMSE; accuracy, Fowlkes-Mallows score, Matthew's correlation coefficient, and F1 score.

3.2 Black-Box Pre-classifier

When choosing a method to act as the pre-classifier, the interpretability of this model is not a concern as the final classification of the data will be using a trusted source. Decisions will be made by the FPT classifier, which the expert has deemed reliable, or by the expert themselves. Therefore, we use XGBoost as our pre-classifier [3] in our experiments. Gradient boosting greatly increases the accuracy of classification at a loss of intrinsic interpretability, which is not a concern for our pre-classifier.

Combining multiple different ML through meta-classification, such as a stacking classifier which combines the outputs of different ML approaches, has shown great results [5]. However, our approach does not combine the outputs of two different ML models but instead uses them sequentially.

Our approach also differs from outlier detection. The black-box pre-classifier is trained to remove data points which FPTs struggle in classifying, not on cases which differ greatly from the rest of the training data. However, as the FPT classifier should struggle with outliers anyway, it should be the case that outliers are removed through this pre-classification process without explicitly doing outlier removal.

4 Experimental Setup

4.1 Pre-classification

We used XGBoost as our black box classifier. The hyper-parameters were optimised using a simple grid search approach using random runs selected from the Australian and German credit benchmarks. The hyper-parameters used were: max depth of 8, learning rate of 0.2 and 1,000 rounds of boosting. All other parameters were left as default.

The score of all cases were ranked and all the misclassed cases or the bottom 20% of scores, whichever was lower, were labeled. If numerous cases tied at the 20% cut-off score they were also included, potentially allowing for slightly more than 20% of cases to be labeled. These were the labels used for the XGBoost classification. The number of cases removed by the XGBoost pre-classifier was recorded.

4.2 GE Parameters

The full SGE experimental parameters are seen in Table 1. The maximum tree depth is set to 7 and reflects the depth at which FPTs have previously been shown to lose their interpretability. 50 runs were performed.

Table 1. List of the main parameters used to run SGE.

Parameter	Value	Parameter	Value
Total Generations	50	Population	500
Elitism	5	Selection	Tournament (3)
Crossover	0.9	Mutation	0.1
Max Tree Depth	7	Min Tree Depth	2

4.3 Fitness Function

The full list of fitness functions used during the evolution of the FPTs is shown below.

$$\text{FF}_{\text{Accuracy}} = 1 - \frac{TP + TN}{P + N} \tag{1}$$

$$FF_{F_\beta} = (1 + \beta^2) - \frac{(1 + \beta^2) * TP}{(1 + \beta^2) * TP + \beta^2 * FP + FP} \tag{2}$$

$$\text{FF}_{\text{RMSE}} = \sqrt{\sum_{i=1}^{n} \frac{(\hat{y}_i - y_i)^2}{n}} \tag{3}$$

$$\text{FF}_{\text{Fowlkes-Mallows}} = 1 - \sqrt{\frac{TP}{TP + FP} * \frac{TP}{TP + FN}} \tag{4}$$

$$\text{FF}_{\text{MCC}} = 1 - \left(\frac{TP * TN - FP * FN}{\sqrt{(TP + FP)(TP + FN)(TN + FP)(TN + FN)}} \right)^2 \tag{5}$$

4.4 Benchmarks

The experiments are run on six binary classification benchmark datasets, all of which can be found online in the UCI repository and are described in Table 2. They range in size and complexity from 748 instances and 4 variables, Transfusion, to over 41,000 instances and 20 variables, Bank Marketing.

5 Results

The experimental results are summarized in Table 3 showing the mean best test performance from 50 runs of SGE utilising the various fitness functions, described above.

The first five columns show the results for SGE using Eqs. 1–5, respectively. The sixth column shows the results for best black box classification method on these benchmarks, reported elsewhere [13]. Wilcoxon signed rank statistical tests were performed on each pair of fitness functions, with a p-value of 0.05 chosen to decide significance. All underlined scores signify that the fitness function was not

Table 2. Benchmark datasets for the classification problems, taken from the UCI repository.

Datasets	Short	Class	Vars	Instances
Australian	Austr	2	14	690
German Credit	Credit	2	20	1,000
Bank Marketing	Bank	2	20	41,188
Pima	Pima	2	8	768
ProRepublica Recidivism	Recid	2	52	7,214
Transfusion	Trans	2	4	748

significantly outperformed by any other function. No fitness function was able to produce better mean FPT performance than the best black-box classifier. This performance disparity ranged from 1%, Australian, Bank Marketing, Recidivism and Transfusion, to 5%, German Credit.

Accuracy, perhaps unsurprisingly, achieved the best accuracy of all the fitness functions investigated as it was trained to optimise this value. Accuracy was not outperformed by any other fitness function on any benchmark. The worst performing fitness function was F1 score, being outperformed by at least two other fitness functions on every benchmark except Australian. RMSE lagged behind Accuracy on two benchmarks, Bank Marketing where it was outperformed by less than 1% and Recidivism where it was outperformed by 2%. Interestingly, these were the two largest datasets experimented with. Both FMS and MCC showed inconsistent performance. Both attained best, or very close to best performance on all benchmarks bar one. MCC attained the worst performance on the German Credit benchmark, over 8% worse than Accuracy and RMSE. More surprisingly, FMS only reached 55% accuracy on the Recidivism problem well below the 73% achieved by Accuracy and MCC fitness functions.

Table 3. Test classification performance comparison of each SGE setup, showing the classification accuracy on the test data for the best solution found averaged across 50 runs. Underlined numbers indicate that this method was not significantly outperformed by any other. The final column, Best, contains the results from the best black-box classifier approach, reported elsewhere.

Dataset	Acc	F_1	RMSE	FMS	MCC	Best
Austr	0.85 (0.03)	0.85 (0.03)	0.85 (0.02)	0.85 (0.02)	0.85 (0.02)	0.86
Credit	0.71 (0.02)	0.64 (0.03)	0.71 (0.02)	0.70 (0.02)	0.63 (0.03)	0.76
Bank	0.90 (0.00)	0.88 (0.00)	0.89 (0.00)	0.90 (0.02)	0.88 (0.01)	0.91
Pima	0.74 (0.02)	0.70 (0.03)	0.74 (0.03)	0.65 (0.03)	0.72 (0.03)	0.77
Recid	0.73 (0.01)	0.70 (0.02)	0.71 (0.02)	0.55 (0.00)	0.73 (0.01)	0.74
Trans	0.76 (0.02)	0.71 (0.04)	0.76 (0.01)	0.76 (0.07)	0.73 (0.03)	0.77

Achieving high accuracy is not the ultimate goal of these experiments how-ever, it is to investigate which fitness function is the most suitable to use with a pre-classification method. The results of each fitness function post classification are shown in Table 4. The best results are highlighted in bold for readability and, as before, Wilcoxon signed rank statistical tests were preformed on each pair of fitness functions. RMSE was seen to leapfrog Accuracy as the best fitness function, achieving the best score in three benchmarks and only being statisti-cally significantly outperformed on one problem, German Credit. RMSE saw a performance increase of 6% on the Bank Marketing dataset, allowing it to over-take Accuracy on this problem which only attained a 4% increase. Accuracy, which seeing improvement on each, problem, was outperformed on three prob-lems but did attained best performance on the Pima and Recidivism problems. The largest performance jump was seen using FMS on the Recidivism problem. Pre-classification was able to boost performance by just under 15%, from 55% to 70%. While still below the best performing fitness function on the problem, Accuracy at 76%, it does bring FMS closer to all other fitness function on this benchmark.

Table 4. Test Classification performance comparison of SGE with pre-classification, showing the classification accuracy on the test data for the best solution found averaged across 50 runs. Underlined numbers indicate that this method was not significantly outperformed by any other. Best numbers are highlighted in bold.

Dataset	Acc	F_1	RMSE	FMS	MCC
Austr	0.88 (0.03)	0.87 (0.03)	**0.89 (0.02)**	0.86 (0.04)	0.87 (0.04)
Credit	0.76 (0.03)	0.73 (0.04)	0.75 (0.02)	**0.79 (0.03)**	0.70 (0.05)
Bank	0.94 (0.00)	0.94 (0.00)	**0.95 (0.00)**	0.94 (0.00)	0.94 (0.01)
Pima	**0.76 (0.02)**	0.73 (0.03)	**0.76 (0.03)**	0.74 (0.04)	0.75 (0.03)
Recid	**0.76 (0.01)**	0.75 (0.02)	0.75 (0.02)	0.70 (0.05)	**0.76 (0.01)**
Trans	0.78 (0.03)	0.76 (0.03)	0.79 (0.02)	**0.80 (0.02)**	0.77 (0.03)

Every fitness function on every benchmark was seen to improve performance when used with a pre-classifier. This improvement was such that every fitness function had at least three benchmarks in which it had better performance than the black-box classifier. The best performance on each benchmark was seen by FPTs, not the black-box classifiers. These results are run on different test datasets so a direct comparison is not possible but it does point towards the large effect pre-classification had. If the performance of these black-box classi-fiers was deemed good enough to deploy with no interpretability, FPTs with pre-classification offers a more accurate alternative with complete interpretabil-ity. This would allow for a safer deployment of such a model.

While the performance increases show the considerable rise pre-classification may have on FPTs, it needs investigating what overhead this comes with. The pre-classification training model was given the bottom 20% of cases or all mis-classed individuals, whichever was lower. However, if a fitness function was poor at separating it's errors it may lead to a model which removes far more/less than 20% of the test data. The average percentage of the test data removed is shown in Table 5. Accuracy was seen to remove the least amount of data, followed by RMSE. MCC removed over 20% of test data on two benchmarks, Australian and German Credit, while FMS removed over 20% on three problems, German Credit Pima and Recidivism. Both Accuracy and MCC removed the least amount of test cases on the Recidivism benchmark, 9.6% and both achieved best perfor-mance. This problem also saw the largest percentage of cases removed, with the pre-classifier for FMS removing on average 32.6% of the test data.

Table 5. Test Points removed through use of the pre-classification model.

Dataset	Acc	F_1	RMSE	FMS	MCC
Austr	7.9%	7.3%	8.5%	15.9%	22.0%
Credit	16.2%	22.7%	11.9%	21.8%	23.5%
Bank	7.8%	11.2%	9.5%	8.2%	10.4%
Pima	12.1%	12.8%	11.4%	22.7%	11.5%
Recid	9.6%	14.5%	11.8%	32.6%	9.6%
Trans	14.9%	17.9%	14.8%	15.9%	15.9%

The reason for this large removal of test data points and striking jump in performance of the FMS fitness function on the Recidivism problem was inves-tigated. A density plot of the scores from the evolved solutions using FMS, Accuracy and RMSE can be seen in Fig. 4.

FMS evolved simple classifiers which exhibit clear trimodal behaviour. It shows behaviour which is confident and correct (far right peak), confident and incorrect (far left peak) or unsure (peak around 0) in its classifications. In stan-dard classification this is inappropriate and is reflected in it's very poor original test accuracy on the benchmark of 55%. However, when used with a pre-classifier this jumped all the way to 70%, performance which is approaching acceptable levels. This is due to the clear separation of data, which allows the pre-classifier to easily identify and remove these blind spots. This drastic performance increase is not seen for both Accuracy and RMSE, which exhibit more subtle and general performance and improve by 3% and 4% respectively. It can be seen that RMSE has a much steadier distribution, which includes many instances less than 0. Accuracy, however, shows a spike around 0, meaning it is unsure and therefore removing it's "blind spots" will be more difficult.

Density Plot for Recidivism Benchmark

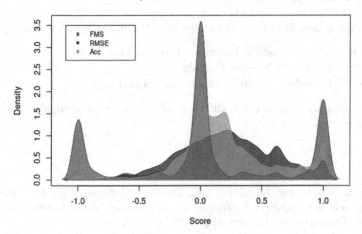

Fig. 4. Density Plot of score for three classifiers on the Recidivism Benchmark. Plot is averaged across each of the 50 runs. FMS is shown in red with 3 spikes in its distribution. Accuracy, green, appears bi-modal and RMSE, blue, is the most smooth of the three classifiers shown. (Color figure online)

6 Conclusion

We investigated the performance effects of Fuzzy Pattern Tree classifiers when combined with a pre-classification technique. Our framework uses an XGBoost model to identify and remove cases which the Fuzzy Pattern Tree classifier was shown to struggle on and mimics a human-machine collaborative approach. We also investigated which evolutionary fitness functions are most appropriate to use in this framework.

Experiments showed that Fuzzy Pattern Tree classifiers augmented with a pre-classifier attained state-of-the-art performance when compared to previous results on a selection of real world classification tasks. This increase in performance does not come at the sacrifice of Fuzzy Pattern Tree's interpretability. RMSE was seen to be the optimal fitness function to combine with pre-classification, it gave the largest performance boost while limiting the number of test cases which must be inspected by the human.

The next major step in this work is the inclusion of pre-classification in more stages of the evolutionary process. Currently, the XGBoost model is created on the best individual, after evolution has finished. Utilising pre-classification in the evolutionary loop would enable Grammatical Evolution to explicitly evolve individuals which exploit pre-classification best. Investigating our framework with lexicase selection is another intriguing option. Both of these possibilities come with a significantly larger computationally cost, however.

Scientific Validation

This paper has benefited from the remarks of the following reviewers:

- Smita Kasar, Maharashtra Institute of Technology, India
- Ting Hu, Queen's University, Canada
- Penousal Machado, University of Coimbra, Portugal

The conference organisers wish to thank them for their highly appreciated effort and contribution.

References

1. Ali, M.S., Kshirsagar, M., Naredo, E., Ryan, C.: Automated grammar-based feature selection in symbolic regression. In: Proceedings of the Genetic and Evolutionary Computation Conference, pp. 902–910 (2022)
2. Birhane, A., Prabhu, V.U.: Large image datasets: a pyrrhic win for computer vision? In: 2021 IEEE Winter Conference on Applications of Computer Vision (WACV), pp. 1536–1546. IEEE (2021)
3. Chen, T., Guestrin, C.: Xgboost: a scalable tree boosting system. In: Proceedings of the 22nd ACM SIGKDD International Conference on Knowledge Discovery and Data Mining, pp. 785–794 (2016)
4. Chouldechova, A.: Fair prediction with disparate impact: a study of bias in recidivism prediction instruments. Big Data 5(2), 153–163 (2017)
5. Džeroski, S., Ženko, B.: Is combining classifiers with stacking better than selecting the best one? Mach. Learn. 54, 255–273 (2004)
6. Fitzgerald, J., Ryan, C.: Exploring boundaries: optimising individual class boundaries for binary classification problem. In: Proceedings of the 14th Annual Conference on Genetic and Evolutionary Computation, pp. 743–750 (2012)
7. Huang, Z., Gedeon, T.D., Nikravesh, M.: Pattern trees induction: a new machine learning method. Trans. Fuz Sys. 16(4), 958–970 (2008). https://doi.org/10.1109/TFUZZ.2008.924348
8. Kaplan, J., et al.: Scaling laws for neural language models. arXiv preprint arXiv:2001.08361 (2020)
9. Koza, J.R., Koza, J.R.: Genetic Programming: On the Programming of Computers by Means of Natural Selection, vol. 1. MIT Press, Cambridge (1992)
10. Lourenço, N., Pereira, F.B., Costa, E.: SGE: a structured representation for grammatical evolution. In: Bonnevay, S., Legrand, P., Monmarché, N., Lutton, E., Schoenauer, M. (eds.) EA 2015. LNCS, vol. 9554, pp. 136–148. Springer, Cham (2016). https://doi.org/10.1007/978-3-319-31471-6_11
11. Marcus, G.: Deep learning: a critical appraisal. arXiv preprint arXiv:1801.00631 (2018)
12. McKinney, S.M., et al.: International evaluation of an AI system for breast cancer screening. Nature 577(7788), 89–94 (2020)
13. Murphy, A.: Evolving provably explainable fuzzy pattern tree classifiers using grammatical evolution. Ph.D. thesis, University of Limerick (2022)
14. Murphy, A., Ali, M., Dias, D.M., Amaral, J., Naredo, E., Ryan, C.: Grammar-based fuzzy pattern trees for classification problems. In: Proceedings of the 12th International Joint Conference on Computational Intelligence - ECTA, pp. 71–80. INSTICC, SciTePress (2020). https://doi.org/10.5220/0010111900710080

15. Murphy, A., Ali, M.S., Dias, D.M., Amaral, J., Naredo, E., Ryan, C.: Grammar-based fuzzy pattern trees for classification problems. In: Proceedings of the 12th International Joint Conference on Computational Intelligence - Volume 1: ECTA, pp. 71–80. INSTICC, SciTePress (2020). https://doi.org/10.5220/0010111900710080

16. Murphy, A., Ali, M.S., Mota Dias, D., Amaral, J., Naredo, E., Ryan, C.: Fuzzy pattern tree evolution using grammatical evolution. SN Comput. Sci. 3(6), 426 (2022)

17. Murphy, A., Laurent, T., Ventresque, A.: The case for grammatical evolution in test generation. In: Proceedings of the Genetic and Evolutionary Computation Conference Companion, pp. 1946–1947 (2022)

18. Murphy, A., Murphy, G., Amaral, J., MotaDias, D., Naredo, E., Ryan, C.: Towards incorporating human knowledge in fuzzy pattern tree evolution. In: Hu, T., Lourenço, N., Medvet, E. (eds.) EuroGP 2021. LNCS, vol. 12691, pp. 66–81. Springer, Cham (2021). https://doi.org/10.1007/978-3-030-72812-0_5

19. Murphy, A., Murphy, G., Dias, D.M., Amaral, J., Naredo, E., Ryan, C.: Human in the loop fuzzy pattern tree evolution. SN Comput. Sci. 3(2), 163 (2022)

20. O'Neill, M., Ryan, C., Keijzer, M., Cattolico, M.: Crossover in grammatical evolution. Genet. Program Evol. Mach. 4(1), 67–93 (2003). https://doi.org/10.1023/A:1021877127167

21. Ryan, C., Collins, J.J., Neill, M.O.: Grammatical evolution: evolving programs for an arbitrary language. In: Banzhaf, W., Poli, R., Schoenauer, M., Fogarty, T.C. (eds.) EuroGP 1998. LNCS, vol. 1391, pp. 83–96. Springer, Heidelberg (1998). https://doi.org/10.1007/BFb0055930

22. Ryan, C., O'Neill, M., Collins, J.: Handbook of Grammatical Evolution. Springer, Cham (2018). https://doi.org/10.1007/978-3-319-78717-6

23. dos Santos, A.R., do Amaral, J.L.M.: Synthesis of fuzzy pattern trees by cartesian genetic programming. Mathware Soft Comput. 22(1), 52–56 (2015)

24. Tetteh, M.K., Mota Dias, D., Ryan, C.: Evolution of complex combinational logic circuits using grammatical evolution with systemverilog. In: Hu, T., Lourenço, N., Medvet, E. (eds.) EuroGP 2021. LNCS, vol. 12691, pp. 146–161. Springer, Cham (2021). https://doi.org/10.1007/978-3-030-72812-0_10

25. Yi, Y., Fober, T., Hüllermeier, E.: Fuzzy operator trees for modeling rating functions. Int. J. Comput. Intell. Appl. 8, 413–428 (2009)

Agro-Ecological Computational Ecosystems

Models for the Computational Design
of Microfarms

David Colliaux[1]([✉]), Pietro Gravino[1,2], Peter Hanappe[1], Julian Talbot[3],
and Pascal Viot[3]

[1] Sony CSL Paris, Paris, France
{david.colliaux,pietro.gravino,peter.hanappe}@sony.com
[2] Sony CSL Rome, Rome, Italy
[3] LPTMC, Sorbonne Université, CNRS UMR 7600, 4, Place Jussieu, Paris, France
julian.talbot@sorbonne-universite.fr, viot@lptmc.jussieu.fr

Abstract. On microfarms, diversified crops are typically cultivated as
densely as possible, and their heterogeneous growth dynamics require
complex design and management of crop rotations. Models in computational agroecology may assist farmers in the maintenance of such farms.
We use a phenomenological model in which the plants are represented
as disks with a growing radius. We show how it can account for the
variability observed in the fields and help visualize the spatiotempo-
ral patterns involved in a microfarm cultivated according to the French
intensive method. In the last part of the paper, we consider monoculture and a mixture of two vegetables with different maximum radii and
growth rates. In the planning strategy, the planting positions and times
are randomly chosen, taking inspiration from models of random sequential adsorption. We describe two different event-driven algorithms (1D
and 2D) to simulate the dynamics of this system. The steady state of the
field consists of disordered configurations of the plants. We study the evolution of the effective planting rate as a function of the nominal planting
rate. When the model plants both vegetables with equal probability, simulations show that the proportion of big plants starts decreasing above a
given threshold. This model and the algorithms describing the planting
strategies may be extended to more species and other planting strategies
to suggest original farm designs.

Keywords: agro-ecosystem · Monte-Carlo simulations · plant growth
dynamics

1 Introduction

Computational agroecology has recently emerged as a set of digital tools dedicated to the design and management of farms cultivated according to agroecological principles [1,2]. It can be organised around three themes: tools, plants, and
people [3]. The first aims at helping the farmer to perform tasks on the field. An
example is a robotic weeder with precise mechanical weeding [4–6]. The second

P. Collet et al. (Eds.): CCE 2023, LNCS 13927, pp. 121–132, 2023.
https://doi.org/10.1007/978-3-031-44355-8_9

is dedicated to the monitoring of culture crops, and their modeling for easing the work of farmers in maintaining their field [7]. The third theme is about people, their knowledge and their know-how. It is focused on gathering knowledge about market farming on small surfaces and creating tools to share this knowledge. In all these aspects, digital technologies may be fruitful [8], and we are particularly interested in the role of computational aspects. Digital tools are deployed mainly in the precision agriculture framework, or agriculture 4.0 [9], but we are interested in some applications which are specific to microfarms cultivating according to the principles of agroecology. For example, the usual context for precision agriculture is that of a large farm in monoculture. In contrast, the methods we are interested in, like the French intensive method [10,11], recommends planting diversified crops as densely as possible. Also, precision agriculture aims at framing agricultural practices within a prespecified environment. Computational agroecology should explore the interactions between the farmer and the plants to reveal their possible dynamics.

Recently, plant phenotyping has rapidly progressed thanks to computer vision and machine learning and is now available in the field. Field phenomics data can be acquired using, for example, a motorised camera mounted on a cable (cablebot), and it is thus possible to monitor on a daily basis the growth of individual plants in a greenhouse [12]. We show below how this data can be integrated into models for the simulation of plant growth in various applications. We first show how to model spatial variability resulting from environmental conditions in a greenhouse. Then, we present the simulations for a plan of culture rotations according to the French intensive method. Finally, we suggest a random planting algorithm optimizing the density of crops for a mixture of lettuces and cabbages.

1.1 Related Work

Models of plant growth are studied both in agronomy, with crop models [13], and ecology, with agent-based models [14]. Crop models include details about the physiology of the plant with distinct compartments for its various organs and corresponding fluxes of chemical components (carbon, nitrogen,...). Agent-based models have a more straightforward description of the growth of each plant but may also include the interactions between neighbouring plants, like competition or facilitation. Coarser modeling is used to design realistic ecosystems at large scale (e.g., for video games [15]). Some recent works propose a multi-scale approach to render realistic architecture at the individual plant level, and spatial patterns for the dispersion of vegetation [16]. A simple model of plants was also used to help manage the pruning and irrigation of a small robotised garden [17].

Models for the intercropping of diverse species are sometimes considered for strip intercropping configurations using patches or strips [18] but don't consider variations in the spatial positions at the individual plant level. The plant arrangements can be approximated as a set of disks with various radii [19]. When considering random plantation times or positions, the model, including growth dynamics, is an extension of the random sequential adsorption model, also known, for the 1D case, as the parking lot model, which describes the dynamics of cars parking randomly on a street [20]. This model is relevant to the study of granular matter with jamming and to the adsorption of proteins on a solid surface, and it has been extended to reversible adsorption [21], bidisperse populations [22,23] and particles having a growth dynamics [24]. For the bidisperse case, it was shown that the selectivity towards a given particle type depends subtly on the pressures of the two populations [25].

2 A Phenomenological Model for Plant Growth

We consider simplified dynamics for the growth of plants, where each plant size is represented by its radius $R(t)$. For salads or cabbages, for example, the plant volume or biomass $M(t)$ can be estimated as that of a half-sphere of radius $R(t)$. In the simplest model, we consider the growth to be linear in time: $R(t) = \alpha(t - t_0)$, with $t_0 < t < t_0 + \tau_h$ when the plant is planted at time t_0 and harvested at $t_0 + \tau_h$. In a more refined model, we consider the growth of the radius to be a sigmoid function of time: $R_t = R_0/(1 + e^{-\alpha(t-t_0)+\beta})$ where α corresponds to the growth rate, β to the offset that is associated with germination and/or slow growth in the first phenological stages of the plant and R_0 the maximal radius at which growth of the plant saturates when reaching maturity.

When modeling the growth of plants, it is important to take environmental parameters into account since plants develop quicker when the temperature is higher. The relevant variable, instead of time, is the accumulated temperature over a threshold T_0 (Réaumur[1] model), growing degree day being a standard measure for estimating the phenological stage [26]. The radius then grows as follows:

$$R_t = \frac{R_0}{1 + e^{-\alpha \int_{t_0}^{t} T(s).H(T(s)-T_0)ds+\beta}}.$$

where H is the Heaviside function so that only the temperatures above T_0 are accumulated and contribute to the growth of the plant.

For a greenhouse, for example, the temperature is maximum at the centre and falls gradually to a minimum at the edge of the greenhouse (see Fig. 1). The model shows a spatial variation in plant sizes similar to those observed in greenhouses [27].

Fig. 1. Simulated culture bed of plants in a greenhouse with a temperature profile depicted on the bottom colour bar. The maximum temperature at the center is 40 °C and the minimum at the borders is 25 °C.

---

[1] René Antoine Ferchault de Réaumur was a French scientist in the XVIIIth century who pioneered the modeling of plant phenology.

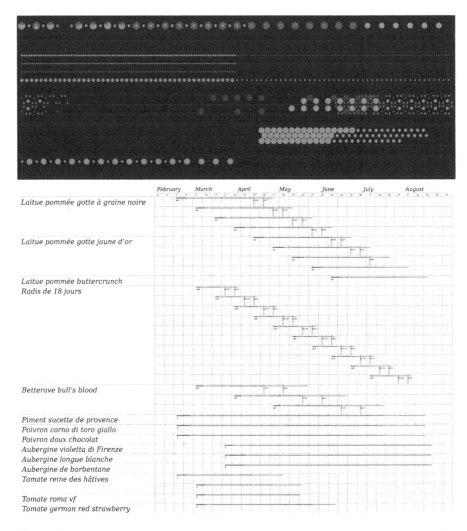

Fig. 2. (Top) Snapshot of a simulation of a microfarm with culture plan according to the French intensive method. Each disk depicts a plant with the different colors corresponding to the species listed in the culture plan. (Bottom) Culture plan for the microfarm: the brown line indicates the sowing period, the blue line indicates the time for germination before transplanting, the green line indicates the growth period in the soil, and the orange line indicates the harvesting period. (Color figure online)

3   Simulation of a Micro-farm Using the French Intensive Method

As a first example of simulations of the growth of plants in a field, we consider a microfarm with five culture beds. The culture plan (Fig. 2), which includes data about the average germination, transplanting and harvesting times, shows the diversity of crops and their intricate interplay. The sowing times follow the recommendation of a recent manual [11] explaining how to cultivate with the principles of the French method. This method is inspired by the practices of Parisian market gardeners of the 19th century [10]. In total, we simulate the culture of 14 species over a time period of 7 months with the linear growth model. Figure 2 shows a snapshot of the field. An animation showing the simulation for the whole season with a simple linear growth model is available online[2].

We observe that the dynamics may be quite complex and that the computational tools may be helpful in forecasting harvest and exploring how changes in the calendar and spatial layout of the plants affect the simulations.

4 Intercropping Lettuces and Cabbages

In order to explore planting strategies, we consider a field planted with lettuces and cabbages. For simplification, for both plants, we consider identical duration before harvesting ($\tau_h = 30$ days) and the same offset $\beta = 4$. On the other hand, the plants have different growth characteristics, like saturation radius ($R_0^c = 0.8$, $R_0^l = 0.3$) and growth rate ($\alpha^c = 0.4$, $\alpha^l = 0.3$).

We start with a 1-dimensional field. Plants are usually planted in a series of batches with regular spacing (Δ). Planting may be synchronised every τ_h or desynchronised so that alternated batches are planted every $\tau_h/2$ with the plants of the new batch being in between the plants of the previous batch (see Fig. 3). For planting both lettuces and cabbages, we may consider two configurations. The first option is to split the field into two parts, one for lettuces and one for cabbages, each planted with the monoculture configuration. Another method is to alternate lettuces and cabbages (see Fig. 3). The latter strategy, intercropping different plants, is often used in market gardening. There are thus four patterns we may consider as reference depending on whether the batches are synchronised or desynchronised and the field being split or intercropped with lettuces and cabbages. In 2D, there are further options depending on the lattice used to position the plants. We use a triangular grid for synchronous monoculture and dual square grids for desynchronised and/or intercropped configurations.

When N plants are planted over a duration t, the effective planting rate, $\rho = N/t$, is helpful in comparing the different configurations. For example, it can be easily calculated that in 1D, the split and intercropped configurations have different effective rates. Also, in 2D, for a monoculture, we can plant more vegetables with the desynchronised configuration as long as $R(\tau_h)/R(\tau_h/2) <$ $\sqrt{2\sqrt{3}} - 1$.

In the following, we will use the desynchronised configuration as a reference both for monoculture and intercropping, except in 2D, for the monoculture of cabbages, where the effective planting rate is higher for synchronised planting.

---

[2] https://www.youtube.com/watch?v=EwrS9HxIqBw.

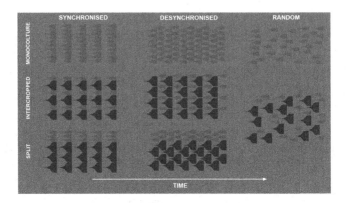

Fig. 3. Reference configurations and samples from the random plantation algorithm.

Table 1. Planting rate for different reference configurations.

		Monoculture		Mixture	
		Lettuces	Cabbages	Intercropped	Split
1D (L = 100)	Synchronised	5.59	2.08	3.04	3.04
	Desynchronised	6.88	2.21	3.32	3.35
2D (L = 20)	Synchronised	43.34	6.02	11.06	10.57
	Desynchronised	56.75	5.89	13.26	10.67

5   A Random Planting Algorithm for Intercropped Lettuces and Cabbages

Although regularly spaced planting strategies are widespread in farming practices, we are willing to explore alternative planting strategies, as they could be implemented by a robot, for example. The most straightforward strategy apart from regular grids is to choose randomly the planting times and positions, as well as the plant species, when considering mixtures, with the constraint that the newly planted individual doesn't overlap with others over the course of its growth. For simplicity, we first consider the planting of crops along a line of length $L = 100$ and then on a plane of dimensions 20×20. We now describe the algorithms for simulating the random planting strategy (see also the detailed description in the boxes below[3]).

---

[3] https://github.com/SonyCSLParis/lettuces_and_cabbages.

Algorithm 1. 1D intercropping algorithm

```
1:  t ← 0
2:  N ← 0
3:  while N < N_p do
4:      φ ← 0
5:      while φ = 0 do
6:          dt ← random time interval (exponential with rate λ)
7:          s ← random species in ['c', 'l'] with probabilities (p, 1-p)
8:          t ← t + dt
9:          φ ← L − Σ σ_i(t, s)
10:     end while
11:     η ← uniform in [0, φ]
12:     k_0 ← max k s.t. φ_k ≤ η
13:     x ← Σ_{k=0}^{k_0} σ_k + η
14:     plants.add(Plant(x, t, s))
15:     Remove plants reaching maturity before t
16:     N ← N + 1
17: end while
```

The algorithm attempts to plant seeds by randomly selecting the species, the planting time and the location at each trial. In fact, three properties can fully describe each plant i: its species s_i (and the associated growth curve parameter for lettuce or cabbage), its planting time t_i, and its planting position ($\mathbf{x_i}$). The species $s_i \in [c, l]$, where l stands for lettuces and c stands for cabbages. For monocultures, only one of the two will be possible. Otherwise, we can draw one of the two with uniform probability. Still, we have two options:

- *mix 1*, where the species is drawn at the beginning of each trial;
- *mix 2*, where the species is drawn at the beginning of each iteration and kept fixed for all trials in this iteration.

In the latter option, the plant population have an equal number of lettuces and cabbages ($N_c = N_l$). After a successful trial, the time for the subsequent trial is drawn from an exponential law of nominal planting rate $r = \frac{\lambda}{\tau}$. So, the time interval between 2 successive planting events is the sum of time intervals sampled overall K trials in an iteration: $t_i - t_{i-1} = \sum_{k=1}^{K} \tau_k$ where τ_k is drawn from the exponential distribution. When there is no rejection, planting events occur as a Poisson process.

The position x_i is sampled with uniform probability in the available space ($1D$) or in the entire space ($2D$). The available space in the $1D$ case is calculated by excluding all the space occupied by plants that are already present but also the place they will occupy in the future and the future size of the plant we should plant. If we consider the generic plant j already sown, the new plant i must be sown at a minimum distance $v_{ij} = R^{s_i}(t_j + \tau_h) + R^{s_j}(t_j + \tau_h)$, which calculates the future size of both plants i and j at the moment when j will be harvested, thus freeing more space. So, each existing plant j has a virtual size v_{ij} that cannot be used to sample position for i. All the intervals $[x_j - v_{ij}, x_j + v_{ij}]$ must be excluded from the available space. In the calculation, we have to take into account that these intervals might be overlapping. After we merge the overlapping intervals, we have a certain number N' of forbidden intervals of generic size σ_f. After we exclude these intervals, the remaining available intervals $[x_j^{min}, x_j^{max}]$ can finally be summed to obtain the available space measure $\phi_N = \sum_{j=1}^{N} \phi_j = \sum_{j=1}^{N} |x_j^{max} - x_j^{min}|$. It is worth noting that the number of available intervals is $N' + 1$, but if we neglect border effects or we consider periodic conditions, the interval number can be considered equal to N'. We then draw a random number η uniformly in $[0, \phi_N]$ and find the interval n_0 so that $\sum_{j=1}^{n_0} \phi_j < \eta < \sum_{j=1}^{n_0+1} \phi_j$ and x_i is then chosen as $x_i = \sum_{j=1}^{n_0} \sigma_j + \eta$, with σ_j the length of the jth forbidden interval. There will be rejections at trial k only if the space is fully occupied, in which case, time is incremented by τ_k, and another sample is drawn (Fig. 4).

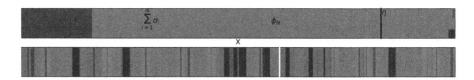

Fig. 4. Position sampling for the 1D model: (Bottom) Each plant is represented by a green interval of width $2R$, with a lighter green extension corresponding to the virtual size. The yellow bar indicates the position which is sampled at this particular iteration. The rectangles surrounded by a red borders show the maximal size of lettuces (light green) and cabbages (dark green) for scale reference. (Top) The occupancy (shown in green) is computed as the sum of occupied intervals (merged overlapping virtual plants). The random number η is chosen uniformly in the remaining space ϕ_N. (Color figure online)

In the 2D simulations, after drawing the position $\mathbf{x}_i$ of plant i uniformly in the space, we compute, for each of its neighbours j, the time t_{ij} at which it will intersect. If t_{ij} is smaller than the harvesting time of plant j, $t_j + \tau_h$, we reject it, increment time, and make another trial.

Let us now analyse the dynamics of the system when the planting ratio is increased. For monoculture in $1D$, for a very low planting rate, there is always available space, so the effective planting rate is equal to the nominal one. Things cannot change before the configuration where the plants are regularly spaced along all L with a gap between pairs of neighbouring plants smaller than $\Delta = 4R$. This will make planting impossible, and all trials will be rejected (even with a lot of unoccupied space, roughly equal to $L/2$). The corresponding effective planting rate is $\rho_{SAT} = \frac{L}{\Delta_{SAT} \tau_h}$ (with $L = 100$, $\rho_{SAT}^l = 2.77$, $\rho_{SAT}^c = 1.04$ and $\rho_{SAT}^{lc} = 1.51$). Even if this scenario is improbable, it marks the beginning of a shift in the dynamics. The average number of rejections in simulations is shown in Fig. 5, and it is 0 before those values. On the other hand, theoretical saturation configurations are shown in Fig. 3, and relative planting ratio values are shown in Table 1. The results tell us that the best reference configuration (desynchronised one) is not achieved, probably because it is a very unlikely one. The effective planting rate seems, in fact, closer to the synchronised configuration.

As shown in Fig. 5, above this threshold, in $1D$, the average number of trials per iteration grows linearly except for the option where species are sampled at every trial (*mix 1*), where the linear relation appears at a much higher rate. For the 2D simulations, Fig. 5 also show how the effective planting rate was measured in simulations for the four conditions. All curves grow in the same manner (linear in $1D$) at a low rate below the threshold identified previously, where the effective rate starts saturating around the reference value computed in the previous section for monocultures and *mix 2* option. In the *mix 1* option, there are two linear regimes before saturation; in the first linear regime, there is almost no rejection, and there is an equal proportion of lettuces and cabbages ($N_c = N_l$). After the first transition point (around the cabbage monoculture saturation point), cabbages start getting rejected. We observe a decrease in the cabbage share until the field is fully covered with lettuce. A snapshot of simulations for the 1D model and the 2D model is shown in Fig. 6 in the *mix 2* option ($N_c = N_l$).

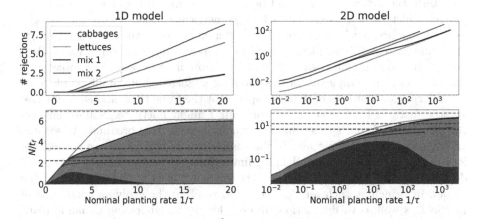

Fig. 5. Measures from the simulations in $1D$ (Left) and $2D$ (Right) with lettuce monoculture in light green, cabbage monoculture in dark green, intercropped culture with species randomly sampled at each trial (*mix 1*) in black or fixed sampled species at each iteration (*mix 2*) in red. The top graphs show the number of rejections before a plant is sown depending on the nominal planting rate ($1/\tau$). The bottom graphs show how the Effective planting rate (N/t) depends on the Nominal planting rate. The regions filled in light and dark green indicate the effective planting rates for lettuces and cabbages with the *mix 1* option. The dashed lines are a visualization of effective planting rate for the reference configurations listed in Table 1. Solid lines are the results of simulations of the ranfom planting strategy. (Color figure online)

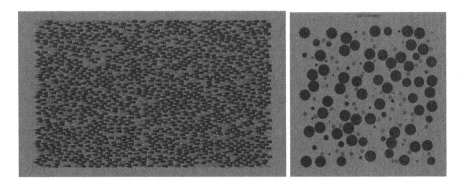

Fig. 6. Simulation of the intercropped field constrained so that $N_c = N_l$: $1D$ on the left and $2D$ on the right.

6 Discussion

Optimising space and time in a farming plan is a task that could appear as an utterly theoretical one. It could be formulated as a tiling or a close-packing problem, just to be solved with a few geometrical considerations. But on the field, things are much more complex. Different areas of the same field might offer different conditions, like humidity or temperature, as shown in Fig. 1. And these conditions might change in time in unpredictable ways (e.g. weather). Furthermore, the complexity of the planning might combinatorially explode as a real farm can host tens of different species at the same time, and each of those species' features (size, maturation time, etc.) might fluctuate. Not to mention the fact that different species might mutually benefit from proximity in sowing, adding an additional constraint to the complexity. In this paper, we present the idea that a priori geometrical planning limitations can be overcome by a dynamic decision-making algorithm, aware of the current status of the field and of the plants. In principle, such an algorithm can react to the evolving conditions of the field as well as to fluctuations in crop features, elaborating dynamic plans that will result in more robustness and flexibility at the same time. To explain this concept, we introduce an algorithm operating in simplified conditions, and we analyse its performance. The algorithms we presented may be helpful in the management of the complex rotation plan, in particular in agroecological microfarms. It may also drive the development of new design strategies. It would be helpful to define an ontology adapted to agroecological principles [7] to have a comprehensive toolbox for the simulation of microfarms.

The distribution of both species in the 1D distribution shows highly correlated patterns, probably existing also in 2D, but harder to spot, which we wish to study in future work.

We conceived a conceptual architecture that will also easily allow the future introduction of more complex scenarios. For example, we plan to add variability in the field condition, seasonality effects, and variable species ratios. All these do not require specific modifications to the algorithm but only to the simulation model. On the other hand, to handle fluctuations in plants' features, the algorithm forecasting capabilities must be improved to take that into account.

Scientific Validation

This paper has benefited from the remarks of the following reviewers:

- Godai Suzuki, Synecoculture Association, Japan
- Tatsuya Kawaoka, Synecoculture Association, Japan
- Takuya Otani, Waseda University, Japan

The conference organisers wish to thank them for their highly appreciated effort and contribution.

References

1. Raghavan, B., Nardi, B., Lovell, S.T., Norton, J., Tomlinson, B., Patterson, D.J.: Computational agroecology: sustainable food ecosystem design. In: Proceedings of the 2016 CHI Conference Extended Abstracts on Human Factors in Computing Systems, CHI EA '16. Association for Computing Machinery, New York, NY, USA, pp. 423–435 (2016)
2. Hanappe, P., Dunlop, R., Maes, A., Steels, L., Duval, N.: Agroecology: a fertile field for human computation. Hum. Comput. **3**(1), 225–233 (2016)
3. Colliaux, D., Minchin, J., Goelzer, S., Hanappe, P.: Computational agroecology: should we bet the microfarm on it? In: Eighth Workshop on Computing within Limits 2022. LIMITS, 21 June 2022
4. Colliaux, D., Hanappe, P.: Lettucethink: a open and versatile robotic platform for weeding and crop monitoring on microfarms. In: EFITA WCCA 2017 Conference (2017)
5. Ditzler, L., Driessen, C.: Automating agroecology: how to design a farming robot without a monocultural mindset? J. Agric. Environ. Ethics **35**(1), 2 (2022)
6. Terra, F., Rodrigues, L., Magalhães, S., Santos, F., Moura, P., Cunha, M.: Pixelcroprobot, a cartesian multitask platform for microfarms automation. In: 2021 International Symposium of Asian Control Association on Intelligent Robotics and Industrial Automation (IRIA), pp. 382–387. IEEE (2021)
7. Darnala, B., Amardeilh, F., Roussey, C., Jonquet, C.: Crop planning and production process ontology (c3po), a new model to assist diversified crop production. In: Integrated Food Ontology Workshop (IFOW'21) at the 12th International Conference on Biomedical Ontologies (ICBO) (2021)
8. Maurel, V.B., et al.: Digital technology and agroecology: opportunities to explore, challenges to overcome. In: Agriculture and Digital Technology: Getting the Most Out of Digital Technology to Contribute to the Transition to Sustainable Agriculture and Food Systems, Number 6 in White Book INRIA, pp. 76–97. INRIA (2022)
9. Sponchioni, G., Vezzoni, M., Bacchetti, A., Pavesi, M., Renga, F.M.: The 4.0 revolution in agriculture: a multi-perspective definition. In: Summer School F. Turco-Industrial Systems Engineering, pp. 143–149 (2019)
10. Orin, M.: French intensive gardening: a retrospective. Accessed 09 Jan 2022

11. de Carné-Carnavalet, C.: Le maraîchage sur petite surface: La French Method : une agriculture urbaine ou périurbaine. Editions de Terran (2020)
12. Sollazzo, A., Colliaux, D., Garivani, S., Minchin, J., Garlanda, L., Hanappe, P.: Automated vegetable growth analysis from outdoor images acquired with a cable-bot. In: Proceedings of the IEEE International Conference on Computer Vision Workshops (2020)
13. Crawford, J.: Mathematical models in agriculture. In: Thornley, J.H.M., France, J. (eds.) Quantitative Methods for the Plant, Animal and Ecological Sciences, 2nd edn, p. 906. Cabi, Wallingford, UK (2007). £150.00. ISBN 0-85199-010-x. Exp. Agric. **44**(1), 139 (2008)
14. Zhang, B., DeAngelis, D.L.: An overview of agent-based models in plant biology and ecology. Ann. Botany **126**(4), 539–557 (2020)
15. Cordonnier, G., et al.: Authoring landscapes by combining ecosystem and terrain erosion simulation. ACM Trans. Graph. (TOG) **36**(4), 1–12 (2017)
16. Makowski, M., Hädrich, T., Scheffczyk, J., Michels, D.L., Pirk, S., Pałubicki, W.: Synthetic silviculture: multi-scale modeling of plant ecosystems. ACM Trans. Graph. (TOG) **38**(4), 1–14 (2019)
17. Avigal, Y., et al.: Simulating polyculture farming to learn automation policies for plant diversity and precision irrigation. IEEE Trans. Autom. Sci. Eng. **19**(3), 1352–1364 (2022)
18. Juventia, S.D., Selin Norén, I.L.M., Van Apeldoorn, D.F., Ditzler, L., Rossing, W.A.H.: Spatio-temporal design of strip cropping systems. Agric. Syst. **201**, 103455 (2022)
19. Ecormier-Nocca, P., Memari, P., Gain, J., Cani, M.-P.: Accurate synthesis of multi-class disk distributions. Comput. Graph. Forum **38**(2), 157–168 (2019)
20. Renyi, A.: On a one-dimensional problem concerning random space-filling problem. Publ. Math. Inst. Hungar. Acad. Sci **3**, 109–127 (1958)
21. Talbot, J., Tarjus, G., Van Tassel, P.R., Viot, P.: From car parking to protein adsorption: an overview of sequential adsorption processes. Colloids Surf. A **165**(1), 287–324 (2000)
22. Hassan, Schmidt, J., Blasius, B., Kurths, J.: Jamming and asymptotic behavior in competitive random parking of bidisperse cars. Physica A: Stat. Mech. Appl. **315**(1–2), 163–173 (2002)
23. Wagaskar, K.V., Late, R., Banpurkar, A.G., Limaye, A.V., Shelke, P.B.: Simulation studies of random sequential adsorption (RSA) of mixture of two-component circular discs. J. Stat. Phys. **181**(6), 2191–2205 (2020)
24. Boyer, D., Talbot, J., Tarjus, G., Van Tassel, P., Viot, P.: Exactly solvable models of irreversible adsorption with particle spreading. Phys. Rev. E **49**, 5525–5534 (1994)
25. Talbot, J.: Analysis of adsorption selectivity in a one-dimensional model system. AIChE J. **43**(10), 2471–2478 (1997)
26. Miller, P., Lanier, W., Brandt, S.: Using growing degree days to predict plant stages. Ag/Extension Commun. Coord. Commun. Serv. Montana State University-Bozeman, Bozeman, MO **59717**(406), 994–2721 (2001)
27. Takayama, K., Morimoto, C., Takahashi, N., Nishina, H.: Distributions of stem diameter and stem elongation rate in a large-scale tomato production greenhouse-measurement of thousand plants. In: International Symposium on New Technologies for Environment Control, Energy-Saving and Crop Production in Greenhouse and Plant, vol. 1037, pp. 721–726 (2013)

Vegee Brain Automata: Ultradiscretization of Essential Chaos Transversal in Neural and Ecosystem Dynamics

Masatoshi Funabashi[1,2]([✉]) [iD]

[1] Sony Computer Science Laboratories, Inc., Tokyo, Japan
`masa_funabashi@csl.sony.co.jp`
[2] Research Division On Social Common Capital and the Future, Kyoto University Institute for the Future of Human Society, Kyoto, Japan

Abstract. Coupled logistic equations and their discretizations are important models in ecology and complex systems science. However, the chaotic dynamics produced by these nonlinear dynamical systems are lumped together, and the mathematical correspondence between continuous and discrete-time systems is not sufficiently clear. The method of ultradiscretization, which has recently been developed in the analysis of nonlinear integrable systems, can discretize both independent variables such as time and dependent variables such as time-evolving quantities in the dynamical system, while providing an analytical basis for the mathematical correspondence with the original continuous system. In this paper, we first show that the ultradiscretization of the logistic equation has the same form as that of a sigmoidal map, which cannot be derived from a customarily used logistic map. Consequently, recursively coupled systems of sigmoidal functions, such as those employed in neural networks, emerge as new candidate models for various dynamics important in agroecology, where both autonomous dynamics of ecosystems and human intervention could be represented. We then explore qualitative correspondences between neural networks and various modes of farming, including chaotic behavior, and propose an ultra-discretized model that serves as the essential underlying element. The newly proposed model has mathematical connectivity with logistic and tent maps, as well as Holling's disc equations, providing interpretations rooted in ecology and neuroscience. The comprehensive results provide a new perspective for extracting the essence of complex agroecology via computation, which has the potential to link the properties of deep learning being studied in neural networks to the complexity of ecological management.

Keywords: Logistic Map · Chaotic Neural Network · Globally Coupled Map Lattices · Ultradiscretizaion · Holling's Disc Equations · Chaotic Itinerancy

1 Introduction

The logistic equation and its coupled Lotka-Volterra equations are a major source of modeling in ecological studies (*e.g.,* [1]). Coupled logistic maps in the form of discrete-time difference equations are also important dynamical systems in understanding the

© The Author(s), under exclusive license to Springer Nature Switzerland AG 2023
P. Collet et al. (Eds.): CCE 2023, LNCS 13927, pp. 133–150, 2023.
https://doi.org/10.1007/978-3-031-44355-8_10

high-dimensional deterministic chaos in complex systems, such as Globally Coupled Maps and Coupled Map Lattices (GCML) [2]. Although discrete-time dynamical systems have been a mathematically informative platform for the analysis of non-linear integrable systems, such as discrete-time solitons [3], the methodology on the derivation of the difference equations from the original differential equations is considered decisive for the feasibility of the analysis; the transformation from continuous to discrete-time dynamical systems should preserve essential dynamics that constitute the complexity of the original model.

For example, the logistic equation and its discretized logistic map are usually described as follows, for the one-dimensional real variable $x(t)$ with time t, environmental capacity K and strength of self-feedback r:

$$\text{Logistic equation } L(x(t)) : \frac{dx(t)}{dt} = rx(t)\left(1 - \frac{x(t)}{K}\right) \tag{1}$$

$$\text{Logistic map: } x(t+1) = x(t) + rx(t)\left(1 - \frac{x(t)}{K}\right) \tag{2}$$

However, the logistic map (2) is known to exhibit complex bifurcation of periodicity and chaotic behavior along with the augmentation of the parameter r [4], which is not observed in the continuous-time model (1). Although the logistic map is useful for investigating coupled chaotic systems, such dynamics could be considered as mathematical by-products resulting from the naive discretization apart from the original ecological implication of the logistic equation. For Eq. (2) to rigorously reproduce the original solution known as the logistic/sigmoid curve, one needs to employ the following model proposed by Morishita [5]:

$$\text{Morishita's logistic map: } x(t + \Delta t) = \frac{(1+a)x(t)}{1+bx(t)}, \tag{3}$$

where $\Delta t > 0$ is the time difference, $a = e^{r\Delta t} - 1$ and $b = a/K$.

The model (2) and (3) could be integrated with a generalized discretization form of (1), using the time difference $l = (m - 1)\tau$ with a positive real number $0 < \tau$ and natural number m, such that

$$x(t + \Delta t) = x(t) + r\Delta t\left(x(t) - \frac{1}{K}x(t)x(t + l)\right) + O(\tau). \tag{4}$$

Since the sigmoid curve $x(t)$ has the upper bound K, so is the variation in (4), i.e., for a sufficiently large τ, $\{x(t + \Delta t) - x(t) - r\Delta t(x(t) - \frac{1}{K}x(t)x(t + l))\}/\tau < K$ holds. By taking the infinitesimal limit $\tau \to +0$, (4) converges to (1) when $l = 0$ and $\Delta t \to +0$; to (2) when $l = 0$ and $\Delta t = 1$; and to (3) when $l = 1$ and $\Delta t \ll 1$. (Note that the actual dynamics of (3) perfectly coincide with the trajectory of (1) with all ranges of $\Delta t > 0$, which is not fully expressed in (4) but these differences converge to the same ultra-discretized model (10).) This means that the choice of the discretization parameters such as l and Δt could influence the nature of discretized dynamics which may not preserve the original characteristics, especially in non-linear systems.

Recently developing analysis on ultradiscretization deals with such challenges to extract essential systems that are discrete not only in time but also the values of variables that are representative of the original complexity and mathematical invariants (*e.g.*, [6, 7]). Since the numerical simulation of non-linear dynamical systems with simple discretization such as the Euler method from (1) to (2) may profoundly alter the characteristics of the model, seeking universal mathematical structure among differential equations, difference equations and ultra-discretized digital equations is essential for the proper computation [8].

2 Ultradiscretization of Logistic Models

2.1 Ultradiscretization of the Logistic Equation

We consider the ultradiscretization of the logistic equation starting from the rigorously discretized form (3) with $\Delta t = 1$ and $a < K$. We focus on the sigmoidal growth of $x(t)$ starting from $x(0) > 0$ and converges to K. Using an arbitrary parameter $\varepsilon > 0$, we consider the following transformation from $x(t)$ to $X(t)$:

$$x(t) = x(0)e^{\frac{X(t)-X(0)}{\varepsilon}} \tag{5}$$

$$1 + a = e^{\frac{R}{\varepsilon}}, R > 0 \tag{6}$$

$$b = e^{\frac{-Q}{\varepsilon}}, Q > 0 \tag{7}$$

We then obtain

$$X(t+1) = X(t) + R - \varepsilon \log\left(e^{\frac{0}{\varepsilon}} + e^{\frac{X(t)-Q-X(0)-\varepsilon \log x(0)}{\varepsilon}}\right), \tag{8}$$

which by taking the limit $\varepsilon \to +0$, converges to the ultra-discretized form

$$\lim_{\varepsilon \to +0} X(t+1) = X(t) + R - \max\left[0, X(t) - Q - X(0)\right]. \tag{9}$$

We choose the representative values A and B ($0 < A < K, 0 < B < K, A + B = K$) for the parameters R and Q that formally express the convergence to the environmental limit K as follows:

$$X(t+1) = X(t) + A - \max[0, X(t) - B]. \tag{10}$$

From the relation between (3) and (4), this result coincides with the ultradiscretization of the limited case of (4) with the specification of parameters $\Delta t = 1, l = 1$ and $\tau \to +0$. The relationships between Eqs. (1), (3) and (10) are depicted in Fig. 1.

2.2 Ultradiscretization of the Neuron Model with a Sigmoid Function

We consider another discrete-time system based on a sigmoid function commonly used in neural network models and show that the ultra-discretized dynamics coincide with that of (10). Let us consider the sigmoid function $S(x; r, \theta, K) := K/(1 + e^{-r(x-\theta)})$ with the parameters $r, \theta, K > 0$, which is known as a basic neuron model with $K = 1$ and also as the solution of (1) in the form of $x(t) := S(t) = K/(1 + e^{-r(t-\theta)})$, where $\theta := \log(K/x(0) - 1)/r$.

We consider a simple element of discrete-time system conventionally used in the self-recurrent neural network models with the time-dependent difference term $\Delta x(t) > 0$ such as

$$x(t + 1) = S(x(t)) = x(t) + \Delta x(t). \tag{11}$$

Using (3), it is known that

$$S(t + \Delta t) = \frac{(1 + a)S(t)}{1 + bS(t)}, \tag{12}$$

and substituting t and Δt with $x(t)$ and $\Delta x(t)$, respectively, we obtain

$$S(x(t) + \Delta x(t)) = S(x(t + 1)) = \frac{(1 + a')S(x(t))}{1 + b'S(x(t))}, \tag{13}$$

where $a' = e^{r\Delta x(t)} - 1$ and $b' = a'/K$. Note that a' and b' are dependent on t and not on Δt. Through the transformation $t + 1 \to t$, we derive a simpler form
***

$$x(t + 1) = \frac{(1 + a')x(t)}{1 + b'x(t)}. \tag{14}$$

We apply the transformation $x(t) = e^{\frac{X(t)}{\varepsilon}}$ for the ultradiscretization, which transforms (14) into the following:

$$\varepsilon \log e^{X(t+1)/\varepsilon} = \varepsilon \log \left\{ (1 + a')e^{X(t)/\varepsilon} \right\} - \varepsilon \log \left\{ 1 + b'e^{X(t)/\varepsilon} \right\}. \tag{15}$$

Performing the parameters transformation $a'' = \varepsilon' \log (1 + a')$ and $b'' = -\varepsilon'' \log b'$ with $\varepsilon' > 0$ and $\varepsilon'' > 0$, and taking the limit $\varepsilon \to 0$ on both sides, we obtain

$$X(t + 1) = X(t) + a'' - max\left[0, X(t) - b''\right]. \tag{16}$$

(i) In the case of $X(t) \le b''$, (16) becomes $X(t + 1) = X(t) + a''$. By definition, $a'' = \varepsilon' r \Delta x(t)$, therefore by taking $\varepsilon' \propto \Delta x(t)^{-1}$, (16) can be described as $X(t + 1) = X(t) + A$ with an arbitrary constant $A > 0$.

(ii) In the case of $X(t) \ge b''$, (16) becomes $X(t + 1) = a'' + b'' = \varepsilon'' \log\left(K\frac{1+a'}{a'}\right)$ by assuming $\varepsilon' = \varepsilon''$. Then by taking $\varepsilon'' = B/\log(K/a')$ with $B = K - A > 0$, $X(t + 1) = K$ remains invariant for all t.

Based on the operations (i) and (ii), taking the limit ε', $\varepsilon'' \to 0$ on (16) results in Ultra-discretized sigmoidal map $S'(X(t))$:

$$X(t+1) = X(t) + A - max[0, X(t) - B], \tag{17}$$

which exactly coincides with (10). This means that the logistic Eq. (1) and the self-recurrent sigmoidal map (11) preserve the same mathematical structure in the ultra-discretized form. From this perspective, it may be more appropriate to use the combination of the sigmoidal map (11) than the logistic map (2) to numerically simulate the mathematical features of coupled logistic equations. The relationship between (11) and (17) is depicted in Fig. 1.

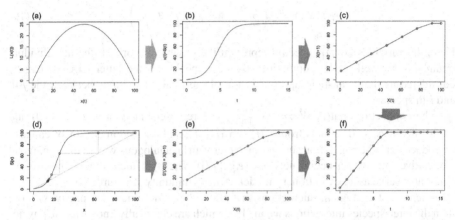

Fig. 1. (a), (b), (c): Relationships between the equations $L(x(t))$ (1), a sigmoid curve $x(t) = S(t)$ and its ultradiscretization (10). (d), (e): relationships between the Eqs. (11) and its ultradiscretization (17). (f): discrete-time development of the ultra-discretized models (10) and (17). Red arrows represent ultradiscretization, and blue arrows correspond to the same coordinate transformation. Example parameters were chosen as $r = 1, x(0) = 1$ for (a) and (b); $r = 0.2, x(0) = 13.83$ for (d); and $K = 100, A = 15, X(0) = 1$ for (c), (e) and (f).

2.3 Analogy Between Neural Network and Agroecological Dynamics

Considering the self-recurrent coupled sigmoidal maps as an essential discrete model of the logistic Eq. (1) opens a way to reinterpret the neural networks from the perspective of the ecological model of interacting species. In this section, we explore ways to express autonomous ecological dynamics and human interventions for its management in reference to discrete-time neural network models such as [9], based on the general modalities used in a wide range of farming methods reviewed in [10].

Crop and weed interactions are important factors in the community dynamics of agroecological systems, which entail symbiotic and competitive relationships that promote and hinder the growth of each species and produce a variety of succession dynamics. The most intuitive way to express such complex interactions is to incorporate the connection functions $V := \{v_{ij}(x_j(t); x_i(t))\}_{i,j=1}^n$ between sigmoidal maps, such as

$$x_i(t+1) = S\left(\sum_{j=1}^n v_{ij}(x_j(t); x_i(t)); r_i, \theta_i, K_i\right), \tag{18}$$

where $S(y; r_i, \theta_i, K_i) := K_i/(1 + e^{-r_i(y-\theta_i)})$, and $v_{ij}(x_i(t), x_j(t)) > 0$ represents facilitation and $v_{ij}(x_j(t); x_i(t)) < 0$ inhibition from $x_j(t)$ to $x_i(t+1)$ using $x_i(t)$ as a parameter. In ecosystems, $v_{ij}(\cdot; \cdot)$ are generally non-linear that are typical in allelopathic interactions between crops and weeds [11], but the simplest linearized form $v_{ij}(x_j(t); x_i(t)) \approx w_{ij}x_j(t)$ converges to the connection matrix of a conventional neural network (*e.g.*, [9]), which provides

$$x_i(t+1) = S\left(\sum_{j=1}^n w_{ij}x_j(t); r_i, \theta_i, K_i\right). \tag{19}$$

Here, the variables $\{x_i(t)\}_{i=1}^n$ could represent the growth rate of n different individual organisms, as well as the population size of n species, in the latter case w_{ij} can be considered as the mean-field approximation of the total interactions between the j-th and i-th species.

The connection matrix $W := \{w_{ij}\}_{i,j=1}^n$ can represent facilitative ($w_{ij} > 0$) and competitive ($w_{ij} < 0$) effects from $x_j(t)$ to $x_i(t+1)$, and the asymmetry in W can also reproduce periodic vegetation succession patterns in an analogous way to the dynamical associative memory in neural network (*e.g.*,[12]). The dynamical modification of W could also serve as an evolutionary model of the community structure.

There exist ecological interactions that affect the environmental capacity K_i more than the inter-species interactions w_{ij} in (19), which are classically known as the physiological optimum of a single species and the ecological optima of a community of multiple species [13]. Such effects could be incorporated as $K_i(\overline{E})$ with the mean environmental condition $\overline{E}$, such as

$$K_i(\overline{E}) := K_i' N\left(\overline{E}; \mu_i, \sigma_i^{opt}\right), \tag{20}$$

where $\overline{E}$ represents the mean environmental parameters that affect plant growth such as temperature, humidity, luminosity, etc., and $N(\cdot; \mu_i, \sigma_i^2)$ is the probabilistic density function of a normal distribution with the mean μ_i and standard deviation σ_i^{opt}. The superscript opt specifies the physiological (*phy*) and ecological (*eco*) optimizations, which is generally known as $\sigma_i^{phy} < \sigma_i^{eco}$, *i.e.*, the relative superiority of ecological optimum in a marginal environment [10]. For the practical fitting of the model, we can choose the constant K_i' according to the unit of measurement such as biomass quantity.

Ecosystems dynamics are dependent on the past states and often exhibit hysteresis such as regime shifts with inherent mechanisms [14]. A general form to incorporate time-delayed feedback in (19) can be expressed as the following:

$$x_i(t+1) = S\left(\sum_{j=1}^n w_{ij}H\left(\{x_j(t-d)\}_{d=0}^t\right); r_i, \theta_i, K_i\right). \tag{21}$$

The hysteresis function $H(\cdot)$ can be approximately decomposed to each past time step using multiple linear regression such as

$$H\left(\{x_j(t-d)\}_{d=0}^{t}\right) \approx x_j(t) + \sum_{d=1}^{t} h'^{(d)x_j(t-d)}, \qquad (22)$$

with a series of coefficients $\{h'(d)\}_{d=1}^{t}$. If we assume a gradual decrease of the past influence, such as $h'(1) > h'(2) > \cdots > h'(t)$, one of the simplest and plausible ways to interpret ecologically important situations (e.g., allelopathic residual effects in the soil [15]) is to express them as the exponential decay such as $h'(d) := h^d$ with the n-th power of the attenuation coefficient $0 \leq h < 1$, which provides

$$x_i(t+1) = S\left(\sum_{j=1}^{n} w_{ij} \sum_{d=0}^{t} h^d x_j(t-d); r_i, \theta_i, K_i\right). \qquad (23)$$

Among the time-delayed feedbacks in (23), self-recurrent negative feedback is especially important to explain the hysteresis such as monocropping failure or replant difficulty (e.g., [16, 17]), which can be expressed as the refractory term of the i-th element that is introduced in a chaotic neuron model [9]:

$$x_i(t+1) = S\left(\sum_{j=1}^{n} w_{ij} \sum_{d=0}^{t} h_f^d x_j(t-d) - \alpha \sum_{d=0}^{t} h_r^d x_i(t-d); r_i, \theta_i, K_i\right), \qquad (24)$$

where α is the scaling coefficient of the refractoriness, and the attenuation coefficient h is distinguished between the feedback and refractory terms as h_f and h_r, respectively. The refractory term can also represent context-dependent human interventions such as thinning harvest, density-dependent weed & pest control (e.g., [18]) and other management strategies that consider the growth history of the target x_i.

A more general and systematic form of human interventions for the management, as well as external periodic factors such as seasonal microclimate changes, can be additionally incorporated as the external inputs term to (24), such that

$$x_i(t+1) = S(\sum_{j=1}^{m} u_{ij} \sum_{d=0}^{t} h_e^d E_j(t-d)$$
$$+ \sum_{j=1}^{n} w_{ij} \sum_{d=0}^{t} h_f^d x_j(t-d)$$
$$-\alpha \sum_{d=0}^{t} h_r^d x_i(t-d); r_i, \theta_i, K_i), \qquad (25)$$

with the interaction matrix $U := \{u_{ij}\}$ between the j-th external input E_j ($j = 1, \ldots, m$) and the i-th element x_i and its attenuation coefficient h_e[1].

The model (25) is one of the simplest linear approximations of complex ecological interactions with the structure of coupled sigmoidal maps, which converges to a neural network with intermittent chaotic behavior [9, 12]. We analogically call it the Chaotic Ecological Network (CEN) and analyze its dynamics from agroecological perspectives in the following section.

---

[1] For simplicity, U was defined as a unit matrix in the simulations of Fig. 4.

2.4   Analysis of the Dynamics in Chaotic Ecological Network

Let us simulate example dynamics of CEN (25) with the parameters $n = 3$, $K_i = K = 100$, $r_i = 0.2$, $\theta_i = \log(K_i/x_i(0) - 1)/r_i = 22.9756$, $h_e = h_f = 0.1$, and the initial values with a relative saturation of $x_1(t)$ such that $(x_1(0), x_2(0), x_3(0)) = (K, 0, -K)$. The values of E_j, α and h_r differ and are specified in each simulation. We define the interaction matrix $W = \left\{w_{ij}\right\}_{i,j=1}^{n=3}$ as follows, to set the ecological niches of $n = 3$ different species (or organisms) as three stable fix points represented with the patterns $K \cdot (p_1^{k'}, p_2^{k'}, p_3^{k'})$, where $\left\{p_{i=1,2,3}^{k'=1}\right\} = (1, 0, 0)$, $\left\{p_{i=1,2,3}^{k'=2}\right\} = (0, 1, 0)$ and $\left\{p_{i=1,2,3}^{k'=3}\right\} = (0, 0, 1)$, based on the definition of the Hebbian learning rule in neural networks [12]:

$$w_{ij} = \frac{1}{3} \sum_{k'=1}^{3} \left(2p_i^{k'} - 1\right)\left(2p_j^{k'} - 1\right). \tag{26}$$

Note that (26) only expresses competitive relationships among $x_i(t)$, because $w_{ij} < 0$ if $i \neq j$. The phase diagrams with the analysis of periodicity, stability and converging niches of the dynamics are shown in Fig. 2, with varying ranges of the refractoriness α and h_r.

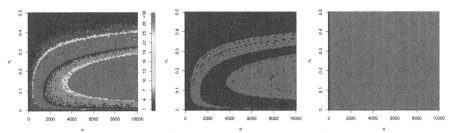

Fig. 2. Periodicity (**Left**), stability (**Middle**) and converging niche patterns (**Right**) of CEN. Refractoriness parameter ranges $h_r = [0, 0.5]$, $\alpha = [0, 10000]$ were used for the simulations, without external inputs *i.e.*, $E_j = 0$. After cutting $t = 10000$ initial steps, the dynamics of additional $t = 1000$ steps were classified with the colors representing periodicity (**Left**, according to the color bar); positive and negative maximum Lyapunov exponents with red and blue, respectively (**Middle**, according to the calculation method in [12]); and the mean value patterns of $x_i(t)$ (**Right**) that showed the dominance of $x_1(t)$ with blue (the mean values of $x_1(t) \geq K/2$, $x_2(t)$ and $x_3(t) < K/2$) and the inferior and competitive growth patterns with red (the mean values of $x_1(t)$, $x_2(t)$ *and* $x_3(t) < K/2$).

Based on the analysis in Fig. 2, it is possible to classify most of the simulated dynamics of CEN into four Areas on the $h_r - \alpha$ plane:

Area 1. Monoculture dominant condition, where a single crop $x_1(t)$ continuously and stably grows more than the others: Periodicity $= 1$; maximum Lyapunov exponents < 0; mean $x_1(t)$ is dominant ($\geq K/2$) over $x_2(t)$ and $x_3(t)(< K/2)$.
Area 2. Monoculture in competition, where a single crop $x_1(t)$ continuously and stably grows but at an inferior level and in strong competition with the other species: Periodicity $= 1$; maximum Lyapunov exponents < 0; mean $x_1(t)$, $x_2(t)$ and $x_3(t)$ remain inferior to $K/2$.

Area 3. Rotational succession, where multiple species form stable limit cycles of varying periods: Periodicity > 1; maximum Lyapunov exponents < 0; mean $x_1(t)$, $x_2(t)$ and $x_3(t)$ remain inferior to $K/2$.

Area 4. Chaotic itinerancy, where multiple species follow unstable chaotic trajectories among different niche patterns: Periodicity > 1000; maximum Lyapunov exponents > 0; mean $x_1(t)$, $x_2(t)$ and $x_3(t)$ remain inferior to $K/2$.

For simplicity, we considered $x_1(t)$ as the growth of the target crop species, $x_2(t)$ and $x_3(t)$ as the competing crop and/or weed species. The dominance of the target crop in Area 1 and the inferior growth in the other Areas qualitatively reflect the magnitude relationship of single-crop productivity between physiological and ecological optima [10]. The complex behaviors of Areas 3 & 4 may correspond to the diversity of vegetation succession important in agroecology, which can be leveraged with human operations for the augmentation of biodiversity and ecosystem functions [19]. Typical dynamics of the four Areas are simulated in Fig. 3.

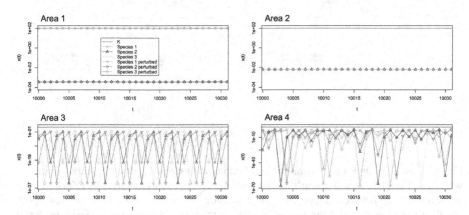

Fig. 3. Typical dynamics of Areas 1–4. Simulated parameters (h_r, α) are: $(0.1, 0)$ for Area 1, $(0.48, 300)$ for Area 2, $(0.155, 3400)$ for Area 3, and $(0.15, 7000)$ for Area 4. The "perturbed" species take the initial values $(K, 0, -K) + 1$ that are slightly different $(+1)$ from the other species. The example of Area 1 represents the successful dominance of a single crop, while that of 2 corresponds to the inferior growth of multiple species under strong competition. The example of Area 3 shows high periodicity (more than 1000) but stability against the perturbation, while that of 4 follows chaotic dynamics where initial perturbations are amplified to the system level.

Although the interaction matrix W is set to be only competitive in (26), the model can still introduce the effect of symbiosis with the use of (20). We can also incorporate symbiotic relationships by modifying the W itself, such as by defining a new interaction matrix $W' = \left\{ w'_{ij} \right\}_{i,j=1}^{n=3}$:

$$w'_{ij} = \frac{1}{2} \sum_{k'=1}^{2} \left(2p'^{k'}_i - 1 \right) \left(2p'^{k'}_j - 1 \right), \qquad (27)$$

where $\left\{p'^{k'=1}_{i=1,2,3}\right\} = (1, 1, 0)$ and $\left\{p'^{k'=2}_{i=1,2,3}\right\} = (0, 0, 1)$, which expresses the symbiosis between species 1 and 2, while species 3 remains competitive.

Furthermore, in analogy to the external inputs that could stabilize chaotic neural networks (*e.g.*, [20, 21]), the effects of external inputs $\{E_j\}$ with agroecological contexts such as harvesting and application of agrochemicals, as well as the time-delayed feedback effects of these interventions, can be investigated.

Examples of these extended features of community structure and responses to feedback inputs are simulated in Fig. 4. The overall results imply the utility of symbiotic interactions and context-dependent negative feedbacks for the amelioration of productivity and stabilization of periodicity in agroecological contexts.

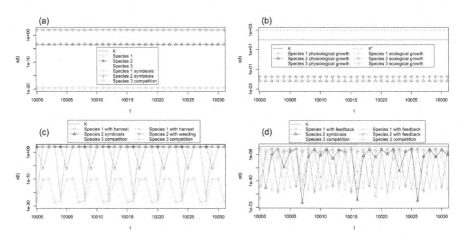

Fig. 4. Typical dynamics with symbiotic interactions and external inputs. (a): Area 1 dynamics with $(h_r, \alpha) = (0.1, 0)$, with competitive interactions W (26) and its modified W' (27) with symbiotic interactions between the species 1 and 2. (b): Area 2 dynamics with $(h_r, \alpha) = (0.48, 300)$ and W, using $K_i = K = 100$ and $K_i = K' = 10K$ for the representation of maximum growth rate of species with physiological and ecological optima, respectively, under a marginal environment in (20). (c): Area 1 dynamics with $(h_r, \alpha) = (0.1, 0)$ and W', with the negative external inputs that represent the thinning harvest of the crop species 1: if $x_1(t) = K$ then $E_1(t + 1) = -4x_1(t)$; and suppression of the weed species 2: if $x_2(t) \geq K/100$ then $E_2(t + 1) = -1.75x_2(t)$; which produce periodic dynamics close to actual harvesting and weeding cycles. (d): Area 4 dynamics with $(h_r, \alpha) = (0.15, 7000)$ with W', with time-delayed negative external inputs to the species 1&2: $E_i(t + 1) = -500(x_i(t) - x_i(t - 1))$, $i = 1, 2$, which increases the stability of the chaotic orbits. The feedback parameters were chosen for the visibility of plots.

3   Elementary Ultra-discrete Automaton

Although it is technically difficult to ultra-discretize CEN (25), the complexity of CEN can be essentially reduced to the dynamics of the single chaotic neuron model [9], which may be possible to further explore essential underlying structure using the ultra-discretized sigmoidal map (17). Here we consider the following ultra-discrete automaton that further incorporates self-recurrent refractoriness in $S'(X(t))$:

Ultra-discretized sigmoidal map with refractoriness $S''(X(t))$:

$$X(t+1) = \mu\Big(X(t) + A - max\big[0, X(t) - B + max[0, X(t) - C]\big]\Big), \quad (28)$$

where $0 < A, B < K, A + B = K, C \geq (\mu - 1)K$. The natural number parameter μ is inspired by the classical tent map that exhibits a fully developed chaotic regime in $\mu = 2$, and we later show that (28) produces orbital instability when $\mu \geq 2$. At the limit of $A \to 0$ with the parameter range $0 < \mu \leq 2$, (28) converges to the tent map on the interval $[0, B + C]$ if $B \geq C$. In the case of $B < C$, a plateau $X(t+1) = \mu K$ exists in the return map (e.g., Fig. 5 (b)), which converges plural orbits of $X(t)$ into a single value μK.

The incorporation of refractoriness in (28) is similar to the nested $max()$ operations proposed in the ultra-discretized model of cryptic oscillations in Lotka-Volterra equations with additional negative feedbacks using Holling's disc equation [22]. Indeed, the type III disc equation is qualitatively similar to the sigmoid function, and the type I disc equation exactly matches the ultra-discretized sigmoidal map (20) (see Fig. 6 Top).

The dynamics of (28) are analyzed in Fig. 5. Typical cases that exhibit unstable limit cycles were simulated with $\mu = 1$ in (a) and $\mu = 2$ in (b), with the periodicity analysis of $\mu = 2$ in (c) and actual dynamics in (d). Since deterministic chaos on the set of real values is known to contain infinite numbers of unstable limit cycles, $i.e.$, the skeleton of chaos [23], the unstable limit cycles that remain in the ultra-discretized models could be considered as the essential mathematical structure of chaos that is preserved in the ultra-discretized limit. In (e), the local temporal stability of a trajectory was judged with an ultra-discrete version of the Lyapunov exponent, namely the one-sided local Lyapunov exponent (LE) defined as follows:

$$LE(X(t)) := \log(|S''(X(t)) - S''(X(t) + 1)|). \quad (29)$$

This means that the one-sided digital perturbation $(+1)$ to the variable $X(t)$ is amplified in $t + 1$ if $LE > 0$, diminished to zero if $LE = -\infty < 0$, and remains invariant if $LE = 0$. Note that $LE = 0$ if $\mu = 1$, and $LE \neq 0$ if $\mu \geq 2$ in (28). Therefore, $\mu \geq 2$ could be also considered as providing an ultra-discretized analog of the logistic map (2), since the smooth interpolation of (28) with a real-value resolution qualitatively converges the dynamics to that of (2). A multi-dimensional spectrum $LE_i(X(t))$ $(1, \ldots, i, \ldots, n)$ can be defined on the vector variable $X(t) = (X_1(t), \ldots, X_n(t))$ and its ultra-discrete map $X(t+1) = F(X(t))$ using the i-th row of the n-dimensional identity matrix I_i, such that

$$LE_i(X(t)) := \log(|F(X(t)) - F(X(t) + I_i)|). \quad (30)$$

Since ultra-discretized models are known to form a max-$plus$ algebra that can be qualitatively considered as the transformation of additions $(+)$ and multiplications $(\times)$ in the original model into the $max(\cdot)$ and $plus$ $(+)$ operations, respectively, the coupled version of (28) could be proposed as follows:

$$F\big(X(t), X^+(t), X^-(t)\big) = max\big[X(t) + A, X^+(t) + A^+\big]$$

$$-max\Big[0, max\big[X(t) - B, X^-(t) - B^-\big] + max[0, X(t) - C]\Big], \quad (31)$$

$$X(t+1) = \max\left[0, \mu F\left(X(t), X^+(t), X^-(t)\right)\right], \tag{32}$$

where $X^+(t)$ and $A^+ > 0$ represent a positively interacting term and $X^-(t)$ and $B^- > 0$ a negative one. An example of (32) producing intermittent dynamics between partially stable and unstable states is simulated in Fig. 6 Bottom, which is qualitatively similar to the chaotic itinerancy reported both in chaotic neural networks [9, 12] and GCML [2, 24], within the constraint of periodicity subject to the possible number of discrete values that $X(t)$ can take on the interval $[0, K + C]$.

The rationale behind the newly introduced models (28) and (32) can be found in relation to the expansion of Holling's disc equations. Through the inverse transformation of ultradiscretization, we can obtain the underlying discrete model of (32) as follows, with the parameters $a, a^+ > 0$ and $0 < b, b^-, c < 1$:

$$x(t+1) = 1 + \frac{a(x(t))^\mu + a^+\left(x^+(t)\right)^\mu}{1 + \left(b(x(t))^\mu + b^-\left(x^-(t)\right)^\mu\right)(1 + c(x(t))^\mu)}. \tag{33}$$

This model reduces to a single uncoupled element that corresponds to the inverse ultradiscretization of (28), such as

$$x(t+1) = \frac{a(x(t))^\mu}{1 + b(x(t))^\mu(1 + c(x(t))^\mu)}. \tag{34}$$

On the other hand, the three types of Holling's disc equations $\mathcal{H}'(\cdot)$ and $\mathcal{H}(\cdot)$ as a discrete-time system of the variable $y(t) \geq 0$ can be formulated as follows (e.g., [25]), using the parameters a, b and K:

$$\text{Type I}: y(t+1) = \mathcal{H}'(y(t)) := \min(K, ay(t)) \tag{35}$$

Type II and III:

$$y(t+1) = \mathcal{H}(y(t)) := \frac{a(y(t))^\mu}{1 + b(y(t))^\mu},$$

$$\text{where} \mu = 1(\text{type II}), \mu > 1(\text{Type III}). \tag{36}$$

The model (34) can therefore be interpreted as the expansion of types II and III incorporating refractoriness at the saturation stage of $y(t)$, which we call type II-R and III-R, respectively:

Type II-R and III-R:

$$y(t+1) = \mathcal{H}_R(y(t)) := \frac{a(y(t))^\mu}{1 + b(y(t))^\mu(1 + c(y(t))^\mu)},$$

$$\text{where} \mu = 1(\text{Type II} - \text{R}), \mu > 1(\text{Type III} - \text{R}). \tag{37}$$

Additionally, we extract a typical non-linear response of single chaotic neuron based on (24) as follows, using $y(t)$ as the internal state of sigmoidal output $x(t)$:

$$y(t+1) = \eta(t+1) + \zeta(t+1), \tag{38}$$

$$\eta(t+1) = h_f\,\eta(t) + wx(t) + w'x'(t),\qquad(39)$$

$$\zeta(t+1) = h_r\,\zeta(t) - \alpha x(t),\qquad(40)$$

$$x(t+1) = S(y(t+1); r, \theta, K),\qquad(41)$$

where w and w' are positive connection coefficients and $x'(t)$ is the output from another neuron.

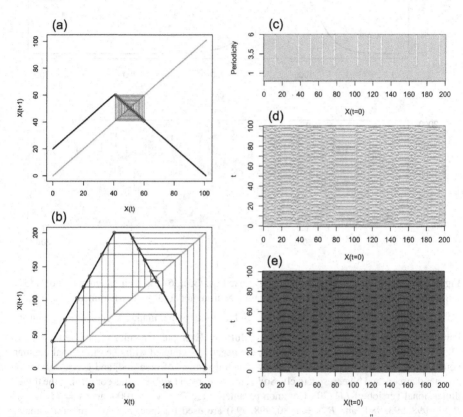

Fig. 5. Dynamics of the ultra-discretized sigmoidal map with refractoriness $S''(X(t))$ (28). Interval maps between $X(t)$ and $X(t+1)$ are depicted in (a): with parameters $(\mu, A, B, C, K) = (1, 20, 80, 0, 100)$ that can be considered as an ultra-discretized analog of the tent map, and (b): $(\mu, A, B, C, K) = (2, 20, 80, 100, 100)$ as that of the logistic map. In (a) and (b), the initial values were taken for all $X(t=0) = [0, 200]$, which converge to unstable limit cycles (red spiderweb plot) and partially stable limit cycles (blue) with respect to the stability $LE(X(t))$. (c): Periodicity of the model (b) with respect to the initial values $X(t=0) = [0, 200]$. (d): Temporal dynamics $X(t)$ of the model (b) from $t = 0$ to 100 and the initial values $X(t=0) = [0, 200]$, with a color gradient from cyan ($X(t) = 0$) to magenta ($X(t) = 200$). (e) The same dynamics as (d) with the color distinction between $LE(X(t)) > 0$ (red) and $LE(X(t)) < 0$ (blue). The blue regions in (e) correspond to the plateau $X(t+1) = \mu K = 200$ in (b), except the right endpoint that gives $LE(X(t)) = 100) > 0$. (Color figure online)

The relationships between type I, II, III, II-R, III-R and the chaotic neuron (38)–(41) are depicted in Fig. 6 Top, which shows qualitative correspondence between type III-R and the chaotic neuron.

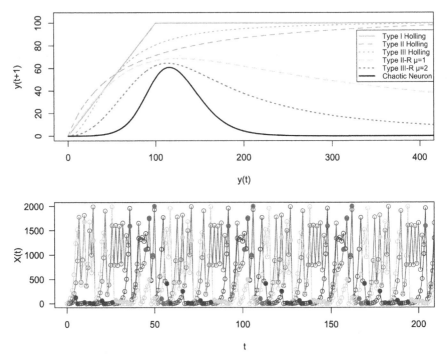

Fig. 6. Top: Relationship between Holling's disc Eqs. (35)(36) and their expanded models (37) (38) corresponding to $S''(X(t))$ (28), and chaotic neuron model (38)–(41). Parameters $h_f = h_r = 0, x'(t) = S\left(y'(t); r, \theta, K\right), y'(t) = r'y(t), r' > 1$ are used for the simulation of the chaotic neuron. Parameter values were chosen for visibility. **Bottom:** Example dynamics of coupled $S''(X(t))$ (32). Three automata (blue, red, and green) are negatively coupled with one-directional circular connections, *i.e.* $A^+ = 0$ and $B^- > 0$, by which dynamics of blue, red, and green negatively affect red, green, and blue, respectively. Solid circles represent stable points concerning the three-dimensional version of *LE* (30). Common parameters are $K = C = 1000$, and $A = (2, 7, 20)$, $B = (998, 993, 980)$ and $B^- = (980, 998, 993)$ are used for blue, red, and green automata, respectively. (Color figure online)

4   Discussion

CEN (25) is presented as the reinterpretation of chaotic neural networks from agroecological perspectives, which essentially employs the same model for different phenomenological classifications of the dynamics such as Area 1–4 in Fig. 2. Only simple linearized interactions were simulated in this article, and it can incorporate other nonlinearity specific to ecosystems using the general form of interactions (18) and (21), such that

$$x_i(t+1) = S\left(\sum_{j=1}^{n} v_{ij}\left(H\left(\{x_i(t-d)\}_{d=0}^{t}\right); H\left(\{x_j(t-d)\}_{d=0}^{t}\right)\right); r_i, \theta_i, K_i\right). \quad (42)$$

In contrast to the differential equation models, the merit of using discrete and ultra-discrete models is the facility of calculation and practicality of incorporation of many realistic processes and interactions, such as the reproduction of individual organisms and the occurrence of human interventions, which are essentially discrete phenomena. Instead of modeling every detail with a real-value resolution, discrete models can reduce non-essential features for the effective abstraction with an appropriate resolution.

On the other hand, proper discretization of a continuous model cannot be *a priori* defined with a fixed formula and requires thorough mathematical comparison. For example, consider a typical Lotka-Volterra equation with a conserved quantity $Q_C :=$ $cx + by - d \log x - a \log y$ as follows:

$$\frac{dx}{dt} = ax - bxy, \frac{dy}{dt} = cxy - dy. \quad (43)$$

Then the following coupled discrete-time maps could be derived using a variant of (4):

$$x(t+1) = \frac{(1 + \Delta ta)x(t)}{1 + \Delta tby(t)}, y(t+1) = \frac{(1 + \Delta tcx(t))y(t)}{1 + \Delta td}. \quad (44)$$

Through the appropriate parameters transformation and the limit operation analogous to (5)–(9), it is possible to derive the following ultra-discretized form:

$$X(t+1) = X(t) + A - \max[0, Y(t) - B],$$

$$Y(t+1) = \max[0, X(t) + C] + Y(t) - D. \quad (45)$$

However, the models (44) and (45) do not reproduce the closed limit cycle of the original differential Eqs. (43), but rather express divergent oscillation (*i.e.*, expanding spirals on x-y and X-Y planes, results not shown) as the discretization time step Δt increases. It is therefore necessary to consider other forms of discretization to examine the property of the integrable system (43) based on the conserved quantity [26].

The difficulty of interpreting discrete models also exists in quantitative analysis, both in temporal scales and variable values. Parameter fitting and its optimization methods need to be explored according to the focus of the research. On the other hand, robust system-level features such as the typology of ecological regime shifts and scale-free phenomena (*e.g.*, [19, 27]) could be more accessible with qualitative analysis, which may further contribute to the management model of essential ecosystem services and hierarchical modeling of the comprehensive biosphere.

The ultra-discrete automaton (32) was actually inspired by unsuccessful attempts to directly ultra-discretize CEN (25). It is proposed as a synthetic model to serve as a stepstone for further investigation, in the same line with the arbitrary modification of dLV to derive a simple ultra-discrete automaton with intermittent dynamics such as in [22]. Nevertheless, the proposed model captures essential characteristics of coupled chaotic systems concerning the intermittent fluctuation of orbital stability commonly reported in coupled logistic maps and chaotic neural networks. It should be noted that the original chaotic neuron model was not based on the rigorous discretization of differential equation neuron model (such as Hodgkin-Huxley and FitzHugh-Nagumo models) either, but rather based on a qualitative observation using *a priori* defined discrete-time formal neuron model [9]. Since the proposed ultra-discrete model (32) conserves essential characteristics of chaos that are generally not integrable, further analysis needs to extend the methodology beyond the conventional framework restricted to the conserved quantity of integrable non-linear systems.

The commonality of dynamics analyzed between neural networks and ecological models could potentially provide a starting point for the integration of knowledge between the vast non-linear classification capacity of deep learning (*e.g.*, [28]) and the complexity of ecosystem dynamics that could provide access to untapped utilities in agroecology.

5 Conclusion

We investigated the relationship between the logistic equation and the sigmoidal map with the light of ultradiscretization that conserves the essential dynamics including chaos. The results suggest that the conventional logistic map (2) may not be appropriate to interpret as a simple discretized form of the logistic Eq. (1), but rather as the one that belongs to a class of model which can be better presented with a self-recurrent sigmoidal function incorporating refractoriness. This insight will further bring clarification in ecological and complex systems modeling on the distinction between technical by-products and computational rationales for mathematically sound simulations. An ultra-discrete model based on the expansion of Holling's disc equations was proposed (32), which qualitatively captured the characteristics of intermittent dynamics known as chaotic itinerancy commonly reported in chaotic neural networks and GCML.

Acknowledgements. Yohei Tutiya, Godai Suzuki and Tatsuya Kawaoka contributed to ameliorating the manuscript.

Scientific Validation
This paper has benefited from the remarks of the following reviewers:
- Tatsuya Kawaoka, Synecoculture Association, Japan
- Godai Suzuki, Synecoculture Association, Japan
- Yohei Tutiya, Kanagawa Institute of Technology, Japan

The conference organisers wish to thank them for their highly appreciated effort and contribution.

References

1. Hugo, F.: From growth equations for a single species to Lotka-Volterra equations for two interacting species. In: Ecological Modelling and Ecophysics, pp. 1–41. IOP Publishing (2020)

2. Kaneko, K.: Overview of coupled map lattices. Chaos **2**, 279 (1992)
3. Hirota, R., Tsujimoto, S., Imai, T.: Difference Scheme of Soliton Equations. In: Christiansen, P.L., Eilbeck, J.C., Parmentier, R.D. (eds.) Future Directions of Nonlinear Dynamics in Physical and Biological Systems. NATO ASI Series, vol. 312. Springer, Boston (1993). https://doi.org/10.1007/978-1-4899-1609-9_2
4. May, R.M.: Simple mathematical models with very complicated dynamics. Nature **261**, 459–467 (1976)
5. Morishita, M.: The fitting of the logistic equation to the rate of increase of population density. Res. Popul. Ecol. **52** (1965)
6. Tokihiro, T.: Ultradiscrete Systems (Cellular Automata). In: Grammaticos, B., Tamizhmani, T., Kosmann-Schwarzbach, Y. (eds.) Discrete Integrable Systems. Lecture Notes in Physics, vol. 644, pp. 383–424. Springer, Heidelberg (2004). https://doi.org/10.1007/978-3-540-403 57-9_9
7. Tokihiro, T., Takahashi, D., Matsukidaira, J., Satsuma, J.: Phys. Rev. Lett. **76**, 3247 (1996)
8. Takahashi, D.: Continuous, discrete, ultradiscrete waves. RIMS Kôkyûroku **1191**, 104–111 (2001)
9. Aihara, K., Takabe, T., Toyoda, M.: Chaotic neural networks. Phys. Lett. A **144**(6–7), 333–340 (1990)
10. Funabashi, M.: Synecological farming: theoretical foundation on biodiversity responses of plant communities. Plant Biotechnol. **33**(4), 213–234 (2016)
11. Belz, R.G.: Allelopathy in crop/weed interactions-an update. Pest Manag. Sci.Manag. Sci. **63**(4), 308–326 (2007)
12. Funabashi, M.: Synthetic modeling of autonomous learning with a chaotic neural network. Int. J. Bifurcation Chaos **25**(04), 1550054 (2015)
13. Putman, R.J., Wratter, S.D.: Principle of Ecology. University of California Press, USA (1984)
14. Beisner, B., Haydon, D., Cuddington, K.: Alternative stable states in ecology. Front. Ecol. Environ. **1**(7), 376–382 (2003)
15. Xuan, T.D., Tawata, S., Khanh, T.D., Chung, I.M.: Decomposition of allelopathic plants in soil. J. Agron. Crop Sci.Agron. Crop Sci. **191**, 162–171 (2005)
16. Lü, L.H., Srivastava, A.K., Shen, Y.L., Wu, Q.S.: A Negative feedback regulation of replanted soil microorganisms on plant growth and soil properties of peach. Not Bot Horti Agrobo **47**(1), 255–261 (2019)
17. Tang, B., et al.: Crop rotation alleviates replant failure in Panax notoginseng (Burkill) F.H. Chen by changing the composition but not the structure of the microbial community. Plant Soil Environ. **66**, 493–9 (2020)
18. Shyu, E., Pardini, E.A., Knight, T.M., Caswell, H.: A seasonal, density-dependent model for the management of an invasive weed. Ecol. Appl. **23**, 1893–1905 (2013)
19. Funabashi, M.: Augmentation of plant genetic diversity in synecoculture: theory and practice in temperate and tropical zones. In: Nandwani, D. (ed.) Genetic Diversity in Horticultural Plants. SDB, vol. 22, pp. 3–46. Springer, Cham (2019). https://doi.org/10.1007/978-3-319-96454-6_1
20. Shibasaki, M., Adachi, M.: Response to external input of chaotic neural networks based on Newman-Watts model. In: The 2012 International Joint Conference on Neural Networks (IJCNN), Brisbane, QLD, Australia, pp. 1–7 (2012)
21. Yamamoto, S., Ushio, T.: Robust stabilization of chaos via delayed feedback control. In: Hashimoto, K., Oishi, Y., Yamamoto, Y. (eds) Control and Modeling of Complex Systems. Trends in Mathematics. Birkhäuser, Boston (2003)
22. Willox, R., Ramani, A., Grammaticos, B.: A discrete-time model for cryptic oscillations in predator-prey systems. Physica D D **238**(22), 2238–2245 (2009)
23. Cvitanović, P.: Periodic orbits as the skeleton of classical and quantum chaos. Physica D D **51**(1–3), 138–151 (1991)

24. Balmforth, N.J., Jacobson, A., Provenzale, A.: Synchronized family dynamics in globally coupled maps. Chaos **9**, 738 (1999)
25. Dawes, J.H.P., Souza, M.O.: A derivation of Holling's type I, II and III functional responses in predator–prey systems. J. Theor. Biol.Theor. Biol. **327**, 11–22 (2013)
26. Hirota, R., Iwao, M., Ramani, A., Takahashi, D., Grammaticos, B., Ohta, Y.: From integrability to chaos in a Lotka-Volterra cellular automaton. Phys. Lett. A **236**(1–2), 39–44 (1997)
27. Funabashi, M.: Human augmentation of ecosystems: objectives for food production and science by 2045. NPJ Sci. Food **2**, 16 (2018)
28. Amari, S.: Any target function exists in a neighborhood of any sufficiently wide random network: a geometrical perspective. Neural Comput.Comput. **32**(8), 1431–1447 (2020)

Modeling Ecosystem Management Based on the Integration of Image Analysis and Human Subjective Evaluation - Case Studies with Synecological Farming

Shuntaro Aotake[1,2](✉) [iD], Atsuo Takanishi[3] [iD], and Masatoshi Funabashi[1,4](✉) [iD]

[1] Sony Computer Science Laboratories, Inc., Tokyo, Japan
{aotake,masa_funabashi}@csl.sony.co.jp
[2] Department of Advanced Science and Engineering, Waseda University, Tokyo, Japan
[3] Waseda Research Institute for Science and Engineering, Waseda University, Tokyo, Japan
[4] Research Division on Social Common Capital and the Future, Kyoto University Institute for the Future of Human Society, Kyoto, Japan

Abstract. The challenge for biodiversity restoration and augmentation is to find effective indicators for ecosystem management without discarding too much of the complexity that contributes to functionality. Many technical challenges lie ahead in setting up information measures to manage dynamically changing ecosystems in the real world. It is expected that image analysis features such as edge, texture, color distribution, etc. will provide clues, but methods to evaluate their effectiveness in the context of integrated management have not been sufficiently studied. Taking synecological farming (Synecoculture™) as a typical example of complex ecosystem management, we investigate the initial steps toward the construction of an evaluation model by incorporating image analysis and empirical knowledge acquired by human managers. As a result, we showed that it is possible to construct a model that connects the features of image analysis and human subjective evaluation with consistency according to the level of the evaluators and proposed a cycle that would refine both the evaluation model and associated human capacity. We also presented an interface for utilizing collective knowledge in ecosystem management using the proposed model and the prospect of scaling up in conjunction with robotics.

Keywords: Open complex systems · Augmented ecosystems · Inter-subjective objectivity · Image analysis · Interactive machine learning

1 Introduction

Agroecology is concerned with the management of trade-offs between environmental impacts and economic benefits in agricultural production. One of the challenges for biodiversity restoration and augmentation is to find effective indicators for the management of complex ecosystems. However, real-world ecosystems are characterized as

P. Collet et al. (Eds.): CCE 2023, LNCS 13927, pp. 151–164, 2023.
https://doi.org/10.1007/978-3-031-44355-8_11

open complex systems that are difficult to manage effectively with a few limited indicators because the diversity of elements and complexity of interactions play important functional roles [1]. Diverse ecosystem functions are supported by biodiversity, which consists of at least three levels: genes, species, and ecosystem diversity. It is difficult to measure all those interactions and to set unitary criteria of information to manage the system in the presence of environmental variability [3,4,5].

Image analysis such as remote sensing and in-field picture recording such as citizen science has the potential to capture diverse aspects of ecosystems at a relatively low cost, but their effectiveness depends on the method of measurement, evaluation and the database used. For example, the mainstream method for documenting species diversity is species identification based on subjective human evaluation of photographs of species [6]. In addition, research aimed at ecosystem assessment have attempted to combine remote sensing with multiple data on biodiversity and functionality through machine learning to calculate an integrated index of complexity (e.g., [7]). These are gaining credibility as a source of scientific information for conservation purposes, such as restoring natural ecosystems or assessing the impact of conventional agricultural practices. However, as in situations typical of agroecology, they are still insufficient for forecasting and managing small-scale ecosystems where humans frequently intervene with diverse objectives, and where dynamic variability and local specificity are high [3].

Synecological farming is one such example and it is an extreme form of agroecology that constructs and utilizes a high degree of biodiversity. In this method, more than 200 species of useful plants are mixed and densely grown in a small area of about 1,000 sq.m. to create a highly diverse ecosystem. This farming method is defined as an application of complex systems science to agroecology [8]. It can be interpreted as the augmentation of ecosystems by humans and has been shown to be effective in restoring and building useful and functional ecosystems beyond the natural background state, especially in the semi-arid tropics [2]. On the other hand, much of the practice is based on empirical knowledge from a farming manual [9] and direct communication.

To develop synecological farming based on scientific collective knowledge as well as human empirical knowledge, several studies have been conducted to integrate human subjective evaluation and objectively measurable indicators: A study in an urban area has successfully extracted indicators that could be significantly used to promote biodiversity, based on human assessments of biodiversity and sensor measurements of soil composition that do not depend on human evaluation [3]. At a more rudimentary level, in conjunction with image analysis, there are examples of the detection of dominant plants that hinder the growth of useful plants and reduce their diversity in a field [10], as well as the detection of vegetation cover and exposed topsoil [11]. These are only results obtained under limited conditions with a considerable narrowing of the target to be recognized and are insufficient as effective indicators for the comprehensive management of ecosystems.

Other research is underway in robotics to assist management in synecological farming [12]. The implementation of tasks such as driving, seed planting, weed pruning, and harvesting was accomplished by a mobile robotic arm. In addition, a maneuvering system is developed to minimize plant damage due to contact with the robot on the dense vegetation of a variety of plants on a synecological farm. Despite the recent innovation of automation in conventional agriculture, it is technically challenging to fully automate the system to recognize and evaluate the condition of the field with high biodiversity. The open-field management of complex vegetation with the mixture of a large number of crops and naturally occurring plants still requires the robot to be operated remotely by a human operator.

Further advancing these research streams, the promotion of human ingenuity towards the integration of highly internalized empirical knowledge with scientific objectivity will lead to the development of methodologies that provide an effective foundation for managing open complex systems [13]. In this paper, we take synecological farming as an example of complex systems management in agroecology and propose a method to build an effective and reproducible management model to achieve augmentation of ecosystems by integrating subjective assessment and objective indicators based on image analysis. Since ecological situations dynamically evolve in synecological farming along with the refinement of management knowledge, it is necessary to employ an interactive framework in that human evaluation and image analysis mutually improve each other, which requires the dynamical reconfiguration of the model [14]. This article consists of an initial phase of such a workflow towards the stepwise construction of an effective management model on the basis of open systems science [1]. The inputs, outputs and function of the models developed in Sects. 2–5 are summarized in the supplementary material [16]. The databases are limited to case studies on a trial basis and are subject to future expansion.

2 Subjective and Inter-Subjective Human Evaluation of a Synecological Farm

A 4-sq.m. vegetable garden in Machida, Tokyo, Japan, was operated according to the Synecoculture™ manual [9] and 26 photographs were taken from 4 m above during the period from May 2019 to January 2021 (Fig. 1, hereafter the farm M). A subjective evaluation was conducted by 8 experienced persons with different periods of practice of synecological farming, referring only to these photos. The evaluators were divided into four levels based on the number of years they had been engaged in synecological farming and their experience: expert (1 person), advanced (1 person), intermediate (3 people, including one person who played a part in the management of farm M), and beginner (3 people, including one person with no experience at all). "Expert" was a person who had been engaged in the farming for more than 13 years and had trained and produced many practitioners of synecological farming; "advanced" was a person who had been engaged in the farming for more than 8 years; "intermediates" for 3 to 10 years; and "beginners" for less than 3 years.

The indicators of subjective evaluation were defined using the Visual Analog Scale (VAS) scores, which were defined on a scale from 1 to 10 and used to assess human subjective measures with an interval scale such as in web surveys [15]. The three evaluation indicators were defined as follows:

1. **Appraisal Score (AS):** subjective evaluation of how good the field is in terms of synecological farming. As a criterion, 1 refers to the condition of the field that he/she

thinks is not at all suitable for synecological farming, and 10 refers to the condition that has achieved the highest degree of synecological farming imaginable.

2. **Harvest Prediction (HP):** subjective assessment of how much yield, including future potential, could be expected from the plots in that image. The criterion was defined as 1 being a field that was unlikely to yield any useful plants, and 10 being the highest yielding field condition imaginable.

3. **Management Grade (MG):** subjective estimation of the degree to which managers of the field in the image were proficient in synecological farming. The evaluators were asked to respond by referring to the shape of the ridges, the arrangement of plants, and whether appropriate management such as thinning and harvesting had been done, as well as changes over time. The criteria were: 1 to 2.5 is beginner, 2.5 to 5 is intermediate, 5 to 7.5 is advanced, and 7.5 to 10 is expert.

All evaluators self-evaluated their levels, and only one of them was concerned with the management of farm M. By examining the correlations between these indicators, it is possible to determine the degree to which intersubjective reproducibility is ensured between the ratings of each level. The results of the correlation analysis between the evaluation of one expert and the indicators averaged for each level from beginner to advanced are shown in Table 1.

The average of three indicators (AS, HP, and MG) showed significant correlations with an expert in the order of advanced, intermediate, and beginner averages. MG alone showed the same tendency of correlations but not in AS and HP. In addition, correlation values using the averages of the three indicators for the seven non-experts showed the highest correlations for almost all indicators, suggesting the validity of group knowledge rather than individual years of experience.

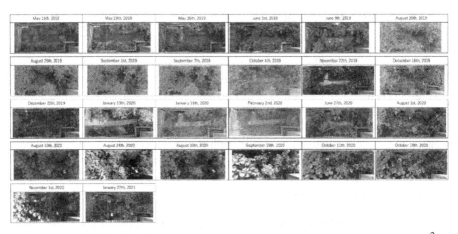

Fig. 1. Date and the top view images of a synecological farm in Machida (farm M), 4 m^2.

As shown in the results of Table 1, the analysis of subjective indicators can be used to estimate competence compared to expert, while the internal model of the evaluator, backed by knowledge and experience, remains a black box. Since subjective indicators

Table 1. Correlation coefficients of VAS ratings (AS, HP, MG) between an expert vs. the average at each level of practitioners in synecological farming. The p-values of all Pearson Product-Moment Correlation Coefficients of AS, HP, and MG were less than 0.01 with the test of no correlation.

	vs. Advanced(n=1)(A)	vs. Intermediates(n=3) (I)	vs. Beginners (n=3)(B)	vs. I&B(n=6)	vs. A&I&B(n=7)
Appraisal Score (AS)	0.74	0.86	0.89	0.90	0.90
Harvest Prediction (HP)	0.90	0.93	0.91	0.95	0.95
Management Grade (MG)	0.90	0.71	0.52	0.74	0.74
3 Indicator Average	0.85	0.83	0.77	0.87	0.86

alone do not include objective criteria, it is impossible to determine quantitatively any mistakes or biases that may have occurred. In fact, the model uses one expert as the highest criterion for subjective evaluation and does not evaluate whether the collective knowledge of the other seven could achieve more effective management. This has been pointed out as a drift of intersubjectivity in subjective evaluation and tying it to objective indicators is essential to remove the bias prevalent in collective knowledge [13].

3   Objective Classification of Conventional and Synecological Farms Based on Image Analyses

In the management of synecological farming, the degree of established biodiversity is an important indicator [5, 9]. On the other hand, in conventional farming methods that are typically monoculture, the level of biodiversity in the field remains low and there is dominant homogeneity in their landscapes [8]. Through image analysis of these external differences, we attempted to extract features that estimate the degree of achievement of synecological farming.

A total of 280 sq.m. of farmland in Oiso Town, Kanagawa Prefecture, Japan, was operated according to the Synecoculture™ manual, along with a total of 235 sq.m. of conventional farmland on the side. A total of 16 photographs was taken from directly above with a drone over a five-month period from May to September 2021 (Fig. Oiso, hereafter the farms O and C). The distance between farms O, C and M is about 26 km and belongs to the same temperate agroclimatic zone. Farm O is further divided into two parts: O1, 180 sq.m. managed with a diversity and quantity of seed that meets the standards of the Synecoculture™ manual; and O2, 100 sq.m. with a seed quantity of 48.5% of the standard per unit area. The adjacent conventional farm C was divided into two rectangular plots C1 (85 sq.m.) and C2 (150 sq.m.), which were photographed and analyzed in the same way. The reason for splitting C into C1 and C2 is to capture only the productive surface in a rectangle, with as little extraneous material as possible in the image. Therefore, a qualitative relationship of C1, C2 < O2 < O1 was established empirically as the degree of achievement of synecological farming.

Using the programming language Python version 3.9.15, 241-dimensional image features were designed from a set of basic libraries related to image analysis. The library used and the variables set are listed in the supplementary material [16], which mainly focused on the edge, texture, and color distribution of the images. The 16 photos in Fig. 2 were each divided into 100 parts, by dividing the image into 10 vertical and 10 horizontal segments, creating a total of 1600 test data. Note that there is no overlap between divided images. From this dataset, 80% of the divided images were randomly selected to train Random Forest learning methods, and the percentage of correct responses to the remaining 20% was examined using the Random Forest classifier with RandomForest-Classifier() function in the "sklearn" library "ensemble" class. We obtained a 91.2% overall accuracy as the output of the "accuracy_score" function in the "sklearn" library "metrics" class for distinguishing C1, C2 from O1, O2. Using the RandomForestRegressor() in the "sklearn" library "ensemble" class, the coefficient of determination was 0.781. The target variable is given as 0: for conventional and 1: for synecological farming plots. Hyperparameters of RandomForestClassifier() and RandomForestRegressor() are specified in the online supplementary material [16].

Next, we examined what features have gained importance with the initial learning step to assess the ecological plausibility. The five most important features with respect to the output "feature_importances_[]" of RandomForestRegressor() are listed as follows:

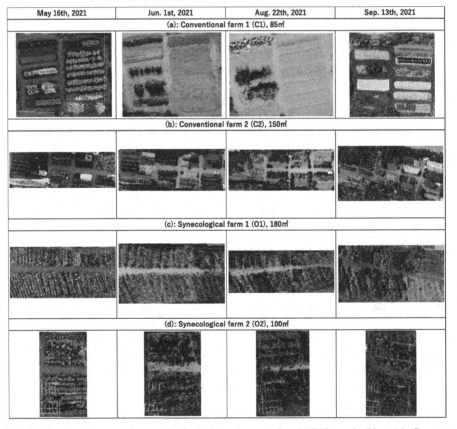

Fig. 2. Top view images of synecological (O) and conventional (C) farms in Oiso. (a): Conventional farm 1 (C1), 85 m². (b): Conventional farm 2 (C2), 150 m². (c): Synecological farm 1 (O1), 180 m². (d): Synecological farm 2 (O2), 100 m².

1. "GLCM1_0 homogeneity," which represents the homogeneity of neighboring pixels
2. "plt_seg_area bmean - rmean," which represents the difference between the mean values of red and blue components of the vegetation area
3. "edge fractal," which represents the fractal dimension of the detected boundaries of the whole image
4. "plt_seg_area hmode - smode," which represents the difference between the mode hue and mode saturation of the vegetation area
5. "plt_seg_area hue median," which represents the median value of the hue of the vegetation area

These indices are related to the complexity of the vegetation shape and the diversity of colors and can be considered as important characteristics to discriminate between conventional and synecological farming, since they may reflect differences in the level of biodiversity.

As a result, if the task is to discriminate between conventional farming and synecological farming as is the case with the certification of the farming method, the classification model is successfully trained with the small data, and the basis of discrimination can be clearly and easily shown as features in image analysis. On the other hand, the generalization capacity and tuning need to be explored to examine the performance of the model in wider and more ambiguous situations. Actually, it is more difficult to find differences that are important for actual human management of synecological farming, such as the difference between O1 and O2, from image analysis alone. It is necessary to search for features that increase the resolution of the model and to provide more teacher data.

4   Integrated Modeling of Ecosystem Management Based on Inter-Subjective Objectivity

To construct a model that complements the features of image analysis and the subjective measures of human VAS scores (AS, HP, MG) in a consistent manner, we propose the "Integrated Inter-Subjective Objective Model (ISOM)" (Fig. 3). In this model, even if there is bias or error in a person's subjective evaluation, the image features serve as an objective anchor and can be corrected quantitatively. Furthermore, it is possible to construct an improvement process that cycles between subjective and objective to weight the effectiveness of objective indicators according to a skilled person's subjectivity and to judge the overall effectiveness of the model.

ISOM first takes the feature values obtained from vegetation images of the field and additional information such as weather as objective data, and the human VAS scores (AS, HP, MG) as subjective data, and trains a Random Forest regression model between the two, as schematized in Fig. 3 (a). By looking at the feature importance of the trained model, we can estimate what features the evaluator is potentially utilizing, but we cannot guarantee how reliable this is. Therefore, we use the evaluator's level information (beginner, intermediate, advanced, expert) and weight the reliability with such empirical knowledge by examining the correlation between the level information and feature importance (b). Note that the results can also be interpreted by the nature of the data features to see if empirical knowledge is consistently developed. The trained model can then estimate VAS scores (AS, HP, MG) from those features alone for new field images (and associated weather information) in a way that reflects the evaluator's level (c). The validity of the estimated results is interpreted considering the actual field operation history (d). The findings will suggest the characteristics of the database that should be expanded and new features that should be analyzed (e). It is also expected that human empirical knowledge can be improved by referring to objective indicators, leading to the refinement of the subjective indicators of the VAS method (f). Such an interactive framework between human and image analysis follows the methodology of open systems science [1] and is an attempt to encapsulate the ever-changing complexity inherent in ecosystem management, which cannot be simply addressed with a fixed set of features and/or without the distinction of human competence. At the same time, a practical application such as the certification of the farming method is supposed to assess the field starting from small initial datasets, in many cases without prior knowledge on other practices, which fits the scope of the initial cycle of ISOM. As ISOM develops through the repetition of feedback cycles (a)–(f), the model is expected to acquire more generalization capacity to novel situations.

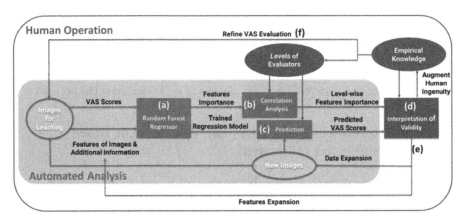

Fig. 3. Integrated Inter-Subjective Objective Model (ISOM). (a, b, c): Learning of and prediction from ISOM. (d, f): Updates of subjective empirical knowledge and VAS methods. (e): Expansion of objective measurement and analytical framework.

Examples of actual analyses for farms M and O (defined in Sects. 2 and 3, respectively) are shown in Fig. 4 and 5, respectively. First, we trained ISOM using 8 people's subjective evaluation of farm M (Table 1) and 26 images (Fig. 1). The same 241-dimensional image features were used as in Sect. 3, which corresponds to the process of Fig. 3 (a). From the trained ISOM, we obtained an estimated model that approximates the internal model implicitly known by the evaluators in terms of image features (Fig. 3 (b)). By choosing the level of the evaluator we want to approximate and giving arbitrary top view images of vegetation, we can obtain estimates of the three subjective ratings (AS, HP, MG) (Fig. 3 (c)). For the estimated output, the evaluation image was divided into $3 \times 5 = 15$ sections, and the VAS score estimates were smoothly color-coded among the 15 sections. An example is displayed in Fig. 4.

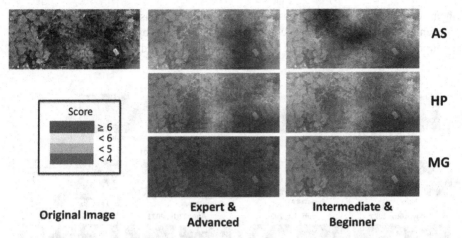

Fig. 4. ISOM outputs of VAS scores prediction (AS, HP, MG) for the evaluation of farm M. The blue-yellow-orange-red color gradient represents the ISOM outputs learned from farm M. Examples based on the picture of Aug. 30th, 2020, in Fig. 1. (Color figure online)

The areas of attention and evaluation differ depending on the level of the evaluator. Therefore, we analyzed the importance of image features for each evaluator's regression model, focusing on the degree of topsoil coverage by vegetation ("plt_seg"), which is particularly important for synecological farming. The average importance of "plt_seg" in the regression model trained on AS was 0.036 for expert and advanced, 0.166 for intermediates, and 0.179 for beginners. In the regression model trained on HP, expert and advanced were 0.052, intermediates were 0.116, and beginners were 0.091. In the regression model trained on MGs, the importance scores were 0.002 for expert and advanced, 0.008 for intermediates, and 0.209 for beginners. Overall, the importance of topsoil coverage in the VAS evaluation tends to decrease with years of experience in farming.

Next, to examine the degree of dependence on features other than topsoil coverage, we examined the standard deviations of the top five feature importance values comprising the learned regression models. If the standard deviation is high, the evaluator relies on specific features and tends to ignore the others, while if low, the evaluation equally refers to all five features. The standard deviations for the regression model trained on AS were 0.018 for expert and advanced, 0.053 for intermediates, and 0.55 for beginners. For the regression model trained on HP, the standard deviations were 0.014 for expert and advanced, 0.027 for intermediates, and 0.027 for beginners. For the regression model trained on MG, the standard deviations were 0.025 for expert and advanced, 0.118 for intermediates, and 0.096 for beginners. Overall, the standard deviations of the five highest feature importance values tended to be higher with years of farming experience, with the five features supporting the decision more evenly.

These results suggest that beginners rely more on easily discernible indicators such as the degree of topsoil cover to make their evaluations, and that the others potentially synthesize other diverse characteristics such as temporal development of images and the forms of vegetation according to the post-survey interview, to make judgments as

160   S. Aotake et al.

their years of experience progress. This is qualitatively consistent with the process of deepening experiential knowledge of managing ecosystems by considering their diverse relationships in a holistic manner [9], which contributes to (d).

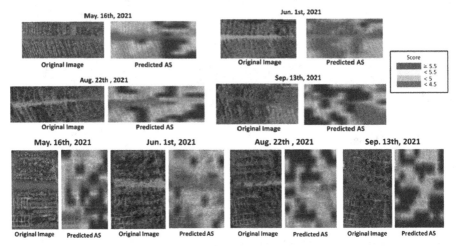

Fig. 5. ISOM outputs of VAS scores prediction (examples of AS) for the evaluation of farm O1 (Top) and O2 (Bottom). The blue-yellow-orange-red color gradient represents the ISOM outputs learned from farm M with 8 evaluators. The red-dominant VAS prediction of Jun. 1st seems to capture the effects of drought in O1. Examples based on the pictures in Fig. 2 (c, d). (Color figure online)

The ISOM learned in farm M was further applied to a larger-scale farm O (Fig. 5). VAS scores (AS, HP, MG) were estimated for each model on top view images taken by drones in two areas: O2, where there is a full-time manager and sufficient seed input and management, and O1, where the amount of seed input and management is about half that of O2. Farm O1 is about 45 times larger and O2 is 25 times larger than farm M to investigate the effectiveness of the model concerning the scale difference. As a general result, the predicted VAS scores showed general superiority in O2 compared to O1. We referred to meteorological data and management information for the field to further assess the validity of the estimation results. One meteorological feature was zero precipitation for the 5 days prior to the observation on June 1, 2021 (data not shown). As a result, fields were dry and growth was poor in O1 than O2 with low seed introduction and management frequency; ISOM predicted worse field conditions on O1 for all indicators AS, HP, and MG for the Jun 1st, 2021, image which was consistent with actual observations of managers.

As a subsequent effect of drought, useful plants declined, and weeds became dominant in O1 during the summer months of August and September. However, the ISOM output estimated higher VAS scores where weeds dominated and did not seem to be able to determine crop growth status. To improve this, it may be necessary to consider further incorporation of features related to the number of crop species and their coverage. In fact, we tentatively trained ISOM on farm M and O images with the number of crop species as additional information and were able to estimate the number of useful plant species with an estimation error of 20% and a coefficient of determination of 0.87 for the farm O input images, which were chosen differently from the training data (results not shown).

These processes are consistent with the dynamical assessment of ecosystems based on open systems science [4,14] and the methodology for capturing significant changes in dynamically changing vegetation succession [3]. In other words, the model is open to constant updating to become more effective as the surrounding environment changes, such as climate change, and as managers' empirical knowledge evolves.

5   Interfaces for Collaborative Robotics

In Table 1, the group that averaged beginners and intermediate members had a higher correlation with the VAS ratings of AS and HP by an expert than an advanced member. Also, a group averaging one advanced member, intermediates, and beginners showed greater correlation with an expert on AS, HP, and averaged scores of the three VAS measures than did an advanced member alone. This suggests that the development of collective knowledge might be more effective in managing synecological farming than the deepening of individual experiential knowledge. More generally, it may be possible that supporting group consensus may be more effective than individual capacity building in overcoming the difficulties of managing complex ecosystems in agroecology. Additionally, in determining whether a field meets the criteria for certification of synecological farming, quality could be assured not only using objective data but also through a combination of inter-subjective review systems by multiple evaluators. In particular, the time scale of the referenced features extends as the level of the evaluator increases to advanced or expert, which is consistent with empirical knowledge where perceptions evolve to include the history of ecological development.

To assist in this cycle of synergistic enhancement of collective and individual experiential knowledge, we considered an interface that provides feedback of the VAS score predicted from ISOM to the individual VAS score (Fig. 6). In this way, the evaluator can recognize under what circumstances his or her VAS evaluation deviates from the VAS estimation by the ISOM that mimics collective knowledge and can learn what new features to pay attention to by examining the image features that contribute to the difference.

The formation of collective knowledge is expected to develop on a larger scale through automation using robotics. Even for complex ecosystems such as synecological farming, robotic management techniques are being developed for areas where vegetation is restricted to a certain height, such as the space under solar panels [12]. Capturing and processing images in conjunction with robotics can scale up the processes (a), (b), (c), and (e) in Fig. 3, and with humans contributing even more deeply to (d) and (f), the development of synergy between human empirical knowledge and robot performance can be expected.

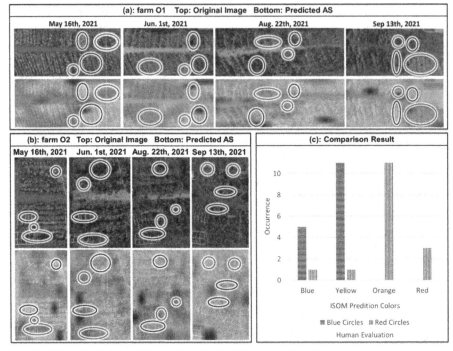

Fig. 6. Estimation of VAS scores on farm O with ISOM learned on farm M and feedback to human evaluation. Prediction of VAS scores (AS, HP, MG) with ISOM learned from the subjective evaluation of 8 evaluators on farm M (the same model as in Fig. 5) are shown with different colormaps in (a): farm O1 and (b): farm O2. The color gradient was adjusted to create two blue and two red areas in each image and is different from Fig. 5. Additionally, an evaluator of intermediate level separately evaluated these images by marking two highest and lowest areas of arbitrary size with blue and red circles, respectively. The number of agreements between the prediction with ISOM (blue, yellow, orange, and red areas) and the human evaluation (blue and red circles) is shown in (c). (Color figure online)

6 Conclusions

In this paper, we proposed a model (ISOM) to connect features of image analysis and human evaluation in a consistent manner, using an example of ecosystem management in synecological farming to detect the information necessary for sustainable management of highly diverse ecosystems. ISOM combines subjective and objective indicators in a complementary manner, enabling the mutual evaluation between the development of empirical knowledge and its objective support. Through the analysis, the open-ended development cycles between human ecological discernment and the discovery and expansion of effective features were suggested, in which interfaces for effective sharing and utilization of collective knowledge and an automatic data expansion process using robotics would help scale-up.

Scientific Validation

This paper has benefited from the remarks of the following reviewers:

- Julian Talbot, Laboratoire de Physique Théorique de la Matière Condensée, France
- Pascal Viot, Sorbonne University, France
- Benjamin Kellenberger, Yale University, USA
- Godai Suzuki, Synecoculture Association, Japan

The conference organisers wish to thank them for their highly appreciated effort and contribution.

Acknowledgements. Members of the Synecoculture Association provided experimental support on the farm in Oiso and contributed to the discussion. Hidenori Aotake and Keiko Aotake provided experimental support on the farm in Machida. Kousaku Ohta, Tomoyuki Minami, Yuji Kawamura, and other members of the Synecoculture project at Sony CSL and Takuya Otani of Waseda University contributed to the experimental design and discussion. Sustainergy Company provided advice on future prospects. Synecoculture™ is a trademark of Sony Group Corporation. Benjamin Kellenberger, Julian Talbot, Pascal Viot, and Godai Suzuki contributed to ameliorating the manuscript.

References

1. Tokoro, M.: Open systems science: a challenge to open systems problems. In: Parrend, P., Bourgine, P., Collet, P. (eds.) First Complex Systems Digital Campus World E-Conference 2015. SPC, pp. 213–221. Springer, Cham (2017). https://doi.org/10.1007/978-3-319-45901-1_25
2. Funabashi, M.: Human augmentation of ecosystems: objectives for food production and science by 2045. NPJ Sci. Food. **2**(16) (2018)
3. Ohta, K., Suzuki, G., Miyazawa, K., Funabashi, M.: Open systems navigation based on system-level difference analysis - case studies with urban augmented ecosystems. Measur. Sens. **23**, 100401 (2022)
4. Funabashi, M., Minami, T.: Dynamical assessment of aboveground and underground biodiversity with supportive AI. Meas. Sens. **18**, 100167 (2021)
5. Funabashi, M.: Augmentation of plant genetic diversity in synecoculture: theory and practice in temperate and tropical zones. In: Nandwani, D. (ed.) Genetic Diversity in Horticultural Plants, Sustainable Development and Biodiversity, vol. 22, Springer, Cham (2019) https://doi.org/10.1007/978-3-319-96454-6_1
6. iNaturalist Homepage, https://www.inaturalist.org/. Accessed 4 Mar 2023
7. SEED Biocomplexity Homepage. https://seed-index.com/. Accessed 4 Mar 2023
8. Funabashi, M.: Synecological farming: theoretical foundation on biodiversity responses of plant communities. Plant Biotechnol. Spec. Iss. Plants Environ. Respon. **33**(4), 213–234 (2016)
9. Funabashi M. (eds.) Synecoculture manual 2016 version (English Version). Research and education material of UniTwin UNESCO Complex Systems Digital Campus, e-laboratory: Open Systems Exploration for Ecosystems Leveraging, vol. 2 (2016)
10. Soya, K., Aotake, S., et al.: Study of a method for detecting dominant vegetation in a field from RGB images using deep learning in synecoculture environment. In: Proceedings of the 49th Annual Meeting of the Institute of Image Electronics Engineers of Japan (2021)
11. Yoshizaki, R., Aotake, S., et al.: Study of a method for recognizing field covering situation by applying semantic segmentation to RGB images in synecoculture environment. In: Proceedings of the 49th Annual Meeting of the Institute of Image Electronics Engineers of Japan (2021)

12. Otani, T., Aotake, S., et al.: Agricultural robot under solar panels for sowing, pruning, and harvesting in a synecoculture environment. Agriculture **13**(1), 18 (2023)
13. Funabashi, M.: Citizen science and topology of mind: complexity, computation and criticality in data-driven exploration of open complex systems. Entropy **19**(4), 181 (2017). https://doi.org/10.3390/e19040181
14. Funabashi, M.: Open systems exploration: an example with ecosystems management. In: Parrend, P., Bourgine, P., Collet, P. (eds.) First Complex Systems Digital Campus World E-Conference 2015. SPC, pp. 223–243. Springer, Cham (2017). https://doi.org/10.1007/978-3-319-45901-1_26
15. Reips, U., Funke, F.: Interval-level measurement with visual analogue scales in internet-based research: VAS generator. Behav. Res. Methods **40**(3), 699–704 (2008)
16. Online supplementary material web link. https://www2.sonycsl.co.jp/person/masa_funabashi/public/20230418_CCE23_Online%20Supplementary%20Material_v-final.xlsx

Security for Complex Computing Systems

On the Provision of Network-Wide Cyber Situational Awareness via Graph-Based Analytics

Martin Husák[1,2]([📧]) [ID], Joseph Khoury[2] [ID], Đorđe Klisura[2] [ID],
and Elias Bou-Harb[2] [ID]

[1] Institute of Computer Science, Masaryk University, Brno, Czech Republic
husakm@ics.muni.cz
[2] The Cyber Center for Security and Analytics, The University of Texas, San
Antonio, TX, USA
{joseph.khoury,dorde.klisura,elias.bouharb}@utsa.edu

Abstract. In this paper, we posit how semi-static (i.e., not changing very often) complex computer network-based intelligence using graph-based analytics can become enablers of Cyber Situational Awareness (CSA) (i.e., perception, comprehension, and projection of situations in a cyber environment). A plethora of newly surfaced cyber security researchers have used graph-based analytics to facilitate particular down tasks in dynamic complex cyber environments. This includes graph-, node- and edge-level detection, classification, and others (e.g., credit card fraudulent transactions as an edge classification problem). To the best of our knowledge, very limited efforts have consolidated the outputs of heterogeneous computer network monitoring and reconnaissance tools (e.g., Nmap) in enabling actionable CSA. As such, in this work, we address this literature gap while describing several use cases of graph traversal, graph measures, and subgraph mining in vulnerability and security state assessment, attack projection and mitigation, and device criticality estimation. We highlight the benefits of the graph-based approaches compared to traditional methods. Finally, we postulate open research and application challenges in graph-based analytics for CSA to prompt promising research directions and operational capabilities.

Keywords: Cyber security · Cyber situational awareness ·
Graph-based analytics · Large and complex network · Network security
management

1 Introduction

Computer networks have become a critical asset in the interconnected world. As such, the sheer number and diverseness of connected devices hinder its security management, deteriorate incident response processes, and ultimately thwart operative Cyber Situational Awareness (CSA) (i.e., situational awareness in

© The Author(s) 2023
P. Collet et al. (Eds.): CCE 2023, LNCS 13927, pp. 167–179, 2023.
https://doi.org/10.1007/978-3-031-44355-8_12

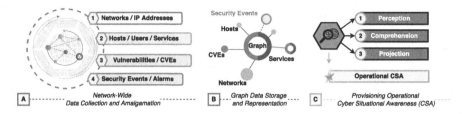

Fig. 1. Provisioning network-wide CSA via graph-based analytics: *(A)* collect and amalgamate network-wide data using heterogeneous tools for computer network monitoring and reconnaissance, *(B)* leverage graph-based analytics to store, visualize, and query the data, *(C)* leverage this data to provision operational CSA for defensive measures, incident responses, and network forensics.

cyberspace). Besides, the constantly changing threat landscape effectively renders network defense a tedious procedure that involves viable CSA coupled with continuous decision-making, actions, and improvements. The concept of CSA defines three levels that need to be achieved to protect the network effectively, *(i)* the `perception` of the elements in the environment within a volume of time and space, *(ii)* the `comprehension` of their meaning, and ultimately *(iii)* the `projection` of their status in the near future [9]. In the context of large and complex networks, graph-based analytics is fairly extensible, can be straightforwardly visualized, and is comprehensible for human analysts, which makes them an excellent choice for the *comprehension* level of CSA. For these reasons, researchers adopted graph-based data representation and storage (e.g., in the form of graph databases) to store data on computer networks, devices, vulnerabilities, and other security-relevant entities.

To that extent, in this paper, we posit the provision of network-wide CSA (and namely its **comprehension** level) via graph-based analytics. Figure 1 illustrates three major steps to achieve this quest. First, in *(A)* we rely on various monitoring and reconnaissance tools (e.g., Nmap [21]) to gather timely information on a computer network and devices (i.e., network/hosts/users/services information, IP addresses, vulnerabilities, Common Vulnerability and Exposures (CVEs), security events). Second, in *(B)* we make use of graph-based analytics (e.g., Neo4j Graph Data Platform [24]) to store and visualize the collected data. Third, in *(C)* we put forward methodical cyber security tasks involving graph-based analytics to achieve operational CSA in practice and ultimately facilitate the preparation of network defenses, planning of preventive actions, and speeding-up incident responses and network forensics.

The remainder of this paper is organized as follows. Section 2 presents background information and summarizes related work. Section 3 presents a selected set of imperative cyber security tasks using graph-based analytics. Section 4 discusses the open issues and formulates the challenges for future work. Section 5 concludes the paper.

2   Background Information and Related Work

Whilst, graph-based analytics are very well known to the cyber security community [1], yet, very limited efforts have been put in the context of semi-static graphs, i.e., graphs where new information is sporadic or recurrent with little to no obvious pattern changes. Attack graphs are one example that has been used for decades to model cyber-attacks and calculate their impact [17,23]). Accordingly, we primarily investigate in this work graph-based analytics for cyber security tasks in the context of semi-static graphs.

The primacy of identifying critical nodes/threats in a network necessitates the usage of advanced graph-based analytics including centrality algorithms (i.e., degree, betweenness, *PageRank*, and closeness). Degree centrality is used to count the edges that connect a node to others [3], while closeness centrality gauges a node's typical separation from every other node in the network. Moreover, betweenness centrality constitutes the extent to which a node lies on the shortest paths between all pairs of nodes in a network [5]. Furthermore, the *PageRank* algorithm ranks nodes according to their significance and is effective in discovering critical nodes in a network [7].

2.1   Tooling and Perception of the Cyber Environment

With the emergence of lateral movement and attacks targeting whole networks, there was a need to grasp complex heterogeneous data on computer networks in a single, comprehensive database. The conceptual works like Cauldron [15] enabled to keep track of hosts, services, users, security events, and other entities in a single database. CyGraph [25] became a well-known implementation of the graph-based approach for cyber situational awareness. CRUSOE [12] is a recently published toolset inspired by CyGraph but based on empirical data provided by common tools instead of perfecting the data structure and analysis.

Such network-wide graphs allow for assessing risks to the organization operating the network, optimizing the network defenses, or facilitating incident response. However, it is still tedious to fill the whole database with exact data, which would allow using all the analytical features. For example, the CRUSOE [12] uses common tools to autonomously monitor the network traffic, actively scan devices in the network, fingerprint running hosts and services, and disclose vulnerabilities. Such data were periodically updated and stored in a joint database along with static information on the network segmentation, organization structure, details on vulnerabilities from external sources, history of cyber security incidents, and other local knowledge.

2.2   Comprehension and Knowledge Building

The graph databases, i.e., graph-oriented NoSQL database management systems, such as Neo4j [24] and specialized graph-querying languages like Cypher and Gremlin and natural choices for storing and querying large graph data.

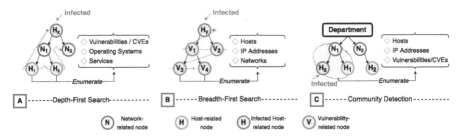

Fig. 2. Graph Traversal and Community Detection Algorithms: *(A)* depth-first search, *(B)* breadth-first search, *(C)* community detection algorithms applied to selected cyber security tasks.

Nevertheless, there is a need to structure them. CRUSOE data model [19] is an example of such a model, independent of the underlying technology.

An interesting observation is that the data about the network stored in a graph are, in essence, knowledge graphs. Likewise, the graph-based data models of CyGraph or CRUSOE can be considered ontologies of the domain. Knowledge graphs allow for reasoning over the data and are the subject of research on artificial intelligence [6,28]. The ontologies allow for understanding the domain and categorizing various attack types and defense options [13,30].

2.3   Existing Surveys

Readers further interested in the outlined topics are kindly referred to several surveys. The earliest one by Akoglu et al. [1] surveyed graph-based techniques for anomaly detection in diverse domains, including network traffic analysis. The attack graphs and their construction were exhaustively covered by Kaynar et al. [17]. The application of graphs in network-wide situational awareness was covered by Noel et al. [26]. Bowman and Huang [4] reviewed the challenges of the application of Graph AI in cyber security. Atzmüller and Kanawati [2] provided an overview of explainability for complex network analysis in cyber security. In the sequel, we discuss selected cyber security tasks using graph-based analytics.

3   Selected Cyber Security Tasks Using Graph-Based Analytics

In this section, we present a selected set of imperative cyber security tasks that is amenable to graph-based analytics. Specifically, we highlight the advantages of these approaches in the context of complex network-related intelligence to achieve operational CSA, namely incident comprehension, prevention, and response. The selected use cases coupled with the graph-based analytic solutions provide a one-way example of addressing these cyber security tasks, particularly, we tailor these instances to the CRUSOE data model [12,19]. Readers are kindly referred to the related work for exact specification of the data and graph construction.

3.1 Finding Similar Hosts in Close Proximity by Graph Traversal

Graph traversal is a simple but efficient method for analyzing graph data, including for cyber security purposes. In a previous work [11], we elaborated on a typical situation in incident response. Let's assume a user reports a machine infected with ransomware. Ransomware infections can spread rapidly and can cause significant harm to the organization, so it is of utmost importance to mitigate it fast. We may start a graph traversal from the node representing the infected device to look up for similar devices in close proximity that are exposed to the infection. Since it may not be clear what type of ransomware infected the device and if it spreads autonomously or via infected files in emails or data storage, we may simultaneously look up devices in the same subnet or location, within the same department, or used by the same user.

Following Fig. 2 *(A)*, we run the Depth-First Search (DFS) algorithm from the infected node (host) H_x. The query looks-up nodes representing other devices within the same network N_1. A constraint on the length of the path between the source and destination node or types of nodes and edges to traverse can be applied. The found devices H_1 and H_2 are then scored by their similarity to the infected one using the enumerated intelligence such as OS and service fingerprint or common history of security incidents [11].

The described query enables fast early warning to users and administrators of devices immediately threatened by ransomware, which may prevent further infections. Later on, when the forensic analysis of the malware returns how it spread, the results can be filtered to include only those with paths related to the attack vector. An alternative use for this approach is network forensics. The recommendation of similar devices in close proximity can direct the investigators in the analysis of an attack involving lateral movement, i.e., an attack technique involving a breach of a third machine to get better access to the actual target.

3.2 Vulnerable Asset Discovery via Graph Traversal

One of the key motivating use cases of the CRUSOE toolset was large-scale vulnerability assessment [12]. The devices in the network are fingerprinted by Nmap or other common tools that generate output in the form of CPE strings, a structured identification of the system's vendor, major and minor version, patches, or edition. The same CPE strings can also be found in vulnerability databases to enumerate vulnerable systems or their specific configurations. Thus, there exists a mapping between a description of a vulnerability and a fingerprint of a device, which can be used to infer which and how many devices in the network are vulnerable.

For example, in CRUSOE, the relation can be represented as a path consisting of an edge between a *Host* and *Fingerprint* and *Fingerprint* and *CVE*, where CVE is a common vulnerability identifier. The nodes and edges in the CRUSOE graph are inserted automatically by tools periodically checking the vulnerability databases and network scanning tools. Figure 2 *(B)* depicts the use of the Breadth-First Search (BFS) algorithm to query and list potential vulnerabilities and CVEs, for instance, V_1, V_2, V_3, and V_4 associated with a recent infection on H_y. By extending the query, one can enumerate how many vulnerable hosts are there in each subnet or under the control of a specific administrator. Such a summary was found to be one of the most valuable features of CRUSOE by practitioners [12]. The advantage of the graph-based approach here is the very low complexity of inserting new connections and queries as simple as enumerating neighbours of the neighbouring node.

An elegant graph-based matching of vulnerable configuration was proposed by Tovarňák et al. [31]. Matching the CPE strings of vulnerabilities and device fingerprints are usually done via a brute-force approach. However, doing so on a large scale calls for more efficient algorithms. The authors decompose the CPE strings into a graph model and provide a query to find all matches between vulnerable CVEs and asset configurations in a single graph traversal.

3.3 Network Segmentation via Community Detection and FSM

Graph-based analytics can also be used to implement network segmentation and an important strategy to isolate malicious entities from a graph network and ultimately restrict the propagation of potential security threats [33]. Figure 2 *(C)* depicts a community detection algorithm, namely, the Girvan-Newman algorithm which is used herein to accomplish network segmentation [8]. Specifically, once a community has been identified with an infected host H_z, its corresponding network N_1 can be isolated by deploying firewalls (or fortifying existing ones) to prevent communication with other communities. As such, this approach can isolate potential security risks and prevent them from spreading throughout the entire network. Additionally, enumerating such communities can help identify and characterize specific vulnerabilities and CVEs associated with the infections.

Furthermore, Frequent Subgraph Mining (FSM) is a subfield of graph mining that can offer additional capabilities for cyber security tasks by identifying frequently occurring patterns in a graph using DFS and BFS algorithms [16]. The application of FSM to graph-based network data offers a wide range of cybersecurity benefits. We might discover, for instance, that a certain set of nodes and edges occurs more frequently than we would anticipate by chance, such as a subgraph representing a collection of devices connecting to a particular server or using a particular resource. Then, by examining these subgraphs, we could look for patterns or motifs that would point to malicious behavior. For instance, if it turns out that a specific subgraph is linked to well-known malware or attack vectors, we may utilize this knowledge to create more specialized detection and prevention strategies, such as adding firewall rules to restrict access to particular servers or resources.

3.4 Node Criticality Estimation via Graph Centrality

A motivating example for using graph centrality measures is a frequent question of network security management - *How important is a particular machine for the organization?* Answering such a question properly requires a knowledge of the

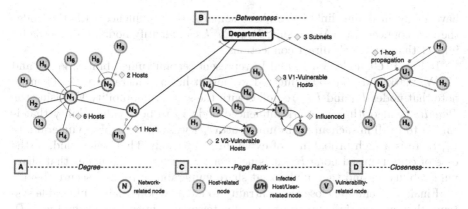

Fig. 3. Graph Centrality Algorithms: *(A)* degree, *(B)* betweenness, *(C)* page rank, *(D)* closeness algorithms applied to specific cyber security tasks.

local environment, which might not be available in large networks and organizations [34]. However, approximations via network measurement help in quickly assessing the importance of a node (device) and aid in identifying a node's role within the network and how that role impacts the network as a whole [20].

To build the network topology graph, multiple hosts in the network use a scanning tool like *Nmap* with the traceroute option to scan the network [21]. Each scan provides a tree structure, with the scanning machine as the host, and these trees are merged into one graph. The more observation points are used, the more is the resulting graph similar to the actual network topology.

The resulting graph can be subjected to a number of centrality measure techniques for understanding the role and impact of different nodes on the network. In the following, we describe four of these techniques, presented in Fig. 3.

To understand the dynamics of a network and select high-value targets, we can identify significant nodes using the degree centrality technique. Nodes with high centrality degrees are crucial to the network's operation and may be potential attack targets [3]. In Fig. 3 *(A)*, we show a scenario where the host H_5 is infected. In this case, we must first isolate the node N_1 as it has the highest centrality degree, that is, is associated with the largest number of nodes (hosts). This will enhance the network security because if N_1 gets compromised, the malicious activity might easily propagate to other nodes and networks in the subnet, all way to the department.

Furthermore, we employ a betweenness centrality approach to find nodes critical to information flow or attack paths via the network [5]. We determine the shortest path between every pair of nodes in the network and subsequently assign a score to each node based on the number of shortest pathways that traverse through it. In Fig. 3 *(B)*, the node *Department* has the highest betweenness centrality as it serves as a bridge between the subnets N_3, N_4, and N_5.

We may also employ the *PageRank* algorithm to measure a node's influence in a network based on the quality of its connections [7]. Influential nodes, which have many incoming links, also share some of their influence with the nodes they are connected to. As a result, *PageRank* can identify nodes with a broader impact than just their direct connections.

In Fig. 3 *(C)*, nodes V_1, V_2 and V_3 represent certain vulnerabilities V_1, V_2 and V_3. We mark node H_4 to be infected we note it has a vulnerability V_1. Then we note that nodes H_3 and H_5 are nodes with the same vulnerability V_1. Using the *PageRank* algorithm we mark influenced node V_3 to be a vulnerability that is similar to V_1. If in such an environment attacker was able to exploit vulnerability V_1, there is a high probability of exploiting V_3 as well. That being said, in the case of compromised node H_4, it is necessary to check all the nodes that share vulnerability V_1 and then nodes that share vulnerability V_3, and secure them.

Finally, we employ closeness centrality to identify potentially vulnerable systems that are in close proximity to a noteworthy threat. As such, Fig. 3*(D)* demonstrates the relevance of closeness centrality in the context of a graph-based network. Specifically, we mark U_1 to be a user node with the highest closeness centrality. Let's say the user opens a fishing email on its local machine U_1 and the machine gets compromised. Then, the malicious propagation can be the fastest to other nodes within the subnet N_5, as it only takes the attacker one hop from U_1 to compromise all other nodes in N_5.

4   Open Issues and Challenges

Herein, we formulate open issues and research challenges that we face in the development and deployment of the tools enabling us to view the network security properties as a complex network.

4.1   Need to Learn a New Paradigm

It is vital to remind that the graph-based or complex network-based view on network security is a novel paradigm for many cybersecurity experts. Just like with the emergence of stream-based data analysis in the past decade, the new paradigm enabled novel views on the problems and ways to resolve them. However, the practitioners had to adopt the principles of stream-based data analytics to make full use of them.

We have already observed a generally very positive attitude towards the graph-based representation of cyber security data [12]; the graph-based visualization is highly comprehensive even without any background knowledge. However, the adoption of new query languages and data processing paradigms can be slow, and the embracement of the methods of graph theory may be even slower among practitioners.

4.2   Dataset

A lack of well-known, high-quality datasets is a common issue of cyber security research. The existing datasets contain mostly network traffic or attack traces, and only a few approach the network defense [22]. A few examples of a dataset created for the needs of CSA research include the MM-TBM [14] and CYSAS-S3 [22]. Nevertheless, the first one contains a simple network topology but focuses on attack traces, while the later one is focused on mission-oriented situational awareness and decision-making rather than the technological background. As far as we know, there is no dataset for preventive or defensive network-wide situational awareness. The closest are the network topologies and scenarios for various cyber competitions [32].

We aim to generate a dataset stored as a graph in our future work. The most viable option at the moment seems to be a graph representation of an existing network topology (e.g., graph storage using combinatorial embedding [18]). Another option includes existing tools such as [12,25] to collect data on a live network. However, such data would require proper anonymization of all entries (e.g., IP addresses, domain names, department names, contacts on users and administrators). Anonymizing the most critical or important nodes in the network would require extreme caution. There is a high risk that any omission would allow the de-anonymizing of the whole dataset and possibly compromise the network in which the dataset was collected.

4.3 Unified Ontology

Since the graph-based representation of the network also serves as a knowledge graph for network defense and the graph-based data models as ontologies, it is important to establish a common ontology to facilitate knowledge transfer and research collaboration and enable the integration of tools. Unfortunately, a mature unified technology in the cyber defense domain is not yet available and widely adopted despite significant research efforts.

So far, the relevant ontologies target specific applications like vulnerability management [29] and cyber threat intelligence [28]. Attempts to develop a unified ontology exist in the form of UCO [30] or STUCCO [13], but have yet to achieve a wider spread in the application domain and remain a research topic. Data models used in CyGraph [25] or CRUSOE [19] are the closest to the topics of this manuscript but are not used as stand-alone ontology outside of the tools they support. Thus, there is still an open call for an ontology.

4.4 Application of Graph Neural Networks and Graph AI

Machine learning is, without a doubt, a significant driving force in research on data analysis, regardless of domain. The graph-based data can be processed by a class of machine learning approaches referred to as graph neural networks (GNNs) or Graph AI. We see an emerging trend of the application of GNNs for intrusion detection [27], vulnerability assessment [10] or reasoning over knowledge graphs [6]. However, applications in the area of CSA are lacking.

At the moment, there is a need to identify promising GNN-based approaches applicable to the available data. Even though the complex graphs representing computer networks contain up to tens of thousands of nodes, the nodes are of certain types and there might not be enough nodes of each type or subgraphs to train the GNNs or Graph AI for a particular purpose. A great benefit would be the use of distributed or federated learning techniques to train the models in multiple networks simultaneously. The privacy considerations of network security management call for such an approach anyway. The graphs are rather static, so the trained models would also not be obsolete that fast as it happens in network traffic analysis, threat intelligence, or other cyber security applications [4]. Nevertheless, explainability remains an open issue [2].

The link prediction, i.e., predicting which entities (nodes) will create a relation (edge), is a widely-used technique worth mentioning here. It suits dynamic graphs, which change rapidly over time. The more static graph representing the computer networks does not offer enough opportunities to observe dynamic changes and to train the ML-based models for link prediction. Therefore, even though we can imagine link prediction for rapid assessment of a newly observed device or vulnerability, we argue such approaches are more suitable for intrusion detection or network traffic analysis.

5   Conclusion

In this paper, we outlined the application of graph-based representation of the data, namely in the form of complex networks, in cyber security with a special focus on cyber defense and cyber situational awareness. In a series of use cases, we illustrated how can we achieve a deeper understanding of a cyber security situation in a network via selected graph algorithms and approaches used in complex network analysis. We illustrated how to provide vulnerability or security state assessment using simple graph traversal and use the results for attack projection and mitigation. Graph centrality measures, link prediction, and subgraph mining were shown to be applicable in advanced security assessment, such as device criticality estimation, prediction of its security state or belonging to a community of common attack targets.

Moreover, we identified several open issues and challenges we may face in future research and development and transferring the research into practice. Namely, we identified the lack of datasets and unified ontology and obstacles practitioners might face when embracing a novel paradigm. On the contrary, we see great potential in the application of graph neural networks in this domain. The open issues will be the subject of our future work, alongside further research and development and empirical evaluation and analysis of the outlined approaches to the presented use cases.

Acknowledgments. This research was supported by OP JAK "MSCAfellow5_MUNI" (No. CZ.02.01.01/00/22_010/0003229).

Scientific Validation. This paper has benefited from the remarks of the following reviewers:
- Pierre Parrend, EPITA Strasbourg, France
- Sofiane Lagraa, Fujitsu, Luxembourg
- Nidà Meddouri, LRE, EPITA, Kremlin-Bicêtre, France

The conference organisers wish to thank them for their highly appreciated effort and contribution.

References

1. Akoglu, L., Tong, H., Koutra, D.: Graph based anomaly detection and description: a survey. Data Min. Knowl. Disc. **29**(3), 626–688 (2014)
2. Atzmueller, M., Kanawati, R.: Explainability in cyber security using complex network analysis: a brief methodological overview. In: Proceedings of the 2022 European Interdisciplinary Cybersecurity Conference. EICC '22, pp. 49–52. ACM (2022)
3. Bavelas, A.: Communication patterns in task-oriented groups. J. Acoust. Soc. Am. **22**(6), 725–730 (1950)
4. Bowman, B., Huang, H.H.: Towards next-generation cybersecurity with graph AI. SIGOPS Oper. Syst. Rev. **55**(1), 61–67 (2021)
5. Brandes, U.: A faster algorithm for betweenness centrality. J. Math. Sociol. **25**(2), 163–177 (2001)
6. Dasgupta, S., Piplai, A., Ranade, P., Joshi, A.: Cybersecurity knowledge graph improvement with graph neural networks. In: 2021 IEEE International Conference on Big Data (Big Data), pp. 3290–3297 (2021)
7. De, S., Sodhi, R.: A PMU assisted cyber attack resilient framework against power systems structural vulnerabilities. Elect. Power Syst. Res. **206**, 107805 (2022)
8. Despalatović, L., Vojković, T., Vukicević, D.: Community structure in networks: Girvan-Newman algorithm improvement. In: 2014 37th International Convention on Information and Communication Technology, Electronics and Microelectronics (MIPRO), pp. 997–1002. IEEE (2014)
9. Endsley, M.R.: Situation awareness global assessment technique (SAGAT). In: Aerospace and Electronics Conference, 1988. NAECON 1988, Proceedings of the IEEE 1988 National, pp. 789–795. IEEE (1988)
10. He, H., Ji, Y., Huang, H.H.: Illuminati: towards explaining graph neural networks for cybersecurity analysis. In: 2022 IEEE 7th European Symposium on Security and Privacy (EuroS&P), pp. 74–89 (2022)
11. Husák, M.: Towards a data-driven recommender system for handling ransomware and similar incidents. In: 2021 IEEE International Conference on Intelligence and Security Informatics (ISI) (2021)
12. Husák, M., Sadlek, L., Špaček, S., Laštovička, M., Javorník, M., Komárková, J.: CRUSOE: a toolset for cyber situational awareness and decision support in incident handling. Comput. Secur. **115**, 102609 (2022)
13. Iannacone, M., et al.: Developing an ontology for cyber security knowledge graphs. In: Proceedings of the 10th Annual Cyber and Information Security Research Conference. CISR 2015. ACM (2015)

14. Ioannou, G., Louvieris, P., Clewley, N.: MM-TBM evaluation datasets (2018). https://dx.doi.org/10.21227/8dt8-gx46, ieee Dataport
15. Jajodia, S., Noel, S., Kalapa, P., Albanese, M., Williams, J.: Cauldron mission-centric cyber situational awareness with defense in depth. In: 2011 - MILCOM 2011 Military Communications Conference, pp. 1339–1344 (2011)
16. Jiang, C., Coenen, F., Zito, M.: A survey of frequent subgraph mining algorithms. Knowl. Eng. Rev. 28(1), 75–105 (2013)
17. Kaynar, K.: A taxonomy for attack graph generation and usage in network security. J. Inf. Secur. Appl. 29, 27–56 (2016)
18. Klisura, Ð.: Embedding non-planar graphs: storage and representation. In: Proceedings of the 2021 7th Student Computer Science Research Conference, p. 57 (2021)
19. Komárková, J., Husák, M., Laštovička, M., Tovarňák, D.: CRUSOE: data model for cyber situational awareness. In: Proceedings of the 13th International Conference on Availability, Reliability and Security. ARES 2018. ACM (2018)
20. Laštovička, M., Čeleda, P.: Situational awareness: detecting critical dependencies and devices in a network. In: Tuncer, D., Koch, R., Badonnel, R., Stiller, B. (eds.) AIMS 2017. LNCS, vol. 10356, pp. 173–178. Springer, Cham (2017). https://doi.org/10.1007/978-3-319-60774-0_17
21. Lyon, G.F.: Nmap network scanning: The official Nmap project guide to network discovery and security scanning. Insecure, Com LLC (US) (2008)
22. Medenou, R.D., et al.: CYSAS-S3: a novel dataset for validating cyber situational awareness related tools for supporting military operations. In: Proceedings of the 15th International Conference on Availability, Reliability and Security. ARES 2020. ACM (2020)
23. Nassar, M., Khoury, J., Erradi, A., Bou-Harb, E.: Game theoretical model for cybersecurity risk assessment of industrial control systems. In: 2021 11th IFIP International Conference on New Technologies, Mobility and Security (NTMS), pp. 1–7. IEEE (2021)
24. Neo4j Inc: Neo4J Graph Data Platform (2023). https://neo4j.com. Accessed 21 Feb 2023
25. Noel, S., Harley, E., Tam, K.H., Limiero, M., Share, M.: CyGraph: graph-based analytics and visualization for cybersecurity. In: Handbook of Statistics, vol. 35, pp. 117–167. Elsevier (2016)
26. Noel, S.: A review of graph approaches to network security analytics. In: Samarati, P., Ray, I., Ray, I. (eds.) From Database to Cyber Security. LNCS, vol. 11170, pp. 300–323. Springer, Cham (2018). https://doi.org/10.1007/978-3-030-04834-1_16
27. Pujol-Perich, D., Suarez-Varela, J., Cabellos-Aparicio, A., Barlet-Ros, P.: Unveiling the potential of graph neural networks for robust intrusion detection. SIGMETRICS Perform. Eval. Rev. 49(4), 111–117 (2022)
28. Sarhan, I., Spruit, M.: Open-cykg: an open cyber threat intelligence knowledge graph. Knowl.-Based Syst. 233, 107524 (2021)
29. Syed, R.: Cybersecurity vulnerability management: a conceptual ontology and cyber intelligence alert system. Inf. Manag. 57(6), 103334 (2020)
30. Syed, Z., Padia, A., Finin, T., Mathews, L., Joshi, A.: UCO: a unified cybersecurity ontology. UMBC Student Collection (2016)
31. Tovarňák, D., Sadlek, L., Čeleda, P.: Graph-based CPE matching for identification of vulnerable asset configurations. In: 2021 IFIP/IEEE International Symposium on Integrated Network Management (IM), pp. 986–991 (2021)
32. Tovarňák, D., Špaček, S., Vykopal, J.: Traffic and log data captured during a cyber defense exercise. Data Brief 31, 105784 (2020)

33. Wagner, N., et al.: Towards automated cyber decision support: a case study on network segmentation for security. In: 2016 IEEE Symposium Series on Computational Intelligence (SSCI), pp. 1–10. IEEE (2016)
34. Zand, A., Houmansadr, A., Vigna, G., Kemmerer, R., Kruegel, C.: Know your Achilles' heel: automatic detection of network critical services. In: Proceedings of the 31st Annual Computer Security Applications Conference. ACSAC 2015, pp. 41–50. ACM (2015)

Metrics for Evaluating Interface Explainability Models for Cyberattack Detection in IoT Data

Amani Abou Rida[1,3(✉)], Rabih Amhaz[1,2], and Pierre Parrend[1,3]

[1] Icube - Laboratoire, des sciences de l'ingénieur, de l'informatique et de l'imagerie UMR 7357, Université de Strasbourg, CNRS, 67000 Strasbourg, France
abou.rida.amani@etu.unistra.fr
[2] ICAM, site de Strasbourg - Europe, 67300 Schiltigheim, France
[3] Laboratoire de Recherche, de L'EPITA (LRE), 14-16 rue Voltaire, 94270 Le Kremlin Bicêtre, France

Abstract. The importance of machine learning (ML) in detecting cyber-attacks lies in its ability to efficiently process and analyze large volumes of IoT data, which is critical in ensuring the security and privacy of sensitive information transmitted between connected devices. However, the lack of explainability of ML algorithms has become a significant concern in the cybersecurity community. Therefore, explainable techniques are developed to make ML algorithms more transparent, thereby improving trust in attack detection systems by its ability to allow cybersecurity analysts to understand the reasons for model predictions and to identify any limitation or error in the model. One of the key artifacts of explainability is interface explainability models such as impurity and permutation feature importance analysis, Local Interpretable Model-agnostic Explanations (LIME), and SHapley Additive exPlanations (SHAP). However, these models are not able to provide enough quantitative information (metrics) to build complete trust and confidence in the explanations they generate. In this paper, we propose and evaluate metrics such as reliability and latency to quantify the trustworthiness of the explanations and to establish confidence in the model's decisions to accurately detect and explain cyberattacks in IoT data during the ML process.

Keywords: Explainability · Trust · ML · Cybersecurity · Cyber-attacks

1 Introduction

Explainability is a crucial factor for establishing trust in ML models [Gui+18]. According to the High-Level Expert Group on Artificial Intelligence (AI) established by the European Union, trust is a critical factor in promoting the development and adoption of AI technologies [AI19a]. Trust is defined as the belief that an AI system will perform as expected and compliant with ethical and legal norms. To achieve trust in AI, the group [AI19a] recommends considering several properties, including transparency, accountability, reliability, safety, and privacy. However, without the ability to understand and interpret the decisions made by the model, trust cannot be established. This is where explainability comes in. It enables users to understand how the model arrived at its decisions, and therefore plays a crucial role in building trust.

In addition, trust and explainability are critical for the effectiveness of ML models in cybersecurity. As cyber threats continue to evolve in IoT data, it is crucial to prioritize explainability since it allows security analysts to comprehend the complex interactions between devices [Mol20], which can be difficult due to the distributed nature of IoT systems. With a better understanding of the reasons behind detection, analysts gain valuable insights which help them improve the detection process. However, achieving explainability using ML models in IoT data can be a complex task. To address this challenge, we extend on the framework for explainability in ML developed by Arrieta [Arr+20]. The framework identifies five key artifacts of explainability that are crucial for ensuring transparency throughout the data analysis process: data traceability [Mor+21], model understandability [Mur+19], output comprehensibility [Fer+19], interface explainability [Fer+19], and human interpretability [Arr+20]. Among these artifacts, interface explainability is the key for building trust and for increasing the adoption of ML systems. While models such as impurity feature importance, permutation feature importance analysis, LIME, and SHAP provide intuitive explanations, they have limitations in offering complete quantitative information and facilitating direct comparisons between explanations.

We therefore propose a novel approach for evaluating the quality of interface explainability models, with a specific focus on reliability of features and latency for providing explanations. We first evaluate existing metrics for interface explainability models, then develop new ones that can improve decision-maker's trust and confidence in the models they select. We aim at providing decision-makers with a solid foundation for selecting and evaluating interface explainability models that are transparent, trustworthy, and effective in making critical decisions. To accomplish this objective, we address the following question: How to evaluate quantitatively the explanations provided by interface explainability models to ensure trust in the data analysis process?

The paper is organized as follows. Section 2 introduces the state of the art, and Sect. 3 shows the benchmark for evaluating the quality of interface explainability models. Section 4 presents the datasets used and the implementation. Section 5 provides the evaluations and Sect. 6 discusses the significance of obtained results. Section 7 concludes this work.

2 State of the Art

2.1 Trusted AI

Definition of Trusted AI. According to the High-Level Expert Group on AI [AI19a], appointed by the European Commission, Trusted AI refers to artificial intelligence systems that meet specific properties and are developed and utilized in a transparent, ethical, and responsible manner.

Properties of Trusted AI. In April 2019, the High-Level Expert Group on AI [AI19a] released Ethics Guidelines for Trustworthy Artificial Intelligence, which outlines seven key properties that AI systems should meet to be considered trustworthy. These properties include respecting human autonomy and fundamental rights, ensuring system robustness and safety, protecting the privacy and data governance, promoting transparency, avoiding bias and discrimination, considering societal and environmental well-being, and holding AI systems accountable for their outcomes. Moreover, the guidelines offer a specific assessment list to verify compliance with each property. This list includes measures such as fundamental rights impact assessments, cybersecurity testing, privacy protection, transparency and explainability, non-discrimination and fairness, and impact assessment tools.

Explainability for Trusted AI. The High-Level Expert Group on AI [AI19a] emphasizes that incorporating transparency and explainability into AI systems is essential for ensuring their trustworthiness and promoting wider societal acceptance. By promoting a greater understanding of how AI systems make decisions and producing more trustworthy outcomes, transparency and explainability increase the social acceptance of AI and mitigate concerns related to issues such as bias, discrimination, and privacy.

2.2   Explainable AI

Definition of Explainable AI. Arrieta [Arr+20] has defined Explainable Artificial Intelligence (xAI) in the context of ML models as follows: "Given an audience, an explainable Artificial Intelligence model produces details or reasons to make its functioning clear or easy to understand."

Artefacts for Explainability in the Data Analysis Process. The data analysis process in ML involves five key components, as identified by Arrieta [Arr+20]: input data, model, output, user interface, and the human element. Input data refers to the information provided to the ML model to produce results. The user interface includes explanations or visualizations that allow humans to interact with and understand how the model works and how the results are derived. The human element involves the people who use the model and interpret the results by making decisions based on the insights generated from the data analysis. To achieve transparency in the data analysis process, Arrieta highlights the importance of incorporating five key artifacts of explainability: traceability, understandability, comprehensibility, explainability, and interpretability [Arr+20]. Traceability ensures the ability to track the origin and lineage of data used to train a model [Mor+21]. Understandability refers to the characteristic of a model to make its function understandable to humans without any need to explain its internal structure [Mur+19]. Comprehensibility is the ability of a learning algorithm to represent its learned knowledge in a way that is understandable to humans [Fer+19]. Explainability is the property of an AI system that enables it to provide an interface between humans and a decision-maker that accurately represents the decision-making process while being understandable to humans [Fer+19]. Interpretability is the ability to explain or provide meaning in understandable terms to a human [DK17].

Interface Explainability Models. Interface explainability models in ML enhance the interpretability and transparency of complex models by providing insights into their decision-making processes. To achieve this, researchers have developed various techniques such as impurity and permutation-based feature importance analysis [AI19b, HMZ21], as well as model-specific methods like LIME [RSG16] and SHAP [LL17]. In this section, we highlight the strengths of these models and explore how they work. We also compare these techniques according to the data they use, the ML models they work on, the type and level of explanation they provide, and their limitations as shown in Table 1. Impurity Feature Importance (FI) and Permutation Feature Importance (PFI) are metrics used to measure feature importance in ML models. Their objective is to identify the most important features in the model's predictions by evaluating their impact on model performance. Impurity FI calculates the reduction in impurity that occurs when a feature is used to split the data and selects the feature with the largest decrease in impurity as the most important [AI19b]. PFI shuffles a feature's values to break its relationship with the target variable and measures the decrease in the model's score, with the feature having the largest drop in score considered the most important [HMZ21]. LIME is a method used to explain black-box ML model predictions locally, by showing the contributions of each feature to the prediction for a specific instance or a subset of the data. It generates new instances by sampling a neighborhood around the instance being explained and applies the model to it, weighting the generated instances based on their distances to the instance being explained. This results in a linear model that provides an understandable explanation of the black-box model's behavior for the instance being explained. The SHAP technique explains ML model output by attributing the prediction to input features, providing a consistent way of computing feature importance globally and locally. It uses Shapley values from game theory to distribute the effect of a feature fairly among all input features, resulting in a feature importance score. By repeating this process for all input features, SHAP provides a final score indicating the relative importance of each feature in the model's prediction.

Metrics for Explainable AI. Metrics are critical for assessing the effectiveness of XAI systems [AI19a]. They allow for a meaningful comparison of how well a model fits the definition of explainability. Arrieta [AI19a] highlights the significance of metrics in evaluating the impact of explanations on the trust and reliance of the audience, as well as the need for concrete tools to compare

Table 1. Compare Interface Explainability models in ML.

Comparison	Impurity Feature Importance (FI)	Permutation Feature Importance (PFI)	LIME	SHAP
Data used	Trained model	Trained model	Any datapoint	Any datapoint
Model types	Only trees - Model specific	Only trees - Model agnostic	Any - Model agnostic	Different explainer's types - Model agnostic
Explainability Level	Global	Global	Local	Global and local
Explainability Type	feature importance, visualization	feature importance, visualization	Simplification, visualization	feature relevance, visualization
Limitations	Computed on training set statistics and therefore do not reflect the ability of feature to be useful to make predictions that generalize to the test set (data), Unsuitable for linear models and for continuous features (only suitable for tree models) (ML model)	Unsuitable to explain time series models or when there are strongly correlated features (data), Do not provide information on how the feature affects the model's predictions for specific instances or subsets of the data (global explanation) (data and output), Does not account for any interactions between features (feature relevance)	Does not provide a complete picture of the model's behavior for the entire dataset (local explanation) (data and output), Depending on the number of fake instances you generate and the kernel width you select this introduces inaccuracies and leads to a loss of information (data and output)	Cannot be used to make statements about changes in prediction for changes in the input (data and output), Difficult to compare explanations from different ml models (each model requires a different type of explainer) (ML model), Large computational time because the training time grows exponentially with the number of features (output)

the explainability between different models. Hoffman [HMKL18] emphasize the importance of developing clear and effective measurement concepts for evaluating the effectiveness of explainable systems. Although their framework identifies key questions about measuring effectiveness, it does not include specific quantitative measures or evaluation methods. Sovrano [Sov+22] provide a qualitative analysis of metrics for evaluating the quality of explainability in AI systems. However, they do not provide specific quantitative measures or thresholds for each metric.

2.3 Explainability for Cybersecurity in IoT Data

Detecting cyber attacks in IoT systems is crucial for maintaining the confidentiality, availability, and integrity of information transmitted over the Internet. ML algorithms are useful in handling the complexity of data generated from various sources and adapting to changing attack patterns [SS20]. However, the lack of explainability of ML algorithms has become a significant concern in the cybersecurity community. As highlighted in [Sri+22], explainability helps cybersecurity experts understand the reasons behind cyber attacks and detect any biases or vulnerabilities in their security systems. However, no research has compared the effectiveness of different explainability models in achieving these goals. Therefore, it is essential to identify and evaluate the most effective explainability model to achieve intuitive explanations of ML models' behavior in cybersecurity.

3   Metrics for Evaluating the Quality of Interface Explainability Models

Reliability Between Different Interface Explainability Models. Reliability is a crucial aspect of interface explainability models, which refers to the consistency and similarity of feature importance scores across different models. If the output of various interface explainability models is consistent and similar, the user can have more confidence in the explanations provided by these models. Conversely, if they are inconsistent or differ widely between models, users may have difficulty interpreting the results and identifying the important features. We propose two metrics to measure the reliability of interface explainability models. The first metric is Top5Ratio, measures the similarity between the top 5 most important feature scores generated by different interface explainability models and is represented according to this formula:

$$\text{Top5Ratio} = \frac{|\text{Top}_5(score(x, m, iexp)) \cap \text{Top}_5(score(x, m, iexp'))|}{5} \quad (1)$$

This metric indicates the similarity between important features across different interface explainability models. The Top5Ratio metric is calculated by identifying the top 5 important features that consistently appear in the top 5 across all interface explainability models based on their feature scores, where x is the data, m is the ML model, $iexp$ and $iexp'$ are different interface explainability models. The top5Ratio metric produces results between 0 and 1, where 1 represents complete agreement between interface explainability models in terms of the top 5 important features and their scores, and 0 represents no agreement. To further assess the consistency of the feature scores across different models, we propose the average reliability metric according to this formula:

$$\text{Average Reliability} = \frac{1}{N} \sum_{i=1}^{N} |score_i(x, m, iexp) - score_i(x, m, iexp')| \quad (2)$$

This metric gives a measure of how much the feature importance scores differ between the two models. Then, computing the absolute distance between the average reliability scores, gives us a measure of how consistent the two models are in terms of their overall reliability. A lower absolute distance between the average reliability of interface explainability models indicates greater consistency, meaning that the two interface explainability models are more similar in terms of their reliability scores. A higher absolute distance indicates that the two models are less reliable.

Latency Between Different Interface Explainability Models. In the context of providing explainability for cyber-attack models, latency refers to the amount of time it takes for the interface explainability model to generate explanations. The objective of the latency metric is to evaluate the efficiency of the explanation model in generating explanations for cyber-attacks. The metric aims to balance the need for quick and accessible explanations with the need for accurate and comprehensive explanations. It measures the time required for the explanation model to generate an explanation, with the time measured in units such as seconds. Local explanations, such as LIME [RSG16], provide insights into the model's decision-making process for each individual data entry in the dataset by analyzing the features that are most important for the model's decision for that specific data entry. The latency metric measures the time taken to generate a local explanation for each data entry in the dataset. The formula below computes the average time taken per instance over the dataset.

$$\text{Latency} = \frac{1}{N} \sum_{i=1}^{N} (T_{end} - T_{start}) \tag{3}$$

where N is the number of instances in the dataset, and T_{end} and T_{start} are the end and start times for generating the explanation for instance i.

For global explanations, we calculate the time taken to generate the explanation for the entire dataset, given by the formula: $\text{Latency} = T_{end} - T_{start}$

This metric measures the average time taken by the interface explainability model to generate explanations for cyber-attacks. A lower value of Latency indicates that the explanation model generates explanations more quickly, while a higher value of Latency indicates slower explanations.

4   Datasets and Implementation

Datasets. To evaluate the explainability of cyber-attacks in ML, we used three datasets created by the Cyber Security Research Group at the University of New South Wales [Boo+21,Kor+19,MS16]. These datasets include TonIoT [Boo+21], BoT-IoT [Kor+19], and UNSW-NB15 [MS16], and contain both normal traffic and various types of cyber-attacks with varying sizes and features.

Implementation. To implement explainability for cyber-attacks in ML, we utilize Jupyter Notebook running on the Larry server of HPE DL385 generation 10+. The server is equipped with two AMD EPYC 7552 48-Core Processors and 3 TB of RAM, providing sufficient computing power to perform the required analyses.

5   Evaluation

Comprehensibility of Output Performance. Comprehensibility of output performance is essential in building trust in ML models, as end-users are more likely to trust and accept the results when they can understand and interpret the output of the model. To ensure the performance output is easily comprehensible, we utilized a range of metrics to evaluate the performance of various multi-classification models, including CART, Random Forrest, XGBoost, and MLP, on the datasets mentioned in Sect. 4. These metrics comprised unbalanced accuracy, MCC, accuracy, precision, recall, F1 score, True Negative Rate (TNR), loss, and multi-classification fit and pred time. Our evaluation revealed that XGBoost achieved the highest accuracy in detecting cyber-attacks in the Ton-IoT and UNSW-NB15 datasets, while CART is the most accurate model for the BoT-IoT dataset. Additionally, CART exhibit the shortest prediction time among all the models evaluated, for all the datasets as shown in Table 2.

Interface Explainability Models. To increase trust in the model's predictions of XGBoost, we used four different interface explainability models: FI, PFI, LIME, and SHAP as shown in Fig. 1. The FI and PFI models provided feature importance scores that contributed to XGBoost's predictions, while the LIME model simplified individual predictions to highlight the most important factors in predicting "MITM" attacks and reveal insights into the model's decision-making process. In contrast, the SHAP model presented a summary plot of the most important features ranked in descending order based on their impact on the prediction for each attack class. These models provided different perspectives on XGBoost's behavior.

Table 2. Comprehensibility of output performance for CART, Random Forrest, XGBoost, and MLP models for different datasets.

Dataset	Ton-IoT (45 features) num of classes = 10				UNSW (45 features) num of classes = 10				BoT-IoT Nb15 (46 features) num of classes = 4			
Learning Models	Random Forest	XGBoost	CART	MLP	Random Forest	XGBoost	CART	MLP	Random Forest	XGBoost	CART	MLP
Precision	0.61369	**0.99991**	0.99981	0.65621	0.72632	**0.87941**	0.85395	0.50275	0.99989	0.99999	1	0.92654
Recall	0.77512	**0.99991**	0.99981	0.0484	0.73545	**0.87858**	0.84999	0.52941	0.99989	0.99999	1	0.84948
TNR	0.16053	**0.99991**	0.99798	0.99581	0	**0.02264**	0.01893	0	0.99987	0.99999	1	0.82715
Accuracy	0.77512	**0.99991**	0.99981	0.0484	0.73545	**0.87858**	0.84999	0.52941	0.99989	0.99999	1	0.84948
F1 score	0.68192	**0.99991**	0.99981	0.01446	0.66093	**0.87161**	0.85185	0.46165	0.99986	0.99999	1	0.86858
Balanced Accuracy	0.38676	**0.99984**	0.99973	0.10115	0.29817	**0.62515**	0.59959	0.23236	0.79865	0.99999	1	0.48904
Mcc	0.55888	**0.99991**	0.99967	0.02514	0.69429	**0.84705**	0.81028	0.41077	0.99953	0.99997	1	0.62287
loss	0.55888	**0.00008**	0.00018	0.95159	0.26454	**0.12141**	0.15001	0.41077	0.00011	0.000005	0	0.15051
Fit time sec	12.4332	483.81	**0.00008**	84.0137	0.25997	1081.45	**1.6835**	53.4782	26.661	104.101	**0.98176**	134.22
Pred time sec	0.93504	0.06234	**0.01611**	0.23403	0.41471	0.056119	**0.01842**	0.10782	0.73737	0.047371	**0.02597**	0.25997

Metrics for Evaluating Interface Explainability Models

Reliability. To evaluate the reliability of different interface explainability models, we first calculate the top5 ratio to determine the similarity of the five most important features in the Ton-IoT dataset, as shown in Fig. 2a. The results indicate that SHAP has a higher ratio compared to FI and PFI, indicating greater feature intersection among the most important features. We further analyze the reliability of these features by calculating the average reliability for each feature across all models, as illustrated in Fig. 2b. When comparing the reliability of different interface explainability models, we calculated the average difference between each model and the rest. The results show that SHAP has the smallest average difference of 0.02 compared to the other interface explainability models, indicating higher reliability. On the other hand, FI has an average difference of 0.116, PFI has an average difference of 0.134, and LIME has an average difference of 0.142 when compared to the other interface explainability models. These findings are depicted in Fig. 3.

Latency. To compare the latency of different interface explainability models, we present a 3D plot that shows the tradeoff latency, accuracy, and time performance. Figure 4 illustrates this tradeoff by showing the latency of the four interface explainability models, with respect to the accuracy and fit time for the four multi-classification models.

6   Discussion

Comprehensibility of Output Performance. The evaluation of the comprehensibility of output performance revealed that XGBoost can accurately detect a large proportion of actual attacks while minimizing false positives, which refer to non-attacks being wrongly classified as attacks. While XGBoost showed superior accuracy, CART was faster and achieved comparable accuracy to XGBoost. This highlights the significance of striking a balance between accuracy and time against cyber-attacks.

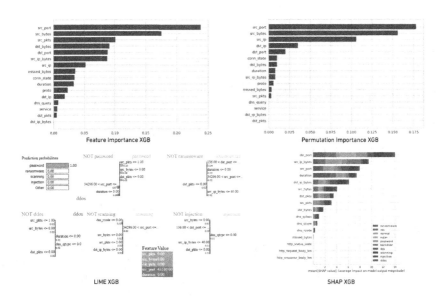

Fig. 1. Interface Explainability Models using XGBoost multi-classification model on Ton-IoT dataset.

Interface Explainability Models. The examination of various interface explainability models has provided distinct perspectives on how XGBoost predicts results. While FI and PFI models offer a global explanation of the overall model performance, they do not provide any insights into the classification of specific classes. On the other hand, LIME provides a local explanation of how the "MITM" class is classified for a particular instance, but not for the entire dataset. In contrast, SHAP provides an XGBoost summary plot that highlights the feature relevance scores. The visualization indicates that the feature "dst port", which is situated at a high level in the plot, resulted in the classification of "Ransomware" more frequently than the other class types. This demonstrates that the feature relevance scores and visualization provided by SHAP offer valuable insights into the model's predictions.

Metrics for Evaluating Interface Explainability Models

Reliability. Despite the variations in methodology and algorithms used by different interface explainability models, we can obtain similar important features when comparing them. This should provide users with confidence in the explainability model they choose. The top5Ratio metric shows that SHAP produces similar most common important features, even though it works differently to compute them. We further analyzed the difference in features between the different models and found that SHAP consistently performed better, indicating that we can rely on it for cybersecurity explanations.

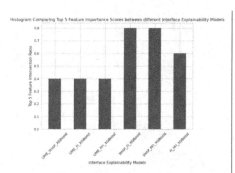 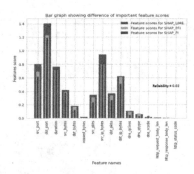

(a) Exploring the Top5Ratio for Common Features in Interface Explainability Models for XGBoost Multi-Classification Model

(b) Average Reliability of SHAP's Feature Scores in Comparison with LIME, FI, and PFI

Fig. 2. Interface Explainability Model Comparison for XGBoost Multi-Classification on Ton-IoT dataset: Top 5 Ratio and Average Reliability Analysis.

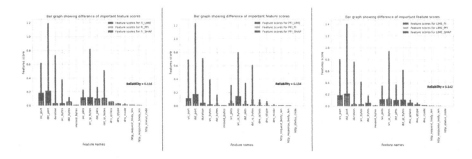

Fig. 3. Average Reliability Comparison of Feature Scores for different Interface Explainability Models.

Latency. Given the time-sensitive nature of cyberattacks, the tradeoff between latency, accuracy, and time performance is crucial for classifying and explaining attacks. While XGBoost has the best accuracy, its latency for detecting an attack is slower compared to other approaches. Similarly, SHAP has a slower latency for providing explanations compared to FI and LIME. It is essential to balance these factors to quickly and accurately classify and explain an attack, allowing incident responders to take appropriate actions in a timely manner.

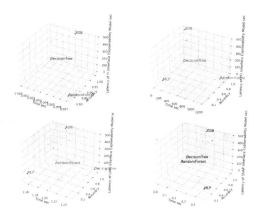

Fig. 4. Latency of different Interface Explainability Models using different multi-classification models on Ton dataset.

7   Conclusions and Perspectives

The reliability and latency metrics proposed in this paper serve as a strong foundation for evaluating interface explainability models in detecting cyber-attacks.

These metrics ensure transparency and trust by demonstrating consistency and similarity in feature scores across various models, and highlighting the tradeoff between accuracy, latency, and time performance. However, to comprehensively evaluate interface explainability models, additional metrics need to be developed in the data analysis process, such as stability when data changes, similarity across ML models with different parameters, and clarity for human interpretability. Moreover, we plan to enhance the data visualization and dashboard for our metrics and provide a more detailed methodology for the training and testing process to facilitate a better understanding of the results and make our research transparent and easily reproducible for other researchers.

Scientific Validation. This paper has benefited from the remarks of the following reviewers:
- Sofiane Lagraa, Fujitsu, Luxembourg
- Mohamed Lamine, University Lumière Lyon2, France
- Nabil El Kadhi, Vernewell Academy, UAE
The conference organisers wish to thank them for their highly appreciated effort and contribution.

References

[AI19a] HLEG AI. High-level expert group on artificial intelligence (2019)

[AI19b] Athey, S., Imbens, G.W.: Machine learning methods that economists should know about. Ann. Rev. Econ. **11**, 685–725 (2019)

[Arr+20] Arrieta, A.B., et al.: Explainable artificial intelligence (XAI): concepts, taxonomies, opportunities and challenges toward responsible AI. Inf. Fusion **58**, 82–115 (2020)

[Boo+21] Booij, T.M., Chiscop, I., Meeuwissen, E., Moustafa, N., den Hartog, F.T.H.: Ton_iot: the role of heterogeneity and the need for standardization of features and attack types in IoT network intrusion data sets. IEEE Internet Things J. **9**(1), 485–496 (2021)

[DK17]   Doshi-Velez, F., Kim, B.: Towards a rigorous science of interpretable machine learning. arXiv preprint arXiv:1702.08608 (2017)

[Fer+19] Fernandez, A., Herrera, F., Cordon, O., del Jesus, M.J., Marcelloni, F.: Evolutionary fuzzy systems for explainable artificial intelligence: why, when, what for, and where to? IEEE Comput. Intell. Mag. **14**(1), 69–81 (2019)

[Gui+18] Guidotti, R., Monreale, A., Ruggieri, S., Turini, F., Giannotti, F., Pedreschi, D.: A survey of methods for explaining black box models. ACM Comput. Surv. (CSUR) **51**(5), 1–42 (2018)

[HMZ21] Hooker, G., Mentch, L., Zhou, S.: Unrestricted permutation forces extrapolation: variable importance requires at least one more model, or there is no free variable importance. Stat. Comput. **31**, 1–16 (2021)

[HMKL18] Hoffman, R.R., Mueller, S.T., Klein, G., Litman, J.: Metrics for explainable AI: challenges and prospects. arXiv preprint arXiv:1812.04608 (2018)

[Kor+19] Koroniotis, N., Moustafa, N., Sitnikova, E., Turnbull, B.: Towards the development of realistic botnet dataset in the internet of things for network forensic analytics: Bot-IoT dataset. Futur. Gener. Comput. Syst. **100**, 779–796 (2019)

[LL17] Lundberg, S.M., Lee, S.-I.: A unified approach to interpreting model predictions. In: Advances in Neural Information Processing Systems, vol. 30 (2017)

[Mol20] Molnar, C.: Interpretable machine learning. Lulu. com (2020)

[Mor+21] Mora-Cantallops, M., Sánchez-Alonso, S., García-Barriocanal, E., Sicilia, M.-A.: Traceability for trustworthy AI: a review of models and tools. Big Data Cogn. Comput. **5**(2), 20 (2021)

[MS16] Moustafa, N., Slay, J.: The evaluation of network anomaly detection systems: statistical analysis of the unsw-nb15 data set and the comparison with the kdd99 data set. Inf. Secur. J. Global Perspect. **25**(1–3), 18–31 (2016)

[Mur+19] Murdoch, W.J., Singh, Kumbier, C.K., Abbasi-Asl, R., Yu, B.: Definitions, methods, and applications in interpretable machine learning. In: Proceedings of the National Academy of Sciences, vol. 116, no. 44, pp. 22071–22080 (2019)

[RSG16] Ribeiro, M.T., Singh, S., Guestrin, C.: "Why should i trust you?" explaining the predictions of any classifier. In: Proceedings of the 22nd ACM SIGKDD International Conference on Knowledge Discovery and Data Mining, pp. 1135–1144 (2016)

[Sov+22] Sovrano, F., Sapienza, S., Palmirani, M., Vitali, F.: Metrics, explainability and the European AI act proposal. Journal **5**(1), 126–138 (2022)

[Sri+22] Srivastava, G., et al.: Xai for cybersecurity: state of the art, challenges, open issues and future directions. arXiv preprint arXiv:2206.03585 (2022)

[SS20] Shah, Y., Sengupta, S.: A survey on classification of cyber-attacks on IoT and IIoT devices. In: 2020 11th IEEE Annual Ubiquitous Computing, Electronics & Mobile Communication Conference (UEMCON), pp. 0406–0413. IEEE (2020)

Education Computational Ecosystems

Machine Learning Model Applied to Higher Education

Cindy Belén Espinoza Aguirre[1,2(✉)]

[1] Departamento de TI, Universidad San Francisco de Quito, Av. Diego de Robles, Quito 170901, Ecuador
cespinozaa@usfq.edu.ec
[2] Computer Science and Engineering Department, Universidad Carlos III de Madrid, Avda Universidad 30, Leganes, 28911 Madrid, Spain

Abstract. Student desertion is one of the main social problems around the world. Consequently, to propose this issue, there are several studies under different circumstances or scenarios. For this reason, this research creates four datasets, which take the common variables of easy extraction to the academic process. These variables have been grouped under common characteristics such as general student profile information, admission process information, financial information, academic information, and academic performance information. Thus, the method used in this research is analytical, since it is intended to analyze each subset of data in order to identify the variables with the greatest impact on university dropout. As a result, have been identified the variables with impact on university dropout, For this, a neural network model has been implemented using Python and Keras. In conclusion, the research evidence that academic information is mostly related to college dropout related to university dropout, while admission, financial, and student profile information are not significant in detecting or predicting college dropout. However, with the data obtained, it has been shown that the prediction is not early but in many cases late, since the notes would have already been delivered to students. Therefore, future research is intended to identify the causes that originate academic problems.

Keywords: dropout · higher education · machine learning · data mining · predictive patterns

1 Introduction

The author uses four different datasets to determine the cause of school dropouts (either financial, academic performance, admission info, or information about the student) uses neural networks to understand school dropouts University desertion cannot be attributed to factors merely extrinsic to the student. For this reason, it is crucial to understand this problem holistically [1]. In this sense, one of the lines of research that address this problem is Science Education and

© The Author(s), under exclusive license to Springer Nature Switzerland AG 2023
P. Collet et al. (Eds.): CCE 2023, LNCS 13927, pp. 195–201, 2023.
https://doi.org/10.1007/978-3-031-44355-8_14

Technology. This problem has been investigated all over the world. Most dropout studies have as a priority to promote student development, leaving out of the analysis the innovation of student retention processes within universities [2,3].

However, today thanks to the application of information technology and the use of data science, we can explain and understand this problem more precisely. In addition, data mining is a powerful technology that can be best defined as the automated process of extracting useful knowledge and information including, patterns, and associations [4]. The main objective of that investigation has been applying neural networks to understand school dropout. Some of them have classified the domains of information for their analysis, such as the case of this research [5]. To mitigate student dropout, it is important to detect university dropouts as soon as possible. Additionally, the machine learning model has been trained with information from a random sample of students to belong to higher education. For this analysis, career changes are not considered. The information analyzed belongs to the students from the period 2008 to 2012.

Hence the structure of the paper is as follows: Section 1 introduction, Sect. 2 state of the question, Sect. 3 methodology, Sect. 4 information dataset, Sect. 5 machine learning techniques, Sect. 6 results, Sect. 7 conclusion, Sect. 8 future works, Sect. 9 discussion and finally references.

2   State of the Question

The university dropout problem can explain and understand this problem more precisely. From the application of information technology and the use of data science. So predictive analytics is the process of forecasting future courses of action by analyzing historical and current facts [6]. A student may be considered a dropout when he or she has not completed his or her academic credits or has dropped out. These studies present different databases or datasets therefore, by applying neural networks, it will be possible to identify the performance of large heterogeneous data sets. Among the studies analyzed are [1] where the K-Nearest-Neighbor algorithm was used to predict dropout in 0.91% taking academic and socioeconomic variables of the students. Also This analysis allows for establishing patterns of association between some variables such as institutional aspects, finding similarities and differences, as well as identifying relevant dropout factors in the population [7]. Also, the premise for reducing dropout rates is to understand the various factors associated with dropping out. The key to reducing dropout rates is to make use of these factors to screen out potential dropout students and take targeted retention measures before the dropout behavior happens [8]. Among the advantages of predictive analytics is forecasting future courses of action by analyzing current and historical events [9,10].

3 Methodology

To develop this research, the Cross Industry Standard Process (CRISP-DM) for Data Mining methodology was applied, whose purpose is to structure data analysis projects. This methodology has six phases for its construction. Therefore, the most relevant activities undertaken for this research are detailed below [11].

In the "Business Understanding" phase, the aim is to understand the problem to be addressed, its motivation as well as the relationship with the data sources and its relationship with the problem addressed, then in the "Data Preparation" phase, the aim is to address the quality of the data through a data dictionary, while in the "Modeling" phase, in order to understand the data model, Python, and Business Analytics tools were used, such as Power BI to work on the data model and Qlik Sense to generate graphics oriented to the visualization of information in an efficient manner. In the first dataset of students called "student" the information of the student file is stored, the second dataset called "admission" contains the information on the admission process, the third dataset called "note" contains the record of grades, the fourth dataset named "finance" contains the finance record and finally, the "academy" dataset contains the academic record information. Student information has a binary classification of two classes, the first being college dropouts and the second non-dropouts.

In the "Evaluation" phase centralized data, it is required to identify the information dataset and the common variables to the academic process, these variables will form part of the data subset. Once the data subset has been generated in the "Deployment" phase, the configuration of the neural network is carried out. However it is worth mentioning that when applying neural networks, the concept of the relu activation function is a transformation that activates a single node if the input is above a certain threshold, as long as the input has a value below zero, the output is zero. For the final layer, the sigmoid function has been used since it allows reducing extreme or outlier values in valid data without eliminating them. And finally, the loss function is used as binary cross entropy to quantify how close a given neural network is to its ideal during the training process.

4 Information Dataset

Unlike previous investigations, in this investigation, the variables that have a unique relationship with the dropout factor, represented by the data subset, have been classified. For this research, the following characteristics were used. The information (refer to Tables 1) For the construction of each data subset, the list of variables and the description of each one is detailed below. It is worth mentioning that these variables are common and applicable to any academic system. Below is an example of the structure of each data set (refer to Tables 3).

Table 1. Distribute each variable to the data subset to which it belongs

Dataset name	Variable's number	Data test	Data training	Sample
Admission,	35	525 - 30%	1222 - 70%	5 dataset
Economic information,	8	525 - 30%	1222 - 70%	5 dataset
Academic information	6	525 - 30%	1222 - 70%	5 dataset
Academic performance	9	525 - 30%	1222 - 70%	5 dataset
Profile information	16	525 - 30%	1222 - 70%	5 dataset

Note: [1]So 1747 students were used, 525 representing 30% of test data and 1222 for model training, representing 70% to generate the data subset.

Table 2. Detail Academic information

Data Set	Num	Variable name	Description
Academy	1	a1	Faculty
Academy	2	a2	Name of Career
Academy	3	a3	Name of Title
Academy	4	a4	Name of Area
Academy	5	a5	Subject Name
Academy	6	a6	Note obtained

Note: [1]The data set that has been used is listed: admission, economic information, academic information, academic performance, and profile information.

To generate each subset of information, the CRISP-DM methodology was applied, after having a centralized database, it was possible to generate unique variables per subset of information. Then the model has been validated with the information belonging to 1747 students who enrolled in the period from 2013 to 2017. Non-dropouts represent 51% of the sample and dropouts 50%. The student dataset contains a total of students who have entered the higher education system in Ecuador for the first time, and a cohort belonging to the 2008 period. The current academic offer consists of 52 undergraduate courses (Table 2).

5   Machine Learning Techniques

The predictive analytics model has been analyzed. In addition, the parameters used to create the neural network in Keras are: 7 layer sequential neural network has been generated, 50 epochs have been created to indicate the number of times all training data has passed through the neural network in the training process and finally the optimizer used is "Adam".

The sklearn package has been used for data preprocessing [12]. The preprocessing package provides several common utility functions and transformer classes to change the raw feature vectors into a representation that is more suitable for downstream estimators.

The data has been divided into batches of 7. Each batch-size partitions have been divide into mini-batches for passing over the network. In Keras, the batch size is the argument indicating the size of these batches to use in the fit() method in one training iteration. After Splitting the dataset have been classified into testing and training, in order to standardize the information, data preprocessing techniques were applied. Once the data set of information has been worked, the sequential-type neural network is generated.

6 Results

For each subset of data, we proceed to generate the model and obtain the result indicators. (refer to Tables 3).

Table 3. Prediction Results

Data Set	Accuracy	Loss
Admission	0.73	0.57
Economic information	0.72	0.56
Academic information	0.98	0.04
Academic performance	0.95	0.14
Profile information	0.55	0.71

Note: [1]The data set that has been used is listed: admission, economic information, academic information, academic performance, and profile information.

For example for admissions we have obtained around 55% prediction, however, when validating the prediction, I have found a minimum confidence level for the data set related to the admission process. Then we carried out the experiment with the note data or academic performance and obtained a precision above 0.95 and a loss of around 0.04 to 0.14. In other words, we can infer that one of the causes of school dropout is related to academic performance during student life. The accuracy of the economic dataset is 0.72 and the loss is 0.56. In addition, an acceptable prediction rate of 99% was used to find the dropouts. Also, an acceptable prediction rate was produced to find the dropouts. It has been made clear that academic performance and academic information are the two causes that have generated school dropouts. While the information of the student prior to entering higher education does not generate significant value when predicting dropout, since it reaches a 70% prediction, that is, it is not efficient. Therefore it is worth mentioning that the academic and academic performance reached high levels of accuracy, it is worth mentioning that this measure relates to the quality of the classifiers.

7 Conclusion

The behavior has been analyzed of factor influencing desertion. Is important to identify the degree of relationship each one has. Because a help us to generate a profile of the deserter student. The results obtained will help to generate early alerts, thus managing to generate permanence strategies and minimizing student dropout.

After carrying out the data analysis, it is concluded that the data related to academics have a greater impact on university dropout since the prediction level obtained for each data set reached a confidence level of over 90% confidence. While admission, economic information does not present a significant prediction.

Despite I have predicted dropout from the student's academic data, this research has served as the basis for generating alternatives that prevent dropout before it is in order. For this research, we were able to predict dropout once the student already had poor academic performance. Therefore, for the following investigations, methods or early warnings were developed at the academic level. Although it does not matter the admission, socioeconomic, or psychological condition of the student or the profile with which they entered, it does not show a clear trend or pattern that is recognized by the machine learning model to label the supervised data and show dropout possibilities.

8 Future Works

Establish a dropout profile considering the domains of information and the variables that have the greatest impact on university desertion. It is intended to analyze if this behavior persists only for those students who enter higher education for the first time. Collect more variables related to financial factors and school performance in order to generate a profile of the dropout.

9 Discussion

The metrics used to assess the level of prediction vary between 0 and 1. The higher, the better. Nevertheless, accuracy is a good measure when the classes of target variables in the data are nearly balanced. Hence the confusion matrix has been applied since we can describe the performance of a supervised Machine Learning model on test data, where the true values are unknown. In this sense, the metric that has been used to monitor the learning (and testing) process in the neural network is accuracy.

In this research, we were able to evaluate the level of prediction achieved by the data subset, in this way we can generate more emphasis on improving the institutional processes that generate the input data of the proposed neural network model.

It is intended to generate mechanisms that manage to determine the origin of the university desertion by taking as reference the academic information of the student. Since the objective is to act as early as possible.

- Shane Tutwiler, University of Rhode Island, USA
- Pedaste Margus, University of Tartu, Estonia
- Ying-Tien Wu, National Central University, Taiwan
- Pierre Collet, Strasbourg University, France

The conference organisers wish to thank them for their highly appreciated effort and contribution.

References

1. Escarria, A.S.: Deserción universitaria en colombia **3**(1), 50–60. Accessed 10 Mar 2023
2. Paura, L., Arhipova, I.: Cause analysis of students' dropout rate in higher education study program **109**, 1282–1286. https://doi.org/10.1016/j.sbspro.2013.12.625. Accessed 12 Mar 2023
3. Breier, M.: From 'financial considerations' to 'poverty': towards a reconceptualisation of the role of finances in higher education student drop out **60**(6), 657–670. https://doi.org/10.1007/s10734-010-9343-5. Accessed 12 Mar 2023
4. Abu-Oda, G.S., El-Halees, A.M.: Data mining in higher education: university student dropout case study **5**(1), 15–27. https://doi.org/10.5121/ijdkp.2015.5102. Accessed 12 Mar 2023
5. Heublein, U.: Student drop-out from German higher education institutions **49**(4), 497–513. https://doi.org/10.1111/ejed.12097. _eprint: https://onlinelibrary.wiley.com/doi/pdf/10.1111/ejed.12097. Accessed 12 Mar 2023
6. Rajni, J., Malaya, D.B.: Predictive analytics in a higher education context **17**(4), 24–33. https://doi.org/10.1109/MITP.2015.68. Conference Name: IT Professional
7. Villarreal, J.O.G., Gómez, L.R.F., Pineda-Ríos, W.: Estimación de las principales causas de la deserción universitaria mediante el uso de técnicas de machine learning **12**(2), 293–311. Accessed 10 Mar 2023
8. Tan, M., Shao, P.: Prediction of student dropout in e-learning program through the use of machine learning method **10**(1), 11. https://doi.org/10.3991/ijet.v10i1.4189. Accessed 12 Mar 2023
9. Ekowo, M., Palmer, I.: Predictive analytics in higher education (2017)
10. Ramos, J.L.C., Rodrigues, R.L., Silva, J.C.S., Oliveira, P.L.S.D.: CRISP-EDM: uma proposta de adaptação do modelo CRISP-DM para mineração de dados educacionais. In: Anais do Simpósio Brasileiro de Informática na Educação, pp. 1092–1101. SBC. https://doi.org/10.5753/cbie.sbie.2020.1092. ISSN: 0000-0000. https://sol.sbc.org.br/index.php/sbie/article/view/12865. Accessed 1 Apr 2023
11. Costa, A.G., Mattos, J.C.B., Primo, T.T., Cechinel, C., Muñoz, R.: Model for prediction of student dropout in a computer science course. In: 2021 XVI Latin American Conference on Learning Technologies (LACLO), pp. 137–143. https://doi.org/10.1109/LACLO54177.2021.00020
12. 6.3. Preprocessing Data. https://scikit-learn/stable/modules/preprocessing.html. Accessed 5 Apr 2023

Satellite and Climate Ecosystems

Modeling El Niño and La Niña Events Using Evolutionary Algorithms

Ulviya Abdulkarimova[1]([⊠])(iD) and Rodrigo Abarca-del-Rio[2](iD)

[1] French-Azerbaijani University, Baku, Azerbaijan
ulviya.abdulkarimova@ufaz.az
[2] University of Concepción, Concepción, Chile

Abstract. Predicting climate variability is challenging. The Pacific Ocean's El Niño-Southern Oscillation (ENSO) affects global climate variability and its complexity. Understanding and mitigating global climate variability requires ENSO episode modeling. Evolutionary Algorithms (EA) are used here to create a library of simple equations to characterize El Niño and La Niña events. The results show that most El Niño events can accurately be modeled with acceptable stability, with the coefficient of determination (R^2) between 0.72 and 0.99 for weak events, 0.84 and 0.98 for moderate events, 0.86 and 0.99 for strong events, and 0.91 and 0.98 for very strong events. For the La Niña events, R^2 was found to be in the range 0.75–0.98 for weak events, 0.74–0.99 for moderate events, and 0.86–0.98 for strong events. The ANOVA test's F-value showed a good model fit with p-values below 0.05 for all events. The study developed a library-database of equations to better understand ENSO events, a methodology that can be applied to other time series or fields.

Keywords: El Niño · La Niña · genetic programming · genetic algorithm · evolutionary algorithm

1 Introduction

The equatorial central Pacific experiences El Niño-Southern Oscillation (ENSO). ENSO atmospheric circulation changes can propagate and irradiate worldwide due to the Pacific Ocean's extent [13,24]. Thus, it drives climate variability [25]. El Niño in a positive ENSO phase causes sea surface temperatures in the eastern Pacific to rise above average and deep waters to upwell less. La Niña has a colder eastern Pacific and more upwelling [6,21,30].

ENSO events occur irregularly and because of their non-linearity [8] are unpredictable [29], and precisely because of its non-linear teleconnections and feedback mechanisms make it hard to predict its events' timing, strength, and evolution [5,7]. ENSO events predictability has been reviewed over the recent years [27,28]. New advances in artificial intelligence have piqued researchers' interest in developing new climate system applications and ENSO prediction methods. Few machine learning methods, including evolutionary algorithms [12,31], have been used to forecast El Niño events [14,22,23]. Other methods include extreme learning machine (ELM) [20] and deep learning [16,26,30].

P. Collet et al. (Eds.): CCE 2023, LNCS 13927, pp. 205–217, 2023.
https://doi.org/10.1007/978-3-031-44355-8_15

This study uses evolutionary methods to model El Niño and La Niña events, according to the most common diversification given its strengths; weak, moderate, strong, and very strong [9]. We intend to create an event equation database to better predict any event's evolution. The equation should be simple, the event parameters interchangeable, such as by changing some parameters from a moderate to a strong event. Thus, instead of deep learning algorithms or other machine learning classifiers, evolutionary algorithms like genetic programming (GP) [18] and genetic algorithm (GA) [15,17] are used.

Genetic Programming (GP) was introduced by Cramer in 1985, and developed by Koza in 1992 [18]. Engineering, medicine, economics, and other fields have used GP successfully. Many applications have yielded human-competitive results [19]. GP is used as a data-fitting method in some applications, like other machine learning methods. GP has an advantage over other machine learning methods because it can also return an equation to describe the mathematical relationship between the independent and dependent variables. It is based on Darwin's theory of natural selection and underpins evolutionary computation, which uses natural evolution terminology. It states that individuals poorly adapted to their environment are less likely to reproduce and pass on their genes. Evolutionary algorithms use this concept to optimize solutions to difficult problems [19].

Since the concept of evolutionary computation is derived from Darwin's theory of natural selection, it uses terminology from natural evolution. It claims that individuals poorly adapted to their environment are less likely to reproduce and pass their genes to the next generation. This concept is being used by evolutionary algorithms for the optimization of solutions to difficult problems [19]. Evolutionary algorithms require individual representation. GAs encode individuals with bit strings or real values. GP uses binary trees to represent the individuals. The search space relies on accurate representations of individuals. GP finds the optimal values for minimizing or maximizing the fitness functions in order to determine the equations that best fit the observed data. The goal of GA, in contrast, is to optimize the variables in a given equation.

2   Data and Methodology

2.1   Data

The only data used in this study is a so-called El Niño index, a time series that allows researchers to trace the evolution of ENSO, the El Niño-Southern Oscillation climate pattern evolution, and whether it is warmer or cooler than average, stronger or weaker [2]. The NOAA Climate Prediction Center's Oceanic Nino Index (ONI) dataset is the most prominent [2]. The running 3-month mean Sea Surface Temperature (SST) anomaly for the Nino 3.4 region in the Pacific Ocean is [5° South 5° North] and [170° West 120° West] [2]. SST anomalies are calculated by subtracting SST climatology from a monthly SST composite [3].

This ONI time series dataset spans 1950-present (Fig. 1). Index values above +0.5 indicate El Niño. La Niña indicates −0.5 or less. El Niño events are identified in at least five consecutive 3-month periods at or above 0.5 °C anomaly,

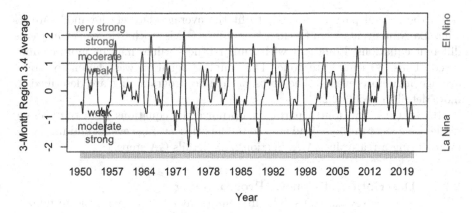

Fig. 1. Oceanic Nino Index (ONI) - 1950-present

while La Niña events are identified at or below 0.5 °C anomaly. After three consecutive 3-month periods of anomalies equaling or exceeding the threshold, these events can be classified as weak, moderate, strong, or very strong. This period saw 26 El Niños and 24 La Niñas.

The threshold for weak El Niño is 0.5–0.9, moderate El Niño is 1.0–1.4, strong El Niño is 1.5–1.9, and very strong El Niño is equal to or greater than 2.0. The threshold for weak La Niña is −0.5 to −0.9, moderate La Niña is −1.0 to −1.4, and for strong La Niña is −1.5 and below.

A typical El Niño and La Niña episode last 9–12 months. Both of them typically begin to develop during the spring months (March-June), peaking during the late autumn or winter (November-February), and weakening during the spring or early summer (March-June) [1].

2.2 Methodology

This section describes the El Niño/La Niña modeling approach. Section 2.2.1 describes this paper's main methodology. Genetic programming and genetic algorithm are described in Sects. 2.2.2 and 2.2.3. Section 2.2.4 discusses GP and GA models. Section 2.2.5 covers evolutionary algorithm software and hardware. Section 2.3 discusses our validation statistics.

2.2.1 Description of the Main Methodology

El Niño and La Niña modeling involves four steps. The first part averaged each El Niño/La Niña event. We extracted 1.5-year data 12 months before and 6 months after the peak for each event type. Next, each event's 1.5-year monthly data was averaged.

In the second part we use GP to fit the average datasets for moderate El Niño/La Niña events from the first step. Since GP is stochastic, each run yields different equations. Equations with similar fitness values may be more complicated. Thus, 30 runs were done. The simplest equation was chosen to model average moderate events. The steps of genetic programming are described in more detail in Sect. 2.2.2.

In the third and fourth parts, we optimize the equations from the average moderate events in the second step to fit the other average events and finally all events using a real-valued GA. Section 2.2.3 details GA steps.

2.2.2 Description of Genetic Programming

GP process has several steps. The first steps involve specifying the terminals, including independent variables and random constants, primitive functions, and fitness function. These instructions assemble potential solutions. Population size, crossover and mutation probabilities, selection pressure, minimum and maximum tree depth, and termination criterion must also be defined to control the run.

This study used GP to randomly generate the initial population using the operators "+," "−," "*," and the "sin" function. Division operator was not included to avoid the complexity of the equation. The problem required only "sin" from elementary functions. The individuals in the population, also referred to as potential solutions, are functions represented by trees. The individuals are evaluated by determining their fitness to the given data. The mean squared error (MSE) was used to evaluate individuals:

$$MSE = \frac{\sum_{i=1}^{n}(x_E - x_O)^2}{n} \tag{1}$$

with x_E the expected value, x_O is the observed value, and n is the sample size.

After evaluation, the parents undergo crossover and mutation operations. This study selects parents using the n-ary tournament [11]. Once the children are created, their fitness values are determined. Tournament selection reduces the parent-child population to its initial size. The steps are repeated until the termination condition is reached.

The run parameters of GP used in this study are as follows: population and offspring size: 50000, number of generations: 500, mutation probability: 0.1, crossover probability: 1, initialization: ramped half-half, maximum tree depth: 6.

2.2.3 Description of Genetic Algorithm

GA differs from GP mainly due to the representation of the individuals. A real-valued GA was used in this study and the individuals are represented by floating points. The steps of GA are explained as follows: GA includes successive steps. Individual representation comes first, followed by individual initialization and evaluation, selection for crossover, mutation, and population reduction. The main run parameters of the algorithm and selection are explained further below.

In the individual representation step, the GA method encodes the parameters of the equation into strings. Each string is referred to as a "chromosome" and is represented by a IEEE754 single precision floating point number, referred to as a "gene".

In the individual initialization step, first, a random population is generated based on the given interval for each parameter. The interval for each variable is chosen using the trial-and-error method. Each individual in the population is the potential solution to the problem. For example, if the equation has four parameters a, b, c, and d to optimize, the individual is represented by a vector of real values $\{a_i, b_i, c_i, d_i\}$, where i represents the individual number.

For evaluating the individuals in GA, the root mean squared error (RMSE) was used:

$$RMSE = \sqrt{\frac{\sum_{i=1}^{n}(x_E - x_O)^2}{n}} \tag{2}$$

where x_E is the expected value, x_O is the observed value, and n is the sample size. Once the individuals are evaluated, they are called parents. Parents are selected to go under crossover with replacement. A parent can be chosen several times at this step. Tournament selection method is used for this purpose.

The crossover step uses a single-point crossover. One child is created from two parents. For example, if the genome of one parent is $\{0.80, 0.20, 0.50, 0.25\}$ and the other parent is $\{0.41, 0.18, 0.35, 0.90\}$, the created child may be either $\{0.80, 0.20, 0.35, 0.90\}$ or $\{0.41, 0.18, 0.50, 0.25\}$ if the crossover point was selected to be in the middle.

An individual is selected for mutation with 0.2 probability, and within each individual, the genes are mutated with 0.6 probability by adding a random uniform value. Manually tuning the added values yields the best result.

Finally, in the population reduction step, the tournament selection method is used to reduce the population size to its original size. Population reduction is done without replacement. The worst of a group is eliminated. The process is repeated until the desired population size is reached.

The algorithm's main parameters are: number of generations: 1000, population and offspring size: 131072, mutation probability: 0.2, crossover probability: 1, selection operator: Tournament 10, reduce parents operator: Tournament 2. This study uses a large population to better explore the search space.

2.2.4   GP and GA Models

The equations obtained by GP and chosen out of several equations to describe average moderate El Niño and La Niña events are in the following general forms, respectively:

$$y = A + Bx + C\sin(D(x + E)^2) \tag{3}$$

$$y = Ax^2 \cdot \sin(Bx^2) + C + sin(Dx^2) \tag{4}$$

GA was used to find the best parameters for each event in Eqs. (3) and (4). The first step is to determine which parameters can be kept constant when moving from average moderate events to weak, strong, and very strong events.

We fixed parameters based on the curves' shape and the equation's nature and tested until the fitness values were optimal.

The GA method lets one fix some equation parameters and vary others to determine how different parameters affect event strengths. Thus, a simple equation with a feasible parameter's transition was found to describe the average weak, moderate, strong, and very strong events. The lowest fitness values determined the best equations. To demonstrate stability, the GA algorithm was run 30 times per average event.

2.2.5 GPU Parallelization

This study used EASEA evolutionary computing [10]. EASEA (EAsy Specification of Evolutionary Algorithms) is a software platform for evolutionary algorithms that automatically parallelizes EAs on parallel architectures ranging from a single GPU-equipped machine to a cluster or several GPU clusters. Non-computer scientists can solve difficult problems with artificial evolution. It generates evolutionary algorithms from problem descriptions. This C-like specification includes genetic operators (crossover, mutation, initialization, and evaluation) and genome structure code. Thus, thanks to the EASEA platform results presented in this paper are reproducible.

The runs were done on PARSEC (PARallel System for Evolutionary Computing) machines [4] that is made of 26 machines hosting two NVIDIA RTX 2080Ti 4352-core GPU cards, meaning that on top of its 8 CPU cores, each machine has access to 8704 GPU cores.

2.3 Statistics

In addition to fitness evaluation in GP and GA, each model was validated through an analysis of variance (ANOVA) test and the following statistics:

The coefficient of determination:

$$R^2 = \frac{\sum_{i=1}^{n}(Y_i - \bar{X})^2}{\sum_{i=1}^{n}(X_i - \bar{X})^2} \tag{5}$$

The standardized standard deviation:

$$\sigma_e = 1 - \sqrt{\frac{\sum_{i=1}^{n}(Y_i - \bar{Y})^2}{\sum_{i=1}^{n}(X_i - \bar{X})^2}} \tag{6}$$

where X and Y are observed and predicted values, respectively.

3   Results and Discussion

3.1   El Niño Results

This section provides the results of the evolutionary algorithm for the El Niño events.

Table 1 shows GP's moderate El Niño equation and GA's weak, strong, and very strong equations. The results show that equations are obtained for the average WE, SE, and VSE events by altering the parameters of the equation derived from the average ME. Figures 2 and 3 show the average event results graphically.

Table 1. The equations for average El Niño events

Average ME	$y = -0.5298154 + 0.7270191x + \sin(1.71968x^2)$
Average WE	$y = -0.529815 + 0.791096x + 0.527520 \sin(1.787091x^2)$
Average SE	$y = -0.529815 + 1.305837x + 1.062371 \sin(1.925856x^2)$
Average VSE	$y = -0.347898 + 1.309794x + 1.361704 \sin(1.719680x^2)$

Table 2 shows the average, best and worst results of the calibrated model for the weak, moderate, strong and very strong events.

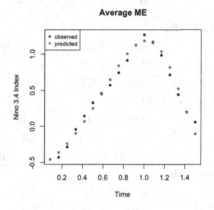

Fig. 2. Average moderate El Niño event predicted by GP

The result for the average moderate event indicates great model performance with R^2 value of 0.98, standardized standard deviation (σ_e) of -0.0269 and a p-value less than 0.05 from the ANOVA test. The results for different moderate events were also great. The worst result was observed to be for the 1994–1995 event, with R^2 of 0.84, σ_e of -0.6382. The best result was for the 1963–64 event, with R^2 of 0.98, σ_e of 0.0144. p-values for all events are less than 0.05, indicating a good fit of the model.

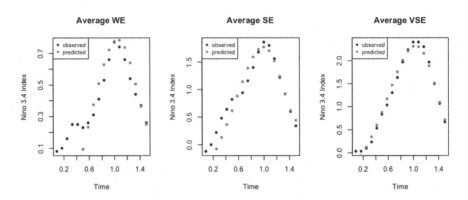

Fig. 3. Average El Niño events predicted by GA

Table 2. Statistical summary of the GA model for all El Niño events over 1.5 year period

Events \ Statistics	R^2	F-value	p-value	σ_e
El Niño				
Weak events (WE)				
average	0.8648	102.3	2.34E−08	0.0420
1969–70	0.7215	41.44	8.21E−06	0.1506
1976–77	0.985	1052	5.02E−16	0.0075
Moderate events (ME)				
average	0.9819	870	2.24E−15	−0.0269
1963–64	0.9798	776.4	5.47E−15	0.0144
1994–95	0.8431	86	7.76E−08	−0.6382
Strong events (SE)				
average	0.9493	299.7	8.74E−12	−0.1798
1965–66	0.988	1318	<2.2e−16	0.0060
1987–88	0.4703	14.21	0.001679	0.3142
Very strong events (VSE)				
average	0.9833	1.19E−15	0.1136	0.0083
1982–83	0.9153	5.39E−10	0.2386	−0.1285
1997–98	0.9845	6.64E−16	0.1341	0.1624

For average weak events, R^2 is 0.86, indicating good model performance. The model fits well with a p-value of less than 0.05 from the ANOVA, σ_e is 0.0420. The results for the different weak events were also good. The worst result was observed for the 1969–70 event, with R^2 value of 0.72, σ_e of 0.1506. The best result was observed for the 1976–77 event, with R^2 of 0.99, σ_e of 0.0075. p-values for all events are less than 0.05, indicating a good fit of the model.

For average strong and very strong events, R^2 shows a great model performance with values greater than 0.95. The F-value from the ANOVA shows a great fit of the models with a p-value less than 0.05. The σ_e is found to be -0.1798 and 0.0083 respectively. For strong events, the fit for 1987–88 was the worst, with R^2 value of 0.47, σ_e of 0.3142. The 1965–66 event was best described by the model with R^2 of 0.99, σ_e of 0.0060. The models fit very strong events well with R^2 values greater than 0.9, p-value < 0.05. The 1997–98 event was best described by the model with R^2 of 0.98, σ_e of 0.1624. The 1982–83 event result was slightly weaker than others with R^2 of 0.92, σ_e of -0.1285.

Overall, the results indicate a great fit of the models for most events. Very strong events had the highest goodness of fit values of all average events.

3.2   La Niña Results

This section provides the results of the evolutionary algorithm for the La Niña events.

Table 3 shows GP and GA equations for average moderate events and weak and strong La Niña events, respectively. Figure 4 provides a visual illustration of the results. As can be seen from the figures, an adequate fit is obtained by the average models.

Table 3. The equations for average La Niña events

Average WE	$y = -0.325334x^2 \sin(1.847927x^2) + 0.139189 - \sin(0.533342x^2)$
Average ME	$y = 0.157304920393981x^2 \sin(4x^2) - 0.07589 + \sin(x^2)$
Average SE	$y = -1.973693x^2 \sin(1.226646x^2) + 0.660145 - \sin(2.656697x^2)$

Table 4 shows the average, worst and best La Niña events' calibrated model results. The results indicate good model performance for the average weak, moderate, and strong La Niña events with R^2 values above 0.95, p-values from ANOVA below 0.05, and standardized standard deviation values $|\sigma_e| < 0.03$.

For weak events, the worst result was found to be for the 2008–09 event, with R^2 value 0.81, σ_e of 0.0288. The model described the 1983–84 event the best with the highest R^2 value, σ_e of 0.0381. The F-value also shows a good fit of the models with a p-value less than 0.05.

For moderate events, the model described the 1955–56 event the worst with R^2 of 0.74, σ_e of 0.1424. The 2020–21 event was best described by the model with R^2 of 0.98 and σ_e of 0.0045. The F-value also shows a good fit of the models with a p-value less than 0.05.

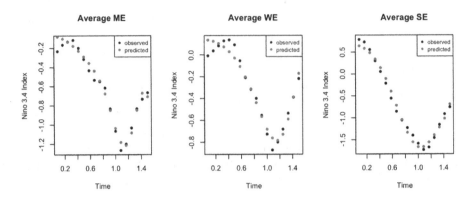

Fig. 4. Average La Niña results

Table 4. Statistical summary of the GA model for all La Niña events over 1.5 year period

La Niña				
Events ⟍ Statistics	R^2	F-value	p-value	σ_e
Weak events (WE)				
average	0.9575	360.8	2.11E−12	0.0288
1983–84	0.9831	931.6	1.31E−15	0.0381
2008–09	0.8009	64.34	5.36E−07	0.2077
Moderate events (ME)				
average	0.9752	630.2	2.80E−14	−0.0256
1955–56	0.7379	45.04	5.00E−06	0.1424
2020–21	0.987	1214	<2.2e−16	0.0045
Strong events (SE)				
average	0.9844	1007	7.06E−16	0.0178
1973–74	0.8633	101.1	2.55E−08	0.1804
1975–76	0.9762	655.2	2.07E−14	0.0125

The model fits all strong events well, with R^2 greater than 0.85. The model described the 1973–74 event the worst with R^2 of 0.86, σ_e of 0.1804. The event for the year 1975–76 was best described by the model with R^2 of 0.98 and σ_e of 0.0125. The F-value also shows a good fit of the models with a p-value less than 0.05.

Overall, the results indicate a good fit of the models for the El Niño and La Niña events. The variability of the results are also studied since the evolutionary algorithms are stochastic. The average best fitness value for the average moderate

El Niño event over 30 GP runs is found to be 0.2112 with a standard deviation of 0.0376. For the average moderate La Niña events, the average best fitness value over 30 GP runs is 0.2736 with a standard deviation of 0.0282. The variability of the results is slightly lower for La Niña case. However, the average best fitness values of the El Niño case are lower than those of La Niña. The variability in the results is acceptable, indicating the stability of the results.

4 Conclusion

This research aimed to outline a methodology for identifying simple models to represent ENSO events using evolutionary algorithms. The results demonstrated that the models found could adequately represent the different kind of occurrences based on 1.5-year (18 months) time series data.

Concerning El Niño, the models for weak, moderate, and strong events had varying levels of success. Weak events had slightly weaker results. Moderate events were well described by the models, with some events having slightly weaker results. The fit was unsatisfactory for some strong events. All very strong events were modeled very well, with high R^2 values and low standardized standard deviation values.

Regarding La Niña, overall, the models were stable and showed acceptable variability. For weak events, the results showed a good fit for most cases, with some events having slightly weaker results than others. The model weakly described some moderate events, but overall, the fit was satisfactory. The model described all the strong events well. Thus, results showed that the models for the La Niña events had better statistical characteristics than those for the El Niño events. Overall, all the models were stable with acceptable variability.

In light of these findings, a library-database of equations has been developed, which can be utilized to better comprehend the evolution of the climatic phenomena being discussed here. This work focused on 1.5-year times series data for El Niño and La Niña 3.4 anomalies. Future works will encompass different flavors and lengthier time series or fields.

Scientific Validation

This paper has benefited from the remarks of the following reviewers:

- Chaitanay Pande, IITM Pune, India
- Kanak Moharir, Banasthali Vidyapeeth University, India
- Francisco Alvial, Universidad de la Frontera, Chile

The conference organisers wish to thank them for their highly appreciated effort and contribution.

References

1. El Niño and La Niña. https://www.unocha.org/fr/themes/el-nino/el-nino-and-la-nina
2. El Niño and La Niña years and intensities. https://ggweather.com/enso/oni.htm

3. Ocean temperature outlooks. http://www.bom.gov.au/oceanography/oceantemp/sst-outlook-skill.shtml
4. Abdulkarimova, U., Leonteva, A., Jeannin-Girardon, A., Collet, P.: The PARSEC machine: a non-Newtonian supra-linear supercomputer. Azerbaijan J. High Perform. Comput. **2**, 122–140 (2019). https://doi.org/10.32010/26166127.2019.2.2.122.140
5. Alexandrov, D., Bashkirtseva, I., Ryashko, L.: How random noise induces large-amplitude oscillations in an El Niño model. Physica D **440**, 133468 (2022). https://doi.org/10.1016/j.physd.2022.133468. https://www.sciencedirect.com/science/article/pii/S0167278922001890
6. Ashok, K., Yamagata, T.: The El Niño with a difference. Nature **461**(7263), 481–484 (2009)
7. Astudillo, H., Abarca-del Rio, R., Borotto, F.: Long-term potential nonlinear predictability of El Niño-La Niña events. Clim. Dyn. **49** (2017). https://doi.org/10.1007/s00382-016-3330-1
8. Astudillo, H.F., Borotto, F.A., Abarca-del Rio, R.: Embedding reconstruction methodology for short time series - application to large El Niño events. Nonlinear Processes Geophys. **17**(6), 753–764 (2010). https://doi.org/10.5194/npg-17-753-2010. https://npg.copernicus.org/articles/17/753/2010/
9. Carreric, A.: ENSO diversity and global warming. Ph.D. thesis, Université de Toulouse (2019)
10. Schoenauer, M., et al. (eds.): PPSN 2000. LNCS, vol. 1917. Springer, Heidelberg (2000). https://doi.org/10.1007/3-540-45356-3
11. Collet, P., Rennard, J.P.: Stochastic optimization algorithms. In: Handbook of Research on Nature Inspired Computing for Economics and Management (2007)
12. De Falco, I., Della Cioppa, A., Tarantino, E.: A genetic programming system for time series prediction and its application to El Niño forecast. In: Hoffmann, F., Köppen, M., Klawonn, F., Roy, R. (eds.) Soft Computing: Methodologies and Applications, pp. 151–162. Springer, Heidelberg (2005). https://doi.org/10.1007/3-540-32400-3_12
13. Diaz, H.F., Hoerling, M.P., Eischeid, J.K.: ENSO variability, teleconnections and climate change. Int. J. Climatol. **21**(15), 1845–1862 (2001). https://doi.org/10.1002/joc.631. https://rmets.onlinelibrary.wiley.com/doi/abs/10.1002/joc.631
14. Dijkstra, H.A., Petersik, P., Hernández-García, E., López, C.: The application of machine learning techniques to improve El Niño prediction skill. Frontiers Phys. (2019)
15. Goldberg, D.: Genetic Algorithms in Search, Optimization and Machine Learning. Addison-Wesley (1989)
16. He, D., Lin, P., Liu, H., Ding, L., Jiang, J.: DLENSO: a deep learning ENSO forecasting model, pp. 12–23 (2019). https://doi.org/10.1007/978-3-030-29911-8_2
17. Holland, J.H.: Adaptation in Natural and Artificial Systems. MIT Press, Cambridge (1992)
18. Koza, J.R.: Genetic Programming: On the Programming of Computers by Means of Natural Evolution. MIT Press, Massachusetts (1992)
19. Koza, J.R., al.: Genetic Programming IV: Routine Human-Competitive Machine Intelligence. Kluwer Academic Publishers (2003)
20. Lima, A.R., Cannon, A.J., Hsieh, W.W.: Nonlinear regression in environmental sciences using extreme learning machines: a comparative evaluation. Environ. Model. Softw. **73**, 175–188 (2015). https://doi.org/10.1016/j.envsoft.2015.08.002
21. McPhaden, M.J., Zebiak, S.E., Glantz, M.H.: ENSO as an integrating concept in earth science. Science **314**(5806), 1740–1745 (2006)

22. Nooteboom, P.D., Feng, Q.Y., López, C., Hernández-García, E., Dijkstra, H.A.: Using network theory and machine learning to predict El Niño. Earth Syst. Dyn. **9**(3), 969–983 (2018)

23. Pal, M., Maity, R., Ratnam, J.V., Nonaka, M., Behera, S.: Long-lead prediction of ENSO Modoki Index using machine learning algorithms. Sci. Rep. **10**, 365 (2020). https://doi.org/10.1038/s41598-019-57183-3

24. del Rio, R.A., Gambis, D., Salstein, D.: Interdecadal oscillations in atmospheric angular momentum variations. J. Geodetic Sci. **2**(1), 42–52 (2012). https://doi.org/10.2478/v10156-011-0025-8

25. Ruzmaikin, A.: Climate patterns: origin and forcing. Am. J. Clim. Change **10**, 204–236 (2021). https://doi.org/10.4236/ajcc.2021.102010

26. Saha, M., Nanjundiah, R.: Prediction of ENSO and EQUINOO indices during June to September using deep learning method. Meteorol. Appl. **27** (2019). https://doi.org/10.1002/met.1826

27. Sharmila, S., Hendon, H., Alves, O., Weisheimer, A., Balmaseda, M.: Contrasting El Niño-la Niña predictability and prediction skill in 2-year reforecasts of the twentieth century. J. Clim. **36**(5), 1269–1285 (2023). https://doi.org/10.1175/JCLI-D-22-0028.1. https://journals.ametsoc.org/view/journals/clim/36/5/JCLI-D-22-0028.1.xml

28. Tang, Y., et al.: Progress in ENSO prediction and predictability study. Natl. Sci. Rev. **5**(6), 826–839 (2018)

29. Timmermann, A., et al.: El Niño-southern oscillation complexity. Nature **559**(7715), 535–545 (2018)

30. Wang, G.G., Cheng, H., Zhang, Y., Yu, H.: ENSO analysis and prediction using deep learning: a review. Neurocomputing (2022)

31. Álvarez, A., Vélez, P., Orfila, A., Vizoso, G., Tintoré, J.: Evolutionary computation for climate and ocean forecasting: "El Niño forecasting". In: Fiemming, N., et al. (eds.) Opertional Oceanography, Elsevier Oceanography Series, vol. 66, pp. 489–494. Elsevier (2002). https://doi.org/10.1016/S0422-9894(02)80055-1. https://www.sciencedirect.com/science/article/pii/S0422989402800551

Geosphere Computational Ecosystems

Estimation of Seismic Phase Delays Using Evolutionary Algorithms

Ulviya Abdulkarimova[1,2(✉)], Franck Latallerie[3], Leyla Gasimova[1], and Alessia Maggi[3]

[1] French-Azerbaijani University (UFAZ), Baku, Azerbaijan
[2] Université de Strasbourg/CNRS, ICUBE, UMR7357 Strasbourg, France
`ulviya.abdulkarimova@ufaz.az`
[3] Université de Strasbourg/CNRS, Institut Terre et Environement de Strasbourg, UMR6073 Strasbourg, France

Abstract. In modern seismology, a comparison between the synthetic seismogram generated using a synthetic model of the Earth and the observed seismogram helps in understanding the structure of the Earth and the difference between the actual structure of the planet and the synthetic structure. The phase delay between synthetic and observed seismograms is one of the sources of such information. The traditional method of calculating phase delay includes translating the seismogram from the time domain to the frequency domain using Discrete Fourier Transform. This research aims to develop a method to find phase delays using Evolutionary Algorithms. We show that phase delays can be estimated using Genetic Algorithm with comparable or better accuracy than Discrete Fourier Transform. It is more flexible, allowing for example to add prior information. This is particularly useful also to avoid the so-called cycle-skip effects (an ambiguity of $\pm 2\pi$ in the recovered phase-delay), a significant drawback with Discrete Fourier Transform methods.

Keywords: Phase delay · Fourier Transform · Genetic Algorithm · Genetic Programming

1 Introduction

Observations such as seismicity and volcanism indicate that the Earth is a dynamic system [10,21,40]. Understanding the Earth's dynamics requires observations of its interior [8,22,26,29]. Seismologists extract the information collected by the seismic waves as they travel through the Earth and derive physics-based equations relating this information to the Earth's structure [9,19,28,38,44,51]. From the measurements, seismologists build models of the Earth's interior using sophisticated inverse methods [3–5,37,42,47,50].

Usually a reference model of the Earth (for example the PREM model from [18]) is used to generate predicted seismograms from which the discrepancy with the observed seismograms is measured. A physics-based relation is then inverted to produce a model of the Earth expressed as perturbations with respect to the reference model. The quality of the Earth's model thus obtained depends on the quality of the measurements used to build it.

In surface-wave tomography, seismologists often use the phase delay between the predicted and observed seismograms to map the velocity of waves within the first few hundred kilometers depth [16,24,31,33,34,39]. One of the conventional ways of calculating phase delay in signal processing is using Discrete Fourier Transform (DFT) to translate the signal from time domain to the frequency domain. The Discrete Fourier Transform is usually calculated with the Fast Fourier Transform (FFT) algorithm. This paper proposes to apply a real-valued Genetic Algorithm to seismic data in order to find the phase difference between two seismograms and compare with the one obtained by Discrete Fourier Transform.

2   Data and Methodology

2.1   Seismograms and Phase Delay

Since the Earth is a finite body, its vibrations can be decomposed into a sum of particular oscillations with each a specific amplitude and frequency: the normal modes [15]. From a reference model of the radial distribution of the elastic properties of the Earth, a set of differential equations can be solved numerically to compute the normal modes. In this study we use the *MINEOS* program to this end [36]. The sum of the normal modes is the seismic wavefield produced by a point source; it is then convolved with the seismic source to obtain the full seismic wavefield. The projection of the seismic wavefield onto a seismograph orientation is then the predicted seismogram for a specific source-receiver pair.

We can write the predicted seismogram as $s(\omega) = A(\omega) \exp^{-i\phi(\omega)}$ and the observed seismogram as $o(\omega) = A^o(\omega) \exp^{-i\phi^o(\omega)}$; where A is the amplitude and ϕ is the phase. For each seismogram the phase is the sum of three components: $\phi = \phi_s + \phi_r + \phi_p$; where ϕ_s and ϕ_r are the phases introduced by the seismic source and receiver respectively. The last component ϕ_p is the phase accumulated during the propagation from the source to the receiver; it is directly related to the Earth's physical properties. Assuming that the characteristics of the source and the receiver are perfectly known, ϕ_s and ϕ_r are exactly the same in both the predicted and observed seismograms.

Therefore, they cancel out when subtracting the phase components of the observed and predicted seismograms, leaving only a perturbation in the propagation component: $\delta\phi = \phi^o - \phi = \phi_p^o - \phi_p$. Note that the phase delay depends on frequency, this is what is called dispersion; and this dispersion is related to the physical properties within the Earth, expressed as perturbations with respect to the reference model.

2.2   Phase Delay Measurement with Discrete Fourier Transform

Most of the approaches to compute the phase delay between two seismograms rely on a Discrete Fourier Transform [17,20,30,32,41]. The results based on the Discrete Fourier Transform approach showed in this study are produced by applying the following processing to the seismograms: bandpass filter in a 10 mHz-large frequency band around a given measurement frequency; multiply with an appropriate time-window to consider only the relevant information; estimate the spectra using the Fast Fourier Transform algorithm [13]; and obtain the phase delay as the difference of the phase components of the spectra. This measurement is repeated in a broad range of frequencies: from 10 to 50 mHz by step of 1 mHz.

The dispersion curve is discontinuous when it reaches $\pm\pi$; making jumps of $\pm 2\pi$ to stay within the $\pm\pi$ range. If the early propagation history of the wave is unknown, one cannot recover a phase delayed or advanced by more than half a phase cycle. This is the so-called cycle-skip. Low frequencies are less likely to have a phase delay greater than $\pm\pi$; therefore correcting the cycle-skip can be done by starting from low frequencies and, for increasing frequencies, adding $\pm 2\pi$ accordingly when a cycle-skip is detected.

Synthetic tests show that this approach leads to acceptable results. However it suffers from some limitations including: sensitivity to noise in the seismogram; misdetection of cycle-skips; frequency-leakage and bias induced by time-windowing; difficult isolation of the relevant information in the time domain, in particular with multi-modal waveforms; and difficult estimation of the measurement uncertainties.

2.3 Evolutionary Algorithms

Evolutionary algorithms are inspired by Charles Darwin's theory of biological evolution, and have been developing around the world since the 1950s [11]. Currently the most widely used types of evolutionary algorithms include: Genetic Programming [14,27], Genetic Algorithm [23,25] and Evolutionary Strategies [43,45]. Evolutionary algorithms have been applied to solve problems and challenges in numerous domains and proved to be successful in many cases [2,46,49]. These algorithms have a lot in common, but the use of one over another is determined by the nature of the problem.

The Genetic Algorithm (GA) produces a sequence of generations over which a population of possible solutions to the problem (individuals) could "evolve". Each generation consists of a population with different individuals randomly initialized. In each generation, the solutions are evaluated based on their "fitness" to the problem, i.e., a quantitative evaluation of how close to the acquired signal is the individual. Using the residual - error between the simulated data using parameters given by the individual, solutions with the smallest fitness value have a higher chance of being selected as a parent to share their genes with other members of the population to produce a child solution (offspring).

In some applications of harmonic analysis, GA has proved to outperform the FFT method. In power sytems harmonic analysis, GA performed better than FFT as it required more sampling per cycle [49]. In an application to harmonic signals coming from Fourier Transform Ion-Cyclotron Resonance Mass Spectrometer, GA was able to determine phase values more accurately than FFT even in noisy signals and required fewer data points than FFT to resolve the peaks in the amplitude spectrum [2].

2.4 Description of the Proposed Algorithm

A seismic signal can be modeled as sum of several sine waves:

$$y = \sum_{i=1}^{N} A_i \sin(\omega_i x + \phi_i) \tag{1}$$

where A is the amplitude, ω is the angular frequency, ϕ is the phase, and N is the number of sines. In this paper, we develop a real-valued GA to determine the main parameters of the sinusoidal function - amplitude, frequency and phase - to best match the seismological data.

Individual Representation

The GA method encodes the amplitude, frequency, and phase of the sines into strings (chromosomes), $\{a, f, p\}$, where each is represented by a IEEE754 single precision floating point number (gene), a is the amplitude, f is the frequency, p is the phase.

Individual Initialization

Initially, the algorithm generates a random population based on an interval of values for amplitudes, frequency, and phase. Since the idea was to compare the results of a genetic algorithm to those of a standard Fourier Transform, the range for the sought values were determined based on the knowledge from the FFT results and used as input for the initialization of the individuals. The range used for amplitude and phase were $[0.0 - 2.0]$ and $[0 - 2\pi]$, respectively.

In addition, we take the advantage of the flexibility of GA by fixing the frequencies that would allow the algorithm to focus on finding the amplitude and phase parameters only to speedup the computation time.

Crossover

The crossover operator is used to create one or more children by combining the genotypes of parents. In this work we use a single-point crossover and make sure that the locus falls in between sines, in order to prevent the crossover from being disruptive. A `child` is created from the values of `parent1` and `parent2`. The reason for the choice of single-point crossover is because the semantics behind the different genes of the genome is well understood.

Mutation

The mutation operation is applied to prevent premature convergence to local minima. The sine is selected for mutation with probability 1 and within the sine a random uniform value is added to all genes with a probability of 0.6. After several runs, it was determined that for this particular problem, 0.6 was the best value for mutation probability. Mutation rate is selected as 1.0 in order to give a chance to all genes to be selected for mutation and to take care of the possibility of not mutating the children.

The values for the basic mutation parameters were tuned by hand so as to get the best performance.

Evaluation

Finally, the evaluation is the Root Mean Squared Error:

$$RMSE = \sqrt{\frac{\sum_{i=1}^{n}(Y_i - \hat{Y}_i)^2}{n}} \tag{2}$$

where Y_i, $\hat{Y}_i$ are the observed and predicted values, respectively, n is the number of data points. The fitness values that are calculated using RMSE were multiplied by 100 for better display.

Main Parameters of the Algorithm

The main parameters of the algorithm are described in Table 1.

Table 1. Genetic Algorithm parameters.

Parameter	Value
Population size	131072
Offspring size	131072
Generations	100
Mutation Rate	1.0
Crossover Rate	1.0
Elite	1
Next generation selection method	Tournament (size 2)
Parent selector	Tournament (size 10)

A very large population size (131,072 individuals) is chosen as it accounts for a very good exploration of the search space.

GPU Parallelization

The proposed algorithm is run on the EASEA[1] (EAsy Specification of Evolutionary Algorithms) [12,35,48] platform which is a software platform designed for non-computer scientists to run evolutionary algorithms. This platform allows automatic parallelization of EAs on NVIDIA GPGPU cards when the source file is compiled with the -cuda option.

---

[1] https://easea.unistra.fr.

Selection

The selection is done in two stages. In the first stage, selection is done for choosing the parents to go under reproduction. Parents are chosen with replacement, allowing the same parent to be chosen several times. As a result of crossover, offspring of the same size as the parents are obtained.

In the second stage, the selection is done to move individuals to the next generation. After the creation of children, the new population consists of parents and children, which is then reduced to the original size of the population. During the population reduction, the selection is done without replacement. n-ary tournament [6,7] selection was used for this purpose. During this stage, n number of individuals are selected and the individual with the worst fitness value is removed. The process is repeated until the population size reaches the original size.

The stopping criteria in the code is the number of generations.

3   Results and Discussion

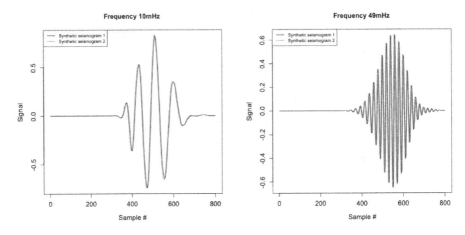

Fig. 1. Synthetic seismograms with high correlation, filtered around 10 mHz (left) and 49 mHz (right).

In this section, we present the results obtained by GA and compare them with the results obtained by DFT.

To evaluate the proposed method, we start with a synthetic test where we use two synthetic seismograms with high correlation: one is the predicted seismogram for a reference model of the Earth and the other one plays the role of the observed seismogram, and is generated using a perturbed version of the reference model where the perturbation decreases linearly with depth. Figure 1 shows filtered synthetic seismograms for frequencies 10 mHz and 49 mHz. Figure 2 shows the results of the phase delay estimation using GA and FFT for the two synthetic

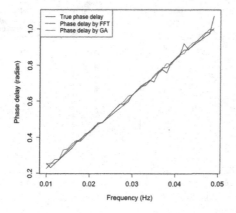

Fig. 2. Phase delay between the two highly correlated synthetic seismograms shown in Fig. 1.

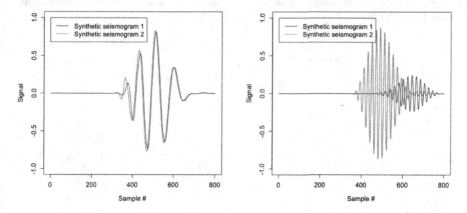

Fig. 3. Synthetic seismograms with low correlation, filtered around 10 mHz (left) and 49 mHz (right).

seismograms. Since both seismograms are synthetic, true phase delay values are known for comparison. The results are quite similar for both GA and FFT to the true phase delay values with correlation coefficients 0.996 and 0.997, respectively.

To evaluate the robustness of our algorithm, we generated another synthetic signal by a more complex model of the Earth to play the role of the observed seismogram. This radial model contains the averaged physical properties, along the source-receiver path, of a 3D model of the Earth. Figure 3 shows the filtered synthetic seismograms for frequencies 10 mHz and 49 mHz. When estimating the phase delay of these seismograms, the FFT method produced a cycle-skip (Fig. 4) that the GA method did not produce. Figure 5 compares the phase delay values obtained by FFT after cycle-skip correction, those obtained by GA, and the true phase delay values. It shows that with a more complex signal, where the correlation between the signals is much lower, the results are still similar to

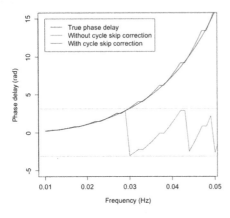
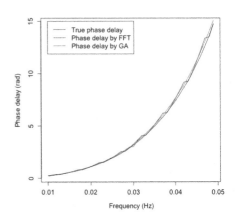

Fig. 4. Cycle-skip effect when measuring phase delay using FFT between the two low correlation synthetic seismograms from Fig. 3.

Fig. 5. Phase delay between the two low correlation synthetic seismograms from Fig. 3 after cycle-skip correction.

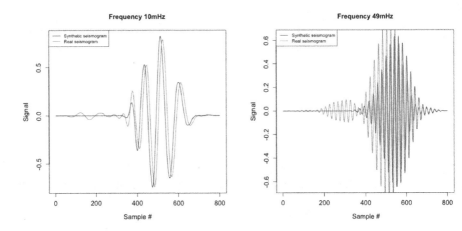

Fig. 6. Synthetic vs real seismograms filtered around frequencies of 10 mHz (left) and 49 mHz (right).

the true phase delay values for both GA and corrected FFT, with correlation coefficients 0.9999 and 0.9993, respectively.

Having validated our proposed method with the synthetic test, we move to a real case where the observed seismogram is now a real one. Figure 6 shows the filtered synthetic and real seismograms for frequencies 10 mHz and 49 mHz. Figure 7 shows that a cycle-skip occurred at a frequency of about 40 mHz when determining the phase delay by FFT between the synthetic and real seismograms from Fig. 6. The comparison between the corrected FFT measurements and the GA measurements are shown in Fig. 8; their correlation coefficient is 0.999.

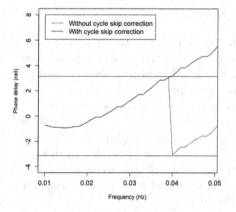 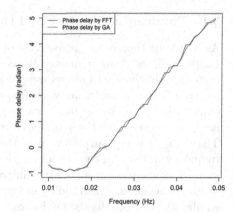

Fig. 7. Cycle-skip effect when measuring phase delay using FFT between the real and synthetic seismograms from Fig. 6.

Fig. 8. Phase delay between the synthetic and a real seismograms from Fig. 6 after correction of the FFT cycleskip.

The results show that GA performs similarly to FFT in determining the phase delays between seismic signals. Since GA is a stochastic algorithm, the algorithm was run 30 times to ensure the stability of the results. The best fitness values were very close (at least 6 digits of precision after the decimal point) across all repetitive runs. The variability of the phase delay values between a synthetic and a real seismogram obtained by GA over 30 runs are shown by violin plots in Fig. 9 for frequencies 10 mHz, 25 mHz, 49 mHz. The standard deviation of the phase delay values for the frequencies 10 mHz, 25 mHz, 49 mHz were 0.00034, 0.00023, 0.00036 radians respectively. The computation time for our algorithm was on average 20 seconds for one run per frequency. The variability of the computation time was less than 2 standard deviations in all runs.

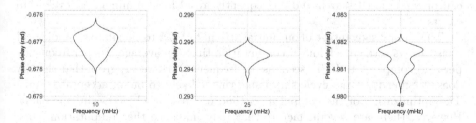

Fig. 9. Variability of phase delays for frequencies 10 mHz, 25 mHz, 49 mHz.

3.1   Physical Interpretation of the Results

As a rule of thumb, the sensitivity of the phase delay to the structure of the Earth shallows as the frequency increases. In the synthetic test, the largest perturbations in the Earth model were at shallow depth, which explains in part the increase in the phase delay with frequency seen in Fig. 2 (another part of the explanation is the larger number of cycles accumulated at higher frequency). It is also expected that the real Earth is more heterogeneous at shallow depths. Therefore, it is not surprising that the dispersion curve is also increasing with frequency in the real case results on Fig. 8. However, the dispersion in this case seems to show more complexities, in particular a lack of increase in phase delay at low frequencies, which indicates that the true and reference Earth models are similar at large depths (beyond about 80 km depth).

3.2   Discussion

In this paper, we showed that GA can be used as an alternative method of determining the phase delays between seismic signals.

There are a number of reasons why using the GA to calculate the phase delays between seismograms might have advantages. A GA is highly flexible because it allows defining the variables of interest and the range of values for the algorithm to find. GA allows fixing known parameters in the equation and have the algorithm focus on determining the other parameters which would decrease the computation time and increase the accuracy of the obtained result.

One of the problems in standard phase-delay measurement in seismology called a cycle-skip, happens when a signal reaches close to $\pm\pi$ and ends up shifting by $\pm 2\pi$, thus seeming either delayed or in advance. GA was able to model the signals and find phase delays accurately regardless of this problem. GA did not suffer from cycle-skip issues because GA is a global search algorithm and is well suited for the harmonic analysis problem whose characteristics are well known. Therefore, by tuning crossover and mutation operators, interesting areas of the search space can be explored. With a large population size, the GA can provide global search and consequently avoid local minima and cycle-skip effects.

The main disadvantage of our initial attempt at GA to calculate seismological phase delays is the much longer computation time (on average 20 s per frequency per run) compared to FFT (seconds per frequency). However, given that the GA doesn't suffer from the cycle-skip issue, this is likely to be an acceptable time. The optimization of the computation time was not an objective in this study. However, there are several factors that may influence the computation time, including population size, number of generations, values initialized for the range of parameters, and the machines used. One of the possible ways to significantly reduce the computation time would be parallelizing over several computers via transfer learning, known as island parallelization [1]. It was shown in [1] that when n islands (machines) are used for parallelization in the island model, the best fitness values are obtained m times faster, with $m > n$.

The further development of using GA for estimating phase delays may include applying a broader filter on seismic signals (this would reduce the signal processing required on the seismological signals).

4 Conclusion

In this paper, we introduced a new approach to estimating phase delays between two seismic signals using Genetic Algorithm. Genetic Algorithm returned approximately the same level of accuracy and precision in estimating phase differences as the Discrete Fourier Transform method, while avoiding the cycle-skip effects that are a drawback of this latter method. We suspect it may also reduce the frequency leakage and depth bias that occurs with Discrete Fourier Transform when time windowing and filtering. Proving these advantages will be the focus of future work.

Scientific Validation

This paper has benefited from the remarks of the following reviewers:

- Conor Ryan, University of Limerick, Ireland
- Jérôme Vergne, Strasbourg University, France
- Olivier Lengliné, Université de Strasbourg, France

The conference organisers wish to thank them for their highly appreciated effort and contribution.

References

1. Abdulkarimova, U., Leonteva, A., Jeannin-Girardon, A., Collet, P.: The parsec machine: a non-newtonian supra-linear supercomputer. Azerbaijan J. High Perform. Comput. **2**, 122–140 (2019). https://doi.org/10.32010/26166127.2019.2.2.122.140
2. Abdulkarimova, U.: SINUS-IT: an evolutionary approach to harmonic analysis. PhD thesis, University of Strasbourg (2021)
3. Backus, G.E., Gilbert, F.: Uniqueness in the inversion of inaccurate gross Earth data. Phil. Trans. R. Soc. A. **266**(1173), 74 (1970). ISSN 2054–0272. https://doi.org/10.1098/rsta.1970.0005
4. Backus, G.E., Gilbert, J.F.: numerical applications of a formalism for geophysical inverse problems. Geophys J. Int. **13**(1–3), 247–276 (1967). ISSN 0956–540X, 1365–246X. https://doi.org/10.1111/j.1365-246X.1967.tb02159.x
5. Backus, G., Gilbert, F.: The Resolving Power of Gross Earth Data. Geophys. J. Int. **16**(2), 169–205 (1968). ISSN 0956–540X, 1365–246X. https://doi.org/10.1111/j.1365-246X.1968.tb00216.x
6. Blickle, T., Thiele, L.: A mathematical analysis of tournament selection, pp. 9–16 (1995)
7. Brindle, A.: Genetic algorithms for function optimisation. Technical Report TR81-2, Department of Computer Science, University of Alberta, Edmonton (1981)

8. Bunge, H.-P., Hagelberg, C.R., Travis, B.J.: Mantle circulation models with variational data assimilation: inferring past mantle flow and structure from plate motion histories and seismic tomography. Geophys. J. Int. **152**(2), 280–301 (2003). ISSN 0956540X, 1365246X. https://doi.org/10.1046/j.1365-246X.2003.01823.x

9. Cara, M., Lévêque, J.J.: Waveform inversion using secondary observables. Geophys. Res. Lett., **14**(10), 1046–1049 (1987). ISSN 00948276. https://doi.org/10.1029/GL014i010p01046

10. Chen, L., Wang, X., Liang, X., Wan, B., Liu, L.: Subduction tectonics vs. Plume tectonics-Discussion on driving forces for plate motion. Sci. China Earth Sci., **63**(3):315–328 (2020). ISSN 1674–7313, 1869–1897. https://doi.org/10.1007/s11430-019-9538-2

11. Collet, P., Rennard, J.P.: Stochastic Optimization Algorithms. Handbook of Research on Nature Inspired Computing for Economics and Management (2007)

12. Collet, P., Kruger, F., Maitre, O.: Automatic parallelization of EC on GPGPUs and clusters of GPGPU machines with EASEA and EASEA-CLOUD, pp. 35–59 (2013). ISBN 978-3-642-37958-1. https://doi.org/10.1007/978-3-642-37959-8_3

13. Cooley, J.W., Tukey, J.W.: An Algorithm for the Machine Calculation of Complex Fourier Series (1965)

14. Cramer, N.L.: A representation for the adaptive generation of simple sequential programs. In: Proceedings of the First International Conference on Genetic Algorithms, vol. 183, p. 187 (1985)

15. Dahlen, F.A., Tromp, J.: Theoretical Global Seismology (1998)

16. Debayle, E., Lévêque, J.J.: Upper mantle heterogeneities in the Indian Ocean from waveform inversion. Geophys. Res. Lett., **24**(3), 245–248 (1997). ISSN 00948276. https://doi.org/10.1029/96GL03954

17. Dziewonski, A., Mills, J., Bloch, S.: Residual dispersion measurement-a new method of surface-wave analysis. Bull. Seismol. Soc. Am. **62**(1), 129–139 (1972). ISSN 1943–3573, 0037–1106. https://doi.org/10.1785/BSSA0620010129, https://pubs.geoscienceworld.org/bssa/article/62/1/129/116997/Residual-dispersion-measurement-a-new-method-of

18. Dziewonski, A.M., Anderson, D.L.: Preliminary reference Earth model. Phys. Earth Planet. Inter. **25**(4), 297–356 (1981)

19. Dziewonski, A.M., Hager, B.H., O'Connell, R.J.: Large-scale heterogeneities in the lower mantle. J. Geophys. Res. **82**(2), 239–255 (1977). ISSN 01480227. https://doi.org/10.1029/JB082i002p00239

20. Ekström, G., Tromp, J., Larson, E.W.F.: Measurements and global models of surface wave propagation. J. Geophys. Res. **102**(B4), 8137–8157 (1997). ISSN 01480227. https://doi.org/10.1029/96JB03729

21. Foulger, G.R.L.: Plates vs plumes: a geological controversy. John Wiley and Sons (2011)

22. Freissler, R., Zaroli, C., Lambotte, S., Schuberth, B.S.A.: Tomographic filtering via the generalized inverse: a way to account for seismic data uncertainty. Geophys. J. Int., **223**(1), 254–269 (2020). ISSN 0956–540X, 1365–246X. https://doi.org/10.1093/gji/ggaa231, https://academic.oup.com/gji/article/223/1/254/5838747

23. Goldberg, D.E.: Genetic algorithms in search, optimization and machine learning. Addison-Wesley (1989)

24. Greenfield, T., et al.: Post-Subduction tectonics of sabah, northern borneo, inferred from surface wave tomography. Geophys. Res. Lett. **49**(3), 1944–8007 (2022). ISSN 0094–8276. https://doi.org/10.1029/2021GL096117

25. Holland, J.H.: Adaptation in Natural and Artificial Systems. MIT Press, Cambridge, MA, USA (1992). ISBN 0-262-58111-6

26. Koelemeijer, P., Schuberth, B.S.A., Davies, D.R., Deuss, A., Ritsema, J.: Constraints on the presence of post-perovskite in Earth's lowermost mantle from tomographic-geodynamic model comparisons. Earth Planetary Sci. Lett. **494**, 226–238 (2018). ISSN 0012821X. https://doi.org/10.1016/j.epsl.2018.04.056, https://linkinghub.elsevier.com/retrieve/pii/S0012821X18302656

27. Koza, J.R.: Genetic Programming: On the Programming of Computers by means of Natural Evolution. MIT Press, Massachusetts (1992)

28. Laske, G., Masters, G.: Constraints on global phase velocity maps from long-period polarization data. J. Geophys. Res. **101**(B7), 16059–16075 (1996). ISSN 01480227. https://doi.org/10.1029/96JB00526

29. F Latallerie, Christophe Zaroli, Sophie Lambotte, and A Maggi. Analysis of tomographic models using resolution and uncertainties: a surface wave example from the Pacific. Geophys. J. Int. **230**(2), 893–907 (2022). ISSN 0956–540X, 1365–246X. https://doi.org/10.1093/gji/ggac095, https://academic.oup.com/gji/article/230/2/893/6544670

30. Lerner-Lam, A.L., Jordan, T.H.: Earth structure from fundamental and higher-mode waveform analysis. Geophy. J. Int. **75**(3), 759–797 (1983). ISSN 0956–540X, 1365–246X. https://doi.org/10.1111/j.1365-246X.1983.tb05009.x

31. Liu, K., Zhou, Y.: Global Rayleigh wave phase-velocity maps from finite-frequency tomography. Geophys. J. Int., **205**(1), 51–66 (2016). ISSN 0956–540X, 1365–246X. https://doi.org/10.1093/gji/ggv555

32. Ma, Z., Masters, G., Laske, G., Pasyanos, M.: A comprehensive dispersion model of surface wave phase and group velocity for the globe. Geophys. J. Int. **199**(1), 113–135, October 2014. ISSN 1365–246X, 0956–540X. https://doi.org/10.1093/gji/ggu246, http://academic.oup.com/gji/article/199/1/113/726797/A-comprehensive-dispersion-model-of-surface-wave

33. Maggi, A., Debayle, E., Priestley, K., Barruol, G.: Multimode surface waveform tomography of the Pacific Ocean: a closer look at the lithospheric cooling signature. Geophys. J. Int., **166**(3), 1384–1397 (2006). ISSN 0956540X, 1365246X. https://doi.org/10.1111/j.1365-246X.2006.03037.x

34. Magrini, F., et al.: Surface-Wave tomography of the central-western mediterranean: new insights into the Liguro-Provençal and Tyrrhenian Basins. JGR Solid Earth **127**(3), 2169–9356 (2022). ISSN 2169–9313. https://doi.org/10.1029/2021JB023267

35. Maitre, O., Lachiche, N., Clauss, P., Baumes, L., Corma, A., Collet, P.: Efficient parallel implementation of evolutionary algorithms on GPGPU cards. In: Euro-Par (2009)

36. Masters, G., Misha, B., Susan, K.: Mineos User Manual v 1.0.2, April (2014)

37. Menke, W.: Geophysical Data Analysis: Discrete Inverse Theory. Academic Press (1989)

38. Montagner, J.P.: Regional three-dimensional structures using long-period surface waves (1986)

39. Moulik, P., et al.: Global reference seismological data sets: multimode surface wave dispersion. Geophys. J. Int. **228**(3), 1808–1849 (2021). ISSN 0956–540X, 1365–246X. https://doi.org/10.1093/gji/ggab418. https://academic.oup.com/gji/article/228/3/1808/6408466

40. Neall, V.E., Trewick, S.A.: The age and origin of the Pacific islands: a geological overview. Phil. Trans. R. Soc. B, **363**(1508), 3293–3308 (2008). ISSN 0962–8436, 1471–2970. https://doi.org/10.1098/rstb.2008.0119

41. Park, J., Lindberg, C.R., Vernon, F.L.: Multitaper spectral analysis of high-frequency seismograms. J. Geophys. Res. **92**(B12), 12675 (1987). ISSN 0148–0227. https://doi.org/10.1029/JB092iB12p12675

42. Parker, R.L.: Understanding inverse theory. Annu. Rev. Earth Planet. Sci., **5**(1), 35–64 (1977). ISSN 0084–6597, 1545–4495. https://doi.org/10.1146/annurev.ea.05.050177.000343

43. Rechenberg, I.: Evolutionstrategie: Optimierung Technisher Systeme nach Prinzipien des Biologischen Evolution. Fromman-Hozlboog Verlag, Stuttgart (1973)

44. Restelli, F., Koelemeijer, P., Ferreira, A.M.G.: Normal mode observability of radial anisotropy in the Earth's mantle. Geophys. J. Int. 233(1), 663–679 (2022). ISSN 0956–540X, 1365–246X. https://doi.org/10.1093/gji/ggac474. https://academic.oup.com/gji/article/233/1/663/6862098

45. Schwefel, H.-P.: Numerical Optimization of Computer Models. John Wiley & Sons, New-York (1981). 1995–2nd edition

46. Slowik, A., Kwasnicka, H.: Evolutionary algorithms and their applications to engineering problems. Neural Comput. Appl. **32**, 12363–12379 (2020). https://doi.org/10.1007/s00521-020-04832-8

47. Tarantola, A.: Inverse problem theory and methods for model parameter estimation. Soc. Ind. Appl. Math. (2005). ISBN 978-0-89871-572-9 978-0-89871-792-1. https://doi.org/10.1137/1.9780898717921

48. Tsutsui, S., Collet, P.: Massively parallel evolutionary computation on GPGPUs (2013). ISBN 978-3-642-37959-8. https://doi.org/10.1007/978-3-642-37959-8

49. Zamanan, N., Sykulski, J., Al-Othman, A.K.: Real coded genetic algorithm compared to the classical method of fast fourier transform in harmonics analysis, pp. 1021–1025 (2006). ISBN 978-186135-342-9. https://doi.org/10.1109/UPEC.2006.367633

50. Zaroli, C.: Global seismic tomography using Backus-Gilbert inversion. Geophys. J. Int. **207**(2), 876–888 (2016). ISSN 0956–540X, 1365–246X. https://doi.org/10.1093/gji/ggw315

51. Zhou, Y., Dahlen, F.A., Nolet, G.: Three-dimensional sensitivity kernels for surface wave observables. Geophys. J. Int. **158**(1), 142–168 (2004). ISSN 0956540X, 1365246X. https://doi.org/10.1111/j.1365-246X.2004.02324.x

Author Index

P. Collet et al. (Eds.): CCE 2023, LNCS 13927, pp. 235–236, 2023.
https://doi.org/10.1007/978-3-031-44355-8

Printed in the United States
by Baker & Taylor Publisher Services